I Joined the Russians

by Johnny Lindner

HEINRICH VON EINSIEDEL

TRANSLATION!
JOHNNY LINDNER

I Joined the Russians

A CAPTURED GERMAN FLIER'S DIARY

OF THE COMMUNIST TEMPTATION

New Haven

YALE UNIVERSITY PRESS / 1953

940.548
V

Preface to the American Edition

A book must speak for itself and this one of mine must be its own justification. It is as direct a record as I can make of a personal experience; it is focused on a problem that has become of universal importance to humanity, and it concerns that area where the life of the individual crosses the general stream of history. In writing it, though, I had the German reader in mind, one who is familiar with the social, psychological, and historical background of what I have to tell. A prefatory note about the background and the method of writing may perhaps help the American reader both to understand my experience and to evaluate my testimony on certain of the historical events in which I participated and which will come under scholarly review.

Germany has been peculiarly responsive to the appeals of authoritarian panaceas and of national pride that have beset our age, and so it is hardly surprising that she is the one major power to have had direct experience of both 20th-century totalitarianisms. My own career has been a kind of internal version of this national development. I was not quite twelve years old in 1933 when the flames of the German Reichstag announced the end of the Weimar Republic. I was brought up by parents whose philosophy of life dated from the era of the Kaiser's Germany and may be characterized as an old-fashioned, respectable conservatism, venerating the traditional symbols of authority and codes of action as foundations of the beloved nation. Without changing their views completely, under the impact of economic crisis and the complete paralysis of governmental authority in Germany they turned to National Socialism. They had been made ripe for this change when their moral and material capital was lost in the collapse of Imperial Germany in 1918 and the inflation that followed. But the illusions produced by Hitler's demagoguery and celebrated with so much enthusiasm and so many torchlight processions in 1933 quickly went to pieces under the shots of June 30, 1934, as Hitler proceeded with the so-called Röhmputsch.

This is my first political memory, this Blood Purge directed by Hitler and one wing of the Nazi party primarily against groups within the party itself, which broadened to include potential political antagonists of all kinds. Among those assassinated were men of conservative, monarchical tendencies with whom my parents were acquainted and in sympathy. Although the historical verdict on the Blood Purge interprets it as a victory for the conservative over the radical wing of the Nazi party, for my family and indeed for many upper middle-class families in Germany the meaning of the event was quite different. The attack upon men of our persuasion and the employment of violence as an official policy against those whom we knew to harbor no revolutionary designs shocked us into a more critical attitude.

What remained after this disillusionment I can best characterize today as a kind of split consciousness that was typical not only of my family but of large middle-class groups in Germany. For Americans this split consciousness is bound to be hard to understand. Yet it is one of the most important aspects of a totally governed state where the sentiment of national pride is steadily exploited in order to compensate for the continued humiliation of being governed by a terrorist clique. This mechanism of repression functions all the better when it actually becomes difficult to distinguish between the justifiable interests of one's own country and the interests of the group in power. Our split consciousness consisted in our approval on the one hand of what the regime was doing to carry out the traditional conservative aims of asserting authority within and national interest abroad, and on the other disapproval of both the agents and the means of that policy. It was obvious in our adoption of two national hymns, the old "Deutschlandlied" and the "Horst Wessel Lied" (the battle song of the SA), and in our adding to the latter of a verse which went: "The nose high, the eyes shut fast, SA marks the quiet steady step; comrades, shot by the SS and the Gestapo, walk in spirit in our ranks." In short, we despised the Nazis and yet served them because they represented the power of Germany.

In 1942 I was twenty-one years old. The whole of my politically conscious life, passed in Nazi Germany, was inevitably marked by this split consciousness. When I found myself in a prisoner-of-war camp at Stalingrad in 1942 I was suddenly forced to come to grips with this phenomenon, only to discover that the bridge which Marxism seemed to build ended by intensifying the division within me. This is the theme of my book. If it were simply a story of the relationship between an individual and totalitarianism it would, in these days, scarcely be noteworthy. Nor would it seem remarkable if it were merely an account of a conflict between an individual's ideals and his duty to his nation. But because it is a case study in a new dilemma which includes both these older ones, my experience may be of some interest. It is the dilemma of an individual faced with two totalitarianisms, each of which claims an exclusive monopoly both of ideals and of national loyalty. The implications may be noted in my own present circumstances, which may be viewed as a kind of ironical conclusion to the story told here. As a former member of both the Hitler Youth and Social Unity party (SED—the Communist party of East Germany) I am doubly barred from the United States; as a *former* member of the SED I am persona non grata to the Russians; and as a former member of the wartime National Committee for Free Germany in the Soviet Union I have come under severe attack by veterans' organizations in Germany itself.

The notion that there can be a moral duty in time of war to wish for and to help bring about the defeat of one's own country, if the leadership of the nation has fallen into the hands of criminals, is a view that is still widely debated today in Germany—and also certainly in Soviet Russia. This battle too has been part of the lively controversy that began with the appearance of my book in Germany.

The diary form which I have chosen for my story and the historical evidence included in it require some explanation. The diary which is the framework is a literary device rather than an actual document. The book was written mainly in the years 1947 and 1948 on the basis of my memory—which is good—and numerous documentary aids in my possession, such as a collection of the newspaper *Free Germany* which we published in Moscow during the war, many leaflets of the Free Germany Committee, minutes of meetings, and personal memoranda which I was able to bring out of the Soviet Union.

For all the material cited verbatim I can give precise documentary support. The Yale University Library has in its possession a microfilm with five hundred photographs of issues of *Free Germany* between July 1943 and November 1945, as well as photographs of leaflets of the committee. Where I have had to rely upon memory I have used the evidence which I have collected as check points and have consulted with friends who were present at the occasions in question. The diary form has been used not only to heighten interest but to make for clarity. I have thought it the best way to assure that the reconstruction of outer events and of my inner development would follow their actual course as closely as possible and to reduce retrospective distortion to a minimum. The reception of the book in Germany attests that this aim has not failed: in all the debate and criticism that the book has aroused there, one reproach has never been leveled against it—that it is untrue or inaccurate. So far as the picture of my own development is concerned, this can only be a matter for my conscience and the reader's judgment.

Introduction

In 1947 when I was released from a prisoner-of-war camp in Russia I met people all over Germany who were interested to hear about my experiences. Germans, Frenchmen, Americans, Russians, Communists and anti-Communists, professors and workers, friends and enemies, all asked so many questions that I was never able to answer any of them fully. I told my story, explained and commented on things as I understood them at the time; and in the end my listeners would suggest that I write a consecutive account of my experiences. This was why I began to write.

I wanted to put things down just as I had been telling them to people on whose friendly understanding and considered judgment I could count, even though what I had to say was not particularly flattering to me or to anyone else. This turned out to be very much more difficult than I had imagined. Things that I had written with the utmost honesty seemed to me, when I read them again a few days later, completely different. At the same time I found myself more and more at odds with the environment I had chosen of my own free will, that of an editor of a Communist newspaper in East Berlin, the *Tägliche Rundschau,* and a member of the Social Unity party. I stopped writing when it finally became clear to me that I would never be able to make a useful record of my experiences while I was living in these conditions and in this psychological state.

Yet the attempt to write had helped me to gain perspective and to revive my powers of judgment which in the last few years had gradually been drugged. Since my attendance at the antifascist school in Moscow in the summer of 1944 I had tried to achieve the impossible: to be a Communist and at the same time retain my inner freedom. In those days at the school I considered the attempt to break my comrades' and my own psychological, moral, and intellectual backbone an incidental accompaniment of extraordinary circumstances, or at least a test which had to be passed if we wanted to enter the circle of the advance guard of the revolution, who had equal rights and were independent in judgment. It would have been easy not to let my resistance be broken if I had realized at the time that the backbreaking was one of the principles of that international terror group which calls itself the Communist party. I would not have rebelled senselessly, but on the other hand neither would I have surrendered. But I had no desire at all for such insight, because the understanding does not easily reject what is hoped for. The Communist party promises to be at the same time the school, the church, the barracks, and the family for the human being who is overcome by apparently meaningless, chaotic, and terrible external events. As one of the most prominent former Communists, Ignazio Silone, recently said: "It is a totalitarian institution in the fullest and purest meaning of the word . . . and it claims the totality of the person who submits to it. In consequence a true Communist, who as it were through a miracle retains his natural power of judgment and uses it in party matters (with good intentions and because he believes he can help the party), exposes himself to the cruel and contradictory fate of the unbeliever; and before he pronounces his final submission or foreswearing he is subjected to spiritual strains of every kind. The very slowness with which a believing Communist appreciates the extent of his deviation is in this respect very significant and has not yet been sufficiently analyzed."

When I resumed work on my manuscript in 1949 after my break with the Communists, it was my intention to illustrate by my own example this psychological process which Silone suggested.

I did not try to write a history of the National Committee for Free Germany. My account of this phenomenon must necessarily be extremely subjective, but I hope that for this very reason it may give valuable hints to an objective historian.

It was never my intention to write a justification of my behavior during imprisonment. I pay my genuine respect to anybody who may be convinced that in identical circumstances he would have behaved more decently, honestly, and correctly than I did. The voice which in 1943 cried to Ulbricht at a meeting in a prison camp, "Even if there are only twelve million of us left, we will fight on till final victory!" can be cited as one of many examples of dash, yet it is in fact no proof of courage but only of that irresponsible attitude which destroyed Europe and opened the gates of Germany to Red fascism. Least of all did such behavior help the prisoners of war in the Soviet Union.

To anybody who is interested in finding out who was responsible for the terrible fate of the German prisoners of war in the Soviet Union my book can give some information, and if it helps to make those men who are so quick to use the words "traitor" or "opportunist" at least honestly face the errors and mistakes of their past, it will have achieved its purpose.

Contents

ILLUSTRATIONS

Sixteen pages of illustrations are grouped between pages 94 and 95.

MAPS

I Joined the Russians

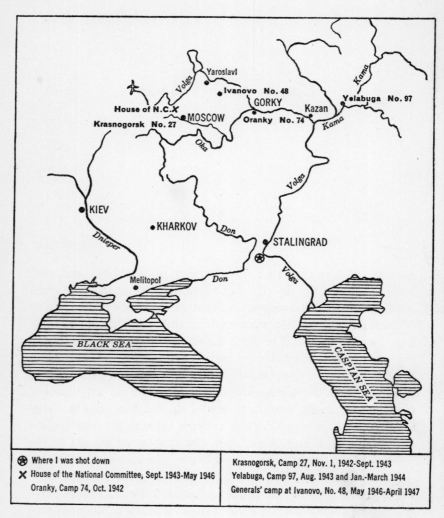

Prisoner-of-war camps

Chapter One / Prisoner

AUGUST 24, 1942. The waters of the Don and the Volga reflected the sky of a day of shimmering heat. A weightless haze lay over the steppes as I circled high above them in my Messerschmitt 109. My eyes scanned the horizon which faded into formless mists. The sky, the steppes, the rivers, and the sea, of which one was aware in the distance, lay as if stretching from eternity to eternity. For a few seconds I gave myself completely to the triumph of flying, that proud intoxication of liberation, speed, and the power of the machine. But this was no time for dreaming. For the expanse beneath me was Stalingrad and it was August 24, 1942, the day on which the battle broke out that was to be the climax of the summer offensive.

Far beneath me, like crisscross lines of ants, I recognized battalions, regiments, divisions; columns, vehicles, tanks: German troops advancing on the Volga, Russian tanks counterattacking on both flanks. A sudden call in my headphone brought me back to reality: "Einsiedel! Over Pitomnik!" The Russians were behind the Stukas. Two Messerschmitts

3

fell like meteors from the sky and crashed on the ground. The space which a moment ago had seemed infinite suddenly shrank. A heavy oily vapor covered the earth. Our airplanes plunged like U-boats into the few square miles of condensed space where Russians and Germans were locked in furious conflict.

Yesterday, when the German combat squadrons began their first daylight mass attack on Stalingrad, not a single Russian plane appeared. The Russians have twenty fighters at Stalingrad to every German one, and yet the city remained undefended, open to destruction. But now the Russian command has seen what is happening. The German offensive began in the early hours of the morning. Neither the Soviet armored mass attacks in the north nor the desperate tank sorties of untrained, badly led workers' regiments from Stalingrad can halt it. At this point the Soviets sent up all their available planes and an air battle developed such as we have had only in the West over the Channel. Every German Stuka, every combat plane was surrounded by clusters of Russian fighters which swarmed behind their own Stormoviks in close formation.

We threw ourselves into the tumult at random. A two-star Rata crossed my track. The Russian saw me, went into a nose dive, and tried to get away by flying low. Fear seemed to have crippled him. He raced seven feet above the ground on a straight course and did not defend himself. My machine vibrated with the recoil of its guns. A streak of flame shot from the gas tank of the Russian plane, which exploded and rolled over on the ground. A broad, long strip of scorched steppe was the last trace of it.

I turned and flew back toward Stalingrad. Suddenly, a few hundred yards to my left, Russian bombers were making a low-level attack on German tanks. Four or five hundred yards behind them were Russian fighters. What I did then was sheer madness: I dived under the very nose of those fighters which could change height into speed. Love of the chase and a sense of indifference had taken possession of me. Flying in a steep curve, I got behind an IL-2. The outline of a Russian machine appeared once more in my sight. I was blinded by the first hits. Hot engine oil spurted out of my opponent's tank and spread in a thin layer from one end of my machine to the other, clouding the view from the cockpit. I turned on the spray which washed the glass. The glimpse I snatched this way was just enough to help me fly over a German tank and steer clear of the flaming IL-2. But my attention was diverted for two or three seconds, and as I turned to look for the Russian fighters I saw their blazing guns ninety yards behind me. There was a terrific explosion and I felt a hard blow on my foot. I twisted my ME and forced it up into a steep climb. The Russian was shaken off. Again I turned to the attack, again I was eighty, sixty, forty yards from a Russian fighter, but my guns were silent. The Russian had put my electric control equipment out of action. I turned westward and continued along the line of advance toward the Don. The line of advance? A broad well-worn track of sand through the steppe grass, without a human being in sight—that was all. Surely the German supply columns should have been moving along it? A machine gun opened up at me. Behind it brown figures crouched in the gun emplacement. So this was the explanation: the German tanks had not yet reached the Volga and they were already cut off.

In my tent at the edge of the airfield the doctor pulled a dozen fragments of explosive bullet from my skin. While he worked leisurely he had me report.

"Yes"—he nodded—"the tanks were cut off at the Volga;

5

just the supply columns with a tank steppe convoy. I'll get you a map of the battle; it has the latest reports of the situation at the front. There's not much change in the south. The Zarepta hills can't be taken. We are still a good twenty-five miles from the Volga."

"And how does it look in the Caucasus?"

"We don't make any real headway there either. The Russian resistance has stiffened a good deal. The Luftwaffe has been reinforced too."

"This time winter seems to begin for the Russians in August!"

"Hold on," laughed the doctor, "one of our advance columns has just started for Leningrad. After Stalingrad and Baku are taken it is Leningrad's turn. We're moving the whole 8th Air Corps there."

"And already sending advance columns?"

"What do you mean, 'already'?"

"Well, I should think spring would be time enough. But perhaps we won't have a chance then."

The doctor got angry. "Don't start that all over again. For God's sake, why are you so pessimistic?"

He put aside his scissors and tweezers and tapped my chest with his finger. "Man, the war is one to zero in our favor. We can't lose. It will be a tie at worst."

"You mean a tie for the referee? How do you figure that? If you got a leave from Vladivostok with a tank convoy?"

"Stop. You are tired out. The first thing you get from me is an order not to fly for a week. After that your machine and your leg will be all right and then we'll talk. What you need is sleep!"

6

AUGUST 28, 1942. I have been flying again. My foot is still bandaged but it does not hurt any more. It was afternoon and the sun was behind us as we flew over the Don at Kalach in the direction of Stalingrad, at a height of eighteen thousand feet. Sixty yards from me a young corporal was flying his machine. He arrived from Germany only this morning and his eyes were bright with enthusiasm and eagerness at being allowed to take part in the day's first flight over enemy territory. Halfway along our course, a few hundred yards higher, a Russian fighter flew toward us. He dropped down behind us and attacked. I have seldom seen Russian fighters start an attack of their own accord; for a single fighter to do it is most unusual. As we moved up in a steep climb to get into attacking position between him and the sun, I looked round in vain for his comrades. The poor fellow seemed to have no experience judging by the slow way he climbed after us.

"You wait," I thought to myself, "and in seconds you'll be hanging onto your parachute—if you're lucky." At this height we were far and away superior to the Russians both in speed and climbing capacity.

But I had misjudged him completely. The man who succeeded in avoiding my attacks through incomparable acrobatics, and who managed two or three times to face me head on so that we flashed past one another at arm's length at a speed of seven hundred miles an hour, was not a novice but an old hand who used his knowledge with calm superiority.

For several minutes we circled each other without result. Grasping the stick with both hands, I tried to force the ME into tighter and tighter circles, following the apparently effortless twists of the Russian. Again and again centrifugal force drove the blood from my head and I blacked out for seconds. At last I made it. The Russian turned a split second too late. I was inside his curve, and he crossed the line of my tracer in-

7

cendiary bullets only twenty yards away, toppled over in a
nose spin, and fell. But he had deceived me again. Two miles
below he pulled out and tried to escape to Stalingrad, flying
low. At 450 miles an hour we chased him and ran into a wild
fire of light flak. I gave my corporal a free hand to attack. He
pounced on his prey like a hunting dog but missed the circling
Russian by yards and in his eagerness got directly in front of
him. The Russian saw his chance instantly, tore after him, fired
—and at the same moment fell a prey to my last, already un-
steady burst. The Russian plane reared up, fell, hit, and exploded.

That was my fourth engagement of the day and that air
battle alone lasted ten minutes. My eyes burned, my head
ached, my shirt stuck to my body. I had had enough and wanted
to get home. But just then I discovered why the Russian had
sacrificed himself. Thirty Russian bombers and about sixty
fighters were over Kalach flying to attack our base. They
would reach it in barely ten minutes. When we had started
out from the base some forty JU-52's, the best part of our
transport fleet supplying the Stalingrad army, was lined up in
close order. A bomb in the middle of these would cut off several divisions. For four to five minutes I raced my machine
all out to cut them off. I gave the alarm continuously over the
radio: "Attention, mass attack on Tusov, mass attack on Tusov.
All planes take off." I could already see over the Don the clouds
of dust raised by the Messerschmitts taking off. We turned and
hurled ourselves among the Russian fighters.

The battle lasted twenty minutes, thirty Germans against
ninety Russians. I had no more ammunition and could do nothing but keep an eye on my novice. The Russians were finally
driven back. Their bombs fell somewhere in the countryside.
They had suffered terrible losses. The flames of crashed aircraft rose everywhere and parachutes swayed in the air. The

ME's spun around chaotically as they landed on the base.

The pilots gathered at the squadron command post and reviewed the engagement. Thirty pilots, their angular, sunburnt faces tense, their hair blowing in the wind, were standing before their commander, "the Prince" as we call him. His head really has something of the look of those statues of medieval princes to be seen in the great cathedrals of the West. The group made a colorful picture in the red glow of the evening sun. One was dressed like a trapper in leather from head to foot, another in fur boots and shorts, a third with a colored scarf and an embroidered Ukrainian cap. One might have thought they looked a little dissipated, if one had not seen the passion and excitement of battle on their radiant boyish faces and known what this motley group had just achieved.

Forty enemy planes are down for certain, and not one of the IL-2's reached its base. I try to imagine this same discussion among the Russians. How often a whole squadron of theirs must fail to return to base. And yet they become more and more numerous and fly better from week to week. How they manage this with such losses is a mystery to me, and an even greater mystery when one sees the captured Soviet pilots who, as a rule, have dull and primitive faces. "The Russians are simply too stupid to run away," Goebbels wrote in the *Reich*. We took this as an insult to the front. But where that country gets its strength, which increases with each day of the war, I do not know. It is like the fairy tale of the clumsy giant who draws his unconquerable strength from his native earth.

This evening our old Commander Lützow took leave of the squadron. He has been appointed fighter commander of the Eastern front. Only a few weeks ago I raced behind him in a fighter-bomber in a low-level attack on the airfield of Lipetsk, north of Voronezh. When we landed I asked him: "Isn't it a strange feeling to repay hospitality this way, sir?" For it was here in Lipetsk, when the Reichswehr was training in the Soviet Union, that like so many of our oldest and most successful airmen he learned to be a fighter pilot. Lützow shrugged his shoulders and did not reply.

Our offensive in the direction of Voronezh was suddenly broken off at that time and diverted to the south toward the Caucasus. Lützow called it another brilliant idea of the Führer's. But when we were unexpectedly ordered to make another left turn, in the direction of Stalingrad, and our ground forces had been successfully separated into three parts, he no longer thought it the inspiration of a genius. And now a fourth part is on its way to Leningrad. In his farewell speech Lützow struck a very different note:

"Gentlemen, flying for fun and seeing who can shoot down the most enemy craft must stop. The position of Germany is more than critical in every respect and the position of the air force is catastrophic. During the next year the heaviest air attacks must be expected in the West. And we have only two fighter squadrons there. Every machine, every drop of gas, every hour's flying is irreplaceable. The easy ground life we are leading is irresponsible; in the air it is even more so. Every shot must go to assist the infantry, if there is no target for it in the air. Every available bomber must be usefully employed at all times."

For the first time a high officer is no longer officially joining in the ready advance distribution of laurels. He is right in what he says both about our flying for the fun of it and about the general situation. But he was not understood. The officers grumbled: "Low-level attack on the Russians? He must be crazy. One hit on the engine and the Russians have you and roast you alive. He can talk, now he does no flying himself. He talks of irreplaceable machines and attacks on Germany, and yet he wants to sacrifice us merely to raise the morale of the ground troops. They should stop hunting five hares at a time when there aren't enough troops to go round." Of course these arguments too have some justification. Low-level attacks when not undertaken in mass formation entail risks quite out of proportion to their effect. But is that a reason to fly home with our ammunition if there is no target in the air? I long ago adopted the practice of chasing transport vehicles in the Russian rear areas, if only to give target practice to the newcomers. But fundamentally the problem is insoluble. It is true that we are hunting five hares at a time: Stalingrad, Leningrad, Baku, El Alamein, and air defense in the West. But Lützow at least tried hard to break up the fog of illusion which clouds the brains of most of us.

AUGUST 30, 1942. Major Ewald, group commander and my squadron leader, gave the signal to start. The two machines raced along the runway like gazelles. After a couple of long, springy hops they were clear of the ground and in the air. Under the wings of my ME two new guns stuck out their long necks. I was curious to know what they could do.

We flew toward the Don. To the north, on the left flank of the 6th Army, the Russians were making fierce mass attacks, but without tactical mobility. Regiment after regiment of infantry was mowed down before the thin German lines. The troops give the impression of being completely demoralized. Numerous deserters paint a hopeless picture of conditions in the Red Army. These are penal divisions which, as disclosed in a captured order, were set up on the model of German penal battalions by direct order of Stalin. The order justifying the measure ran something like this:

"Many millions of our brothers and sisters are already suffering under the German yoke. Vital territories of our mother-land have fallen into the hands of the German fascist conqueror. Further retreat would exhaust the strength of our beloved mother country to the danger point. Therefore we must get rid of the disastrous idea that the surest way to destroy an opponent is to entice him farther and farther into our country and retreat possibly as far as the Urals. Such an attitude betrays only cowardice, faintheartedness, and panic. The enemy is not that strong. Comrades, the time of retreat is past! Not a square yard of our beloved motherland is to be sacrificed to the enemy. He who retreats is a traitor. Death to the German invaders!"

Together with this captured document, which was to be read to the troops as a sign of the imminent collapse of the Soviet Union, we received an order about cutting communications between Stalingrad and Kalach, that loop between the northern and southern arms of the pincers with which we were reaching for Stalingrad. For this engagement, according to the words of our commander, all the tanks and armored vehicles in the region of Stalingrad were to be concentrated—seventy in all.

"One hundred and seventy or seven hundred, sir?" I corrected, certain that he had misread the number.

"Don't contradict me," he snapped, "I can read!"

"I respectfully beg your pardon, sir," I replied, "but I cannot imagine that having reached the climax of all our operations this year and at the peak of the battle for Stalingrad and the Volga, we should have only seventy tanks and armored vehicles at our disposal. Perhaps there has been a mistake in transmission."

But inquiries showed that the figure was correct. The German tank divisions were ordered to take the offensive at the end of June 1942 without their full complement of battle-ready tanks. Moreover, the incredible marches which the Russian

12

retreats have demanded of the German troops, and which Hitler has increased by his hectic rearrangement of divisions from Voronezh to the lower course of the Don and then back again into the great bend of the Don, have further contributed to weaken the German tank force. In addition our tanks as well as planes lack the dust filters which are indispensable both in the sand of the steppes and in the desert. The engagement at El Alamein swallowed up the entire production of filters. As a result engine breakdowns have reached enormous proportions.

In the fighter force this shortage means that a fighter group of forty-two planes rarely has more than ten machines ready for combat. The German fighter force entered the war with only seven incomplete squadrons. Even now it has but slightly above eleven. So Germany, with a squadron strength of 132 planes on paper, is defended at best by five hundred available fighters on an air front of thousands of miles around Europe. The German Plane Spotting Service on the other hand, as early as the spring, counted more than two thousand enemy fighters on the southern coast of England alone.

Now we were over Stalingrad. Excited shouts in my earphones told me that not far from us the air battle had begun again. My eyes scanned the air methodically. Flags with swastikas had been laid out as signals to show us that we were flying over the front. Only ten or twenty miles away, on the other bank of the Volga, lay the Russian airfields. The Russian fighters were already piercing the blanket of clouds in a dive attack on us. One of them seemed to have lost his comrades and arrived right in front of us. Major Ewald needed only to turn in slightly to get into position to shoot. He fired, and a white trail behind the Russian showed that his engine had been hit. But Ewald was already beyond the Lagg so I turned my machine to complete the job with my three guns. The major yelled into the radio, "Leave him to me, leave him to me!" "After you,

13

Major," I replied. There was irony in this because it was not customary for us to address each other by rank when in battle. But this was not the first time that the major had played this game with me, and it was not the first time that he was too late. Before he was able to get into a firing position again, the Russian had made a belly landing and the clouds of antiaircraft fire around us showed that he had not chosen a bad place to land. But Ewald had another idea: "Einsiedel, you have three guns, set him on fire!" The belly landing of the Lagg on his own territory would not count for the major unless the machine were destroyed on the ground. Without his order I was about to attack the plane on the ground. But in my anger over such unnecessary experiments fifty miles behind the front I could not resist asking once more, "Wouldn't you rather yourself, sir . . ."

Then I fired. In the fire of my guns the Lagg broke up on the ground and went up in flames. I pulled up again. On the south side of Stalingrad where the Volga bends sharply toward the southeast, twenty or thirty small, fleet Ratas and still older Russian models swarmed like bees. We could not make out what they were defending on the ground for the Russians are masters of camouflage. There was no sense in our going for these troublesome insects. They fly too low over the dangerous light antiaircraft fire and they are too agile for our fast machines. The risk far outweighs the chances of success. But as we could see no other opponent in the air we attempted a few attacks on the swarm anyway.

The Russians flew even lower, brushed along the Volga cliffs, dived and looped over us, then turned their machines almost on the spot and came at us head on. For an instant the gun mouths flashed before us and it was only by chance that we did not collide. After one of these duels I pulled up my ME to follow a Rata from whose cloth-covered wings my shots

14

had already torn large shreds. Suddenly a stinging smell filled my cockpit. Liquid poured in a broad stream out of my right cooler. A shot had torn it open. I reached for the handle of my cutout, but this old type of machine was not yet fitted with one. Flying at two thousand feet, I could just get over the Zarepta hills. Hot oil and fumes poured out of the engine, the pistons worked harder and harder, and then with a sinister jerk the propeller stopped.

I tried gliding toward the front. One after another the small compact machines of the Russians passed me. Their shots rattled on my rear armor like gravel on a tin roof. Keeping my head down, I kicked the rudder to get out of the line of fire. Every movement meant loss of height. Antiaircraft shells hit the wings. The left gun broke off. The machine was falling. Once more I succeeded with a violent heave on the stick in pulling the plane up a little, then it hit the ground, bounced, crashed, rolled over, and came to a stop in terrifying silence.

Twice my head banged hard against the instrument panel. Half stunned and with great effort, I forced back the roof of the cockpit which had jammed tight, and jumped out onto the ground. Forty yards in front of me lay the fragments of a Russian plane, scattered in the shape of a horseshoe. From the west, against the setting sun, troops in loose formation came over the steppes, apparently infantry detached from their units. From the Russian emergency landing field, on the edge of which I had happened to come down, shots were fired at me. Ground staff came running toward me. I put up my hands.

This was the decisive moment around which our thoughts and fears had so often circled without our being able to picture it clearly.

With raised hands I awaited the Russians. My eyes turned to the west, where the sun was approaching the horizon. There,

15

fifteen minutes' flight away, my comrades would be standing on the landing field waiting for me. That was all over. Here I was alone, exposed to an unknown fate. I looked down at my leather coat, covered with oil, at my worn flying boots and pilot's gloves. Finally, I undid my belt with its pistol and handed them to the first Russian who came toward me; then I raised my hands again. Without a word he emptied my pockets: handkerchief, cigarettes, wallet, gloves—he seemed to have use for them all. Meanwhile a car approached and an officer in pilot's fur boots got out. He held out his hand. A little gold star glittered on his chest. "Comrade," he said, rolling his r's. At last I could put down my hands. Greatly relieved, I took the hand he offered me.

With the air of an expert he examined the wreck of my machine lying forlornly on the sand, with its buckled wings, bent body, and twisted propeller blades. When he saw the little white lines on the controls, and the cockades and Soviet stars, he gave an exclamation of astonishment. He counted them quickly—ten, twenty, thirty, thirty-five—then nodded his head thoughtfully, and forming the figure twenty-two with his fingers pointed to the gold star on his chest and said something in Russian. As I did not understand, he added, "I—hero of Soviet Union." Not realizing that this was an official decoration, given for special merit, I could hardly suppress a smile. But he seemed to take it for a sign of recognition, and laughed with pleasure and pride.

At that moment a truck drove up full of pilots. The men jumped out and rushed at me shaking their fists. One giant as he jumped from the truck tried to land me a blow which might have cost me several teeth, but I ducked and the fellow, carried by his own impetus, fell over me straight into the arms of the "hero" who, taking him by the lapels of his uniform, pushed him aside and gave him a dressing down of the kind one used to hear on a Prussian barrack square.

I had to take a few more knocks and blows before the first excitement died down and their interest turned to "professional" questions. Why did I have to make a forced landing? How many planes had I shot down? What decorations had I received? Was I married and where was my home? All these questions were put in broken German with laughter, astonishment, and childlike curiosity. Finally the group captain gave the order to leave, and I was taken to the command post of the landing field. Here, twenty-three steps underground, the first interrogation took place.

"Name and rank?" The group captain with the gold star put the questions himself. I hesitated. My tunic was back at my headquarters, and I had no badges on my leather jacket, nothing on me which could give away my identity. I wondered if it wouldn't be better to keep quiet about my rank and title. But from either defiance or pride I told the truth. I gave my mother's maiden name as Countess Bismarck. The officer jumped up and shouted, "Bismarck, Bismarck, Reichschancellor? You son of Bismarck?"

I explained laboriously that I was only a great-grandson. He went into the next room and I heard him telephoning, shouting the name Bismarck over and over again. Somewhat puzzled, I awaited further developments. Opposite me a pilot perched on a bench stared at me incessantly. Then he got up, grasped my left hand and raised it to his face as if he wanted to kiss it. It was my signet ring he was after. He transferred it with a quick movement to his trousers pocket, together with my wristwatch. Making a threatening gesture he left, ordering me to keep my mouth shut about this little incident.

The interrogation led to my immediate removal. Blindfolded,

I was pushed into a car, and an officer with a drawn pistol squeezed in beside me as we drove off. I managed gradually to slip the bandage off my eyes a little. The car was moving down the steep bank of the Volga and into the streets of Stalingrad, where dusk was already falling. The streets were empty and lined with smoke-blackened ruins. Through holes which were once windows the dark red glow of distant fires could be seen. In a green patch between the ruins of huge concrete buildings lay a practically undamaged Heinkel 111. I recognized the badge of the Lion squadron and wondered where my comrades had been taken.

I had to stand for hours with my face to the wall in the corner of a dreary office. One Russian offered me a chair, another knocked me off it. They questioned me again in the night. The house shook as bombs fell nearby. At last I was taken into the street where a truck and several soldiers were waiting. "You officer, I officer, we comrades!" said one of them and slapped me on the shoulder. The smell of vodka revealed his condition.

The journey seemed endless through Stalingrad that night, particularly as the Russians had their automatic pistols dug into my ribs, and I was afraid each time the car bumped that one of them would go off.

With a guard on either side I stumbled through dark passages where soldiers and civilians were copulating shamelessly. The next thing I knew I was on the wire mesh of an iron bedstead in the basement of a large tenement house. The officer who smelled of vodka was sitting in front of me. Slit-eyed Mongols and Cossacks sat on the edge of the bed beside me. The Russians were not unfriendly. Two of them spoke broken German. Again I had to answer innumerable questions about my personal life and about Germany. They had the same ideas about us that we had about them. Gradually the conversation took a political turn.

"Why do you attack us? What have we done to you? What do you want at Stalingrad?"

If only I knew, I thought, and said nothing. They waited a little and then repeated their questions. I realized that I could not get out of replying.

"We Germans have nothing against the Russians," I began cautiously. "There has never been any enmity against Russia in Germany. Against the French perhaps, and against the English, on account of the last war, but not against Russia."

"But why do you attack, why destroy everything?"

The question was not to be avoided.

"I think it is a disaster for Germany and Russia to be fighting each other. The only ones to benefit by it are the English and Americans. They have maneuvered Germany into this adventure."

I said this just to slide out of the situation. After all, I didn't want to tell them to their faces that we had come to overrun their land and colonize it. And they wouldn't like to hear of the "Crusade against Bolshevism."

The effect of my words was astounding. I had no idea I had struck a note which for years had been the official line of Soviet propaganda.

The opinion these Russians had of the English in particular didn't seem to be high, mainly on account of the delay in opening the second front. They began to interpret my words to each other and nodded in agreement. They rolled cigarettes for me in strips of newspaper, licking the end and then lighting them for me. For a moment I forgot my position and felt like an explorer who had discovered an interesting native tribe rather than a prisoner with an unknown future.

The officer was the first to disturb the peaceful atmosphere.

He plainly wanted to wipe out the favorable impression my words had made and not let sympathy be aroused for the "fascist." In a curiously singsong voice he said, "Hitler capitalist."

The words fell into the room like stones thrown into calm water. Everyone looked at me with expectation and hostility. The officer leaned toward me, breathing vodka into my face:

"You, you tell what Hitler is!" and he took hold of my coat and rocked me slowly backward and forward.

I tried to laugh and pretend indifference. For all that I care, let Hitler be a capitalist too, I thought, furious that I was to pay the bill for that.

"Oh! Hitler," I said placatingly, "maybe he is a capitalist; I don't know, but I don't think so."

At this the room broke into an uproar. They punched me viciously and pushed me onto the bed. The officer drew his pistol—which I noticed was attached to a German rifle cleaner, as if that were important—and with a face distorted with rage struck out at me.

I closed my eyes. This is the end, I thought, and had no time to be frightened. But suddenly the room was empty. Only the little Mongolian sentry remained at the door with his gun, which, with its fixed bayonet, was twice as large as he. The sight of him made me laugh. I shook with hysterical laughter until I cried.

I did not sober down until the sentry pointed his bayonet at my chest and told me to shut up. A feeling of utter forlornness came over me like lead. I tried to imagine my comrades at the airdrome standing talking about me. Did the major see me make a forced landing and know that I am alive? What will he tell my parents? A new fear seized me. What will my mother say when she hears I am missing? Surely they will all think at home that the Russians have tortured me to death. If only I could get a message through that would give them hope. Is it possible to send letters through a neutral country to Germany? Possibly through Papen in Ankara? I racked my brains. Perhaps I must be a prisoner for years, knowing that my mother is worried to death at home. How long will my imprisonment last? I remember saying in an argument with our doctor, "If we don't take Stalingrad and Baku before this winter, we shall certainly lose the war."

But victory or defeat—when will it end? That is a question I have not thought about at all clearly. "If peace suddenly breaks out," we sometimes said jokingly. For some of the more ardent fighter pilots it wasn't a pleasant prospect. Damn! Now things look quite different. What does imprisonment hold for me? How many prisoners are there already? Are there any at all? Where are the camps? In Siberia? Will we suffer the fate of "the army behind barbed wire" over again, or will it be different this time? Question after question—but no answer.

AUGUST 31, 1942. I was sent for to be interrogated again. It was a dirty barrack room with the floor deep in filth. In the middle were seated a couple of fierce-looking living caricatures of Communists as depicted in the *Völkische Beobachter*. Their caps well back on their heads, their disheveled hair falling over their foreheads, they rolled their cigarette ends from one corner of their mouths to the other. They spat sunflower seeds on the floor, drank vodka, shook their fists, brandished their pistols and whips in the air, and made a terrible din. Through all this they shouted questions at me. When I refused to name my group they slugged me and beat me with a whip. "We'll make you talk, you damned German swine."

This phrase, without the word "German," I heard from a

21

Gestapo official in 1938, when I had to give an account of my leadership of an illegal group of young people. But the Gestapo man added, "when we no longer have to be considerate."

But here they have no need to be considerate. Prisoners are outlaws today. I was a little more careful in answering the next question and no longer directly refused information. I lied, feigned ignorance, and pretended not to understand. In this way I got through comparatively unscathed.

SEPTEMBER 1, 1942. Two guards brought me out of Stalingrad and a ferryboat took us across the Volga. Beneath the trees and bushes in the valley were the Soviet supply columns, well camouflaged. A large number of officers and men gathered around me and again began the questions I already knew so well, questions that were a mixture of garrulity, hate, curiosity, and geniality. Suddenly one of the officers rushed at me and grabbed me by the collar. I did not understand what he said to the others, but roars of laughter were the answer. My guards appeared to protest but they could do nothing. Amid shrieks and bursts of laughter I was shoved into the wood and placed in front of a tree. A platoon armed with automatic pistols was lined up in front of me. Lord God, they meant to shoot me! My first thought was that no one would ever hear of my death. I did not know what to fight against most, tears or a terrible feeling of nausea. Only the hope that they might miss kept me from fainting. There were shouts, an order, the pressing of triggers, and then the world crashed around me.

When I came to, I was still leaning against the tree. I could hear nothing but I could see the coarse, broad faces of people shouting with laughter. Well-intended slaps and prods finally brought me to myself, and I fell to the ground, vomited, and began to cry without being able to stop. The Russians stood around, completely at a loss. Everyone wanted to do something for me. One man brought me water to drink, another produced a piece of melon, a third offered me a cigarette—but I wanted none of these. A feeling of complete indifference came over me. I was not even able to hate these men.

Toward evening our truck rolled over a pontoon bridge which crosses the northern arm of the Volga to Srednaia Akhtuba and over which I often flew when making low-level attacks on the nearby airfield. We stopped in a village street, and one of my companions disappeared into a farmhouse. He returned with a young officer of a type I had not yet seen in Russia, a slender young man with fine features, whose demeanor and dress could not have been better if he had been to a Western military college—a contrast to the majority of slovenly Russians I had so far seen. And he spoke German without an accent. Politely and correctly, even with a touch of friendliness, he invited me into the house. The room he took me into was clean. It had a bowl of flowers on a table, a tidy bed, another table with papers on it, two chairs, and on the wall a framed drawing of Lenin.

He opened his cigarette case. "Please help yourself. You are Count Einsiedel, Group 3, Udet fighter squadron, aren't you?"

"How do you know?" I said, amazed. "I haven't mentioned my unit to anyone."

"Oh, you're not the first of that squadron I've talked to. Your losses over Stalingrad are high."

"That depends on how you look at it," I replied. "For every one we lose we shoot down sixty of yours." This was an exaggeration. The ratio had been that favorable only in 1941. In the winter it had gone down to 1 to 30, and had risen to 1 to 40 in the four months that we had been back at the front.

The Russian shook his head. "You don't even believe that yourself. If it were true, would you have so few fighter planes

23

over Stalingrad? Anyway your figures are misleading. You can't compare your fighter losses with our losses of all types of aircraft. You'd have to count the German losses in bombers, ground attack planes, and transports."

His argument was correct of course. But why should I admit it?

"Well, why have the Germans so few fighter planes at Stalingrad?" he insisted.

"Many or few—you don't expect me to give you information on that point."

"Oh, I don't need military information from you."

He leafed through his papers and read out to me the numbers of squadrons and sections in the Stalingrad area and their average operational strength. Just over one hundred machines at most.

He laughed. "I wouldn't believe those figures at first. But they've been confirmed again and again by prisoners' statements."

"Yes, you have no scruples about interrogating prisoners; you don't draw the line at threats!"

"So you've been beaten? Well, it happens; but most of your people are so scared of being shot in the back, as Goebbels told them they'd be, that they tell everything without being asked. Actually the Germans are hardly in a position to appeal to international law!"

For a moment the officer was silent. "We'll talk about it later. Let's get back to the hundred fighters. That's very few, don't you agree?"

"It's apparently enough," I said, pointing to the open window, through which for the past few minutes the roar of engines, rattle of firing, and thunder of light antiaircraft guns could be heard, proof that yet another violent air battle was taking place in the dusk over Srednaia Akhtuba. "Over our air bases some fifty or sixty miles behind the front such things don't happen. When some ninety of your machines headed for our base recently, only twelve miles behind the front, not a bomb hit the target. And you lost forty bombers and fighters."

The Russian gestured to me to be silent. "Your army reports lie," he said.

"What army reports don't? But I took part in that particular battle and it was not the only one of its kind."

"Don't let's quarrel over such things, but answer me one question. Do you think Germany is winning the war? Think about it, for we shall talk again tomorrow."

With this I was led away with a guard on either side.

My quarters for the night were a tumble-down goat shed without roof or door, only four broken mud walls around a small square of hard earth.

September nights are bitterly cold on the steppes, but I was not allowed to move about to get warm. Once when I tried to the guards raised the butts of their guns at me. I began to feel feverish. My skin was burning and itching all over, the aftereffect of the tetanus injection I had received after my shell wound. I had spent hundreds of nights before this in the open air—from one on the northern flank of the Piz Palü at 14°F to fourteen days and nights in the hills of Lapland, in wet clothes and tormented by thousands of mosquitoes. As a boy of eleven I was sent at night to walk twelve miles through a mountain forest without map or flashlight, almost dying with fear at the sound of my own footsteps. Compared with this night, those were paradise . . .

The cold of the universe seemed to stream down upon me, concentrated from the infinite spaces of the black firmament, and the stars looked down upon me hard and aloof. ". . . the starry heavens above and the moral law within me"—my lips involuntarily formed Kant's words. Then I made a face at the stars. My teeth chattered, hunger raged in me, my body burned, and all my limbs hurt. And ideas raced ceaselessly through my brain. What an unusual young officer that was. The sort one could want for a friend. Had the Soviets many such? I was really looking forward to continuing the conversation. But what should I say to him? Of course it is the natural and obvious duty of a soldier to believe in his cause and its victory, or at least to appear to when confronted with an enemy. Most of my comrades really believed in it. But did I? And if I had doubts could I admit them? Wouldn't the Russian merely think I was trying to keep on his right side? But I wanted to know what this man, who clearly belonged to the Soviet elite, had to say to all these questions, the answers to which I didn't really know myself. To hell with regulations. This was a situation which hadn't been foreseen. I would speak as the moment dictated.

Suddenly I imagined that I saw before me the phalanx of automatic pistols, the coarse, dull faces which reflected joy at having a defenseless being in their power, the distorted mouth behind a drawn pistol, the fists and huge horsewhips of the interrogating commissars.

How would it all end? How long could it last? If only I could send a message. If only those damned stars up there could at least serve for that. Suddenly I felt the vast globe, on whose back I lay shaking and trembling, racing senselessly through black nothingness. I jumped up. Let the sentries knock me down. I had to move, get warm, and change my thoughts or I couldn't stand it any longer.

The sentries cursed and shouted and threatened me with the butts of their rifles and bayonets. I began to scream too, waved my arms about, stamped my feet, and stormed like a madman.

At this they let me alone and stood in the doorway suspiciously watching my nocturnal dance.

SEPTEMBER 2, 1942. With the rising sun came warmth, the courage to go on living, and refreshing sleep. My conversation with the young lieutenant was not resumed until the afternoon.

"Well," he began, "what do you think about the war? Will Germany win? Is it really a just war?"

I tried to think of a fitting reply.

"You must have given the war some thought. A man like you doesn't fight at the front for years without thinking about the meaning and aims of this struggle."

"The meaning and purpose of this war is to give Germany a place among the nations corresponding to her size, population, and achievements!" I finally said.

"And is war the only way to do that?"

"Apparently."

"Do you believe Germany has no choice but to make war, attack other countries, occupy and plunder all Europe—all in order to take her rightful place in the world? Do you believe that making war is Germany's mission?"

"No, I certainly do not believe that, but . . ." I named the factors which to my mind had led Germany into the Third Reich and into the war: the failure to respect her claims to equality at Versailles, unemployment, debt, overpopulation, and the inability of the Weimar regime to deal with these problems.

After I had finished he asked:

"Have you ever considered that in America, where there was no enforced Versailles Treaty, where there is a much lower density of population, where they have inexhaustible sources of raw materials and overseas export markets, they have still suffered periods of crisis as severe as those in Germany? Production fell almost as much, unemployment rose just as much. Did the Americans make a Hitler their leader because of it and begin a war?"

"No, they didn't," I admitted. "Those very facts gave them greater possibilities of overcoming their crisis."

"So you believe that the war was inevitable and necessary?"

"Whether it was inevitable and necessary I cannot say. After all, I'm not an economist or a politician. But the facts I mentioned explain it."

"So your war is a just one? You have invaded Soviet territory justly? You have justly bombarded Stalingrad, Voronezh, Rotterdam, Belgrade, and London? Justly you murder Jews, Poles, Ukrainians, Frenchmen, Yugoslavs? Or . . . ?"

"No. The war is one thing, the murders another."

"You are an officer?"

"Yes."

"A fighter pilot?"

"Yes."

"You have been in battle?"

"I have."

"How many enemy planes have you shot down?"

"Thirty-five."

"Why?"

I might have said "For Germany." But I couldn't get it out. It was too trite. No, not even trite. It was simply impossible for me to say it. But in my mind I continued this conversation started by the Russian. For Himmler and Ley? Or perhaps for Göring, in his blue silk plus fours or red boots made of Russian leather with their golden spurs? For the Reichstag fire? For June 30 or the concentration camps, or for the Gestapo and the party officials? Or for the deportation of Jews and murder of hostages? For what? Why? I didn't know the answer, and suddenly it was clear to me that I had never known it. I was twelve in 1933. As a boy I heard a great deal at home about the "Thousand-year Reich" which did not exactly increase my respect for its "great men." The conflict between the free Youth Movement and the Hitler Youth, as well as my love of criticism and taking the opposite side, did their part to produce in me a kind of basic opposition to the Nazi system.

War as an adventure and war as a political fact however were two very different things to me, about which I had never thought at one and the same time. But how was I to explain all this to the man in front of me?

The Russian watched me silently, but my eyes avoided his. It was he who broke the silence.

"Well, you have no answer. But do you think Hitler is winning the war?"

"I fear not."

"You *fear* not, so you would like him to win it?"

"A lost war is not exactly fun for any country."

"Do you suppose it would be fun for other countries if Hitler won the war?"

I shrugged my shoulders. Suddenly the whole discussion revolted me. What did this fellow really want from me? War was war; there have always been wars and always will be; just wars and unjust, wars run well and run badly. A German fights for Germany, a Russian for Russia, a Briton for the empire. It had never occurred to me to ask a captured RAF officer what he was fighting for and why. But we had drunk whisky with them and run races in the evenings with them around our bases. They were soldiers and we were soldiers, bitter enemies in the air but comrades on the ground, with a respect for each other which was taken for granted. Why wasn't it that way here? The Russian asked a few more questions. I didn't answer any more. Then he had me led away—in a perfectly matter-of-fact manner, without changing his expression, without triumph, but I felt his contempt. I returned to my four mud walls, depressed and ashamed, furious with myself, with the Nazis, with the war, and with the Russians.

Again the night seemed cruel and never-ending. I felt feverish. A painfully irritating rash had spread over my body. In the morning I managed to explain to the guard that I was sick. A medical orderly arrived with a thermometer, pills, and hair clippers, objects which I was amazed to see existed here. Then I laughed at myself. If they possessed airplanes, tanks, automatic pistols, and mowing machines, they obviously would have thermometers and hair clippers.

But when the Russian applied his clippers to the back of my neck and never stopped until he reached my forehead, I jumped up to defend myself, cursing and yelling. It was no use. I lost all my hair. Thoroughly upset, I passed my hand over my bald head. It was just as though I had been crippled and it was hours before I recovered my composure. I remembered Samson and Delilah. Now I understand why for centuries all captives have had their hair shorn, and why corporals of all armies sense mutiny when a recruit defends his hair against their hatred. Rob a man of his hair and you deprive him of a part of his personality and his self-respect.

SEPTEMBER 4, 1942. Another cross-examination. A fat, bald man, evidently a high-ranking officer, asked me to take a seat.

"Well, how do you like being with us?" he inquired ironically.

"I preferred the other side," I snapped out.

30

I did not feel at ease with this man. He might well have been a public prosecutor, one of those who enjoy crime because it gives them an opportunity to bask in the reflection of their own power. At the same time he had about him something of the monk one sees on advertisements of Bavarian breweries, his hands folded across his stomach and his tiny, laughing eyes in his round face looking out at the world with an air of self-satisfaction and piousness. By the way his inferiors addressed him I gathered that this was Colonel Tulpanov.

"Well, we didn't exactly invite you," he continued sarcastically. "As an unwanted guest, you must take what you are given."

Unshaven, dirty as I was, my hair shorn, my stomach aching with hunger, this mockery made me all the angrier.

"In the lead mines of Siberia you will have plenty of time to think about all this," he continued unrelenting.

I was tempted to say that I had hardly expected anything else, but I kept myself under control. Discretion seemed to me the better part of valor when one was up against this type of man. After this he asked particulars about me and my family; he wanted to know what relation I was to Bismarck. Then followed questions about my education, my military training, and other such matters. All of a sudden he asked what I knew about Karl Marx. I recalled vaguely that somewhere in my early school years, before 1933, Karl Marx had been mentioned in history classes. But I remembered little more than that he lived in the last century, that he was a Jew and the father of communism. The ironical smile of the fat fellow at this point maddened me. Here was I taking part in a crusade against Bolshevism, and I had no idea what it was all about. The fat, bald fellow continued his cross-examination.

"Do you read a great deal? What have you read?"

I mentioned what came to my mind: Wiechert, Binding,

Rilke, Hermann Hesse, Jünger, Beumelburg, Dwinger. Then I thought for a moment: Russian literature? I mentioned "Taras Bulba," some short stories by Lermontov and Pushkin, but Krasnov's *From the Double Eagle to the Red Flag* I preferred to leave out.

"I'm surprised how little you know of world literature," he said.

I had no time then to reflect on how unexpected it was to have a Bolshevik, of all people, examine me on my literary knowledge. But I was furious at the persistence of the man. What did he expect? I was twenty-one, with three years in the service—what should I know of world literature? I would have liked to know if Russian air force lieutenants had read any more. The few captured pilots I had seen and the stupid officers at the head of the prisoners' columns certainly didn't give that impression.

"Do you know what Bismarck thought about war with Russia?"

"Several things; at any rate he thought it would be very risky."

"Do you think he was right?"

"In his time, certainly."

"And today?"

"Very likely today, too."

"So you think Hitler will lose the war?"

"That depends on you."

"How?" he asked.

"If the war in the East is not over this year, Hitler has lost it!"

"Do you think that it will be over?"

"I can't tell what effect the possible fall of Stalingrad and Baku will have on your ability to go on fighting, but I regard it as out of the question that the war will be over."

32

"In that case, why are you fighting?"

"What has that to do with it? The German nation is fighting and believes in victory. I have known only five or ten people in Germany who didn't believe in a victory for Hitler, and my comrades simply laughed at me when I doubted it."

"Do you want to write a letter home?"

"Of course, but how can you get it there?"

"As a leaflet, if you will express your doubts about Hitler's victory in it."

"I won't do that."

"Why not?"

"It hardly needs explanation."

"You never expressed your doubts at home?"

"Among my companions, yes."

"Then why not now?"

I didn't reply. Well, why not now? It was against all military codes. But the news that I was missing would soon reach home, and then what? The last surviving son missing in the Soviet Union! It was worse than to have fallen in battle.

The man opposite me interrupted my thoughts.

"Well, if you don't want to do it, no one will force you."

I asked for time to think it over.

The guard led me back to my mud hole of a hut and left me to my thoughts. A leaflet? It would be high treason. Return to Germany so long as Hitler remained in power would be impossible after that. This was a decision which would affect my whole life. In the last war this sort of thing was unheard of. An officer of the Kaiser would not have thought twice about such a suggestion. But how could one make the comparison? In those days the Reichstag existed; peace resolutions, strikes, and antiwar demonstrations were still possible.

What would you have done ten days ago, I asked myself, if you had heard of a plot to overthrow Hitler's army? Would

33

you have denounced the men concerned? What a question! Was I to play the martyr for those madmen, those drug fiends and drunkards, for those adventurers who had become megalomaniacs, with stupidity written on their faces? I remembered how my stepfather, to the horror of the assembled family, while hanging a cheap over-life-size painting of Hitler on the wall gazed thoughtfully at it a long while and burst out: "Can't you see, all of you, how cretinous and greasy and low this fellow looks?"

And yet only five days ago I had been fighting under Hitler's flag, with the swastika on my uniform. What would the Russians think if I turned against it all now, as a prisoner of war?

I had no further time to reflect. The guard had come to take me to the room where my interrogators were waiting.

"Well, what is your decision?"

I was still uncertain. What was I to do? I couldn't tell whether it was shame or rage or my fever that was raising my temperature. Was it perhaps my own fault that there were such possibilities?

Why was there no postal arrangement for prisoners of war? Why didn't they write us off completely? Hadn't I a perfect right to do or not do whatever I thought best, now that I was entirely my own master, with no rights or laws to bind me and with no protection from my Fatherland? Even to say or write whatever I chose, in order to give my mother a little consolation and a little hope?

The Russian had put his question again and I made my decision:

"Yes, I will write it."

I sent greetings to my parents and to my friends; I said that so far I had been treated correctly; that I was of the opinion

34

that Germany would lose the war and that Bismarck's warning against a war with Russia had once again been confirmed.

As I left the room the Russian gave me his hand: "Auf wiedersehen," he said.

I did not reply.

Chapter Two / Antifascists

OCTOBER 1, 1942. I tried to keep my balance on the rough path through the boggy wood, bent double by the weight of an extremely heavy sack. There were twelve Italian officers in front of me, all equally laden, equally tired, equally miserable and weary. Behind me walked the guard with the butt of his gun raised, swearing furiously. "Son of a bitch! Get going, faster!"

Red rings began to dance in front of my eyes. The blood hammered in my temples and the infected wound which I had received on August 24 was very painful. I thought I would count another hundred steps and then throw my sack into the bog and myself with it. But then I found myself counting another hundred and yet another. Finally we reached the edge of the wood and dragged ourselves up a little hill. The leader of the convoy ordered, "*Stoi!*—Halt!"

With a sigh of relief the thirteen of us sank to the ground. We closed our eyes and gulped air into compressed chests. It was some time before the first one pulled himself up to roll a cigarette with tobacco leaves and a tiny strip of newspaper. Again we felt the pains of hunger—violent, cruel pangs which made some of the men chew anything green they could get their hands on and swallow it.

I had met the Italians on September 7 at a transit prisoner-of-war camp on the Volga, after a three-day march of 110 miles. I spent the night in the ice cellar of the camp together with two other pilots who were also suspected of trying to escape.* The following day the first group was marched away: two hundred men in columns of four, the twelve Italian officers—majors, captains, lieutenants—at the head of the columns, and in front of them all myself, the only German officer. In this way we marched straight onto the steppes, surrounded by thirty to forty heavily armed Red Army men. They drove us fifty miles in twenty-four hours. Then followed a few hours of rest in the middle of the road and a further twenty-five miles in twelve hours. Thus we reached the Astrakhan-Saratov railway line.

We lay for three days about the railway station waiting for a train. Then fifty men were squeezed into every freight car. Most of us had already contracted dysentery, and death had begun to gather its harvest. During the whole month of our move we had received only a chunk of bread the size of a fist every other day and what sugar you could balance on the tip of a knife. If we were lucky, on the train we had a mug of oily water from the engine. The dense traffic of Soviet supplies was formidable on this stretch. Our train often had to stand for hours in sidings. Trains packed with troops, arms, tanks, and other war material continually rolled past the crack of the sliding doors through which the toilet bucket was pushed.

I reproached myself for not having taken greater interest

* Fliers were especially suspect by the Russians of harboring intent to escape. *Trans.*

in ground tactics at the military academy. But even without this I was able to figure out for myself that a giant army was being transported into the Stalingrad region.

Finally this morning the officers were unloaded. There were only a few seconds to say goodby or to try to note an address or a name; then the car door was shut with a bang and our comrades rolled on. The train was taking them north, the direction in which we had been heading for the past three weeks. We had no idea where we were now. According to my calculations it ought to have been somewhere west of the Volga, but the others insisted that if this were so we would have been bound to notice when we crossed the river.

Having left the freight train, we continued a few hours in a passenger train, but soon we were all told to get out again. The guards gave us their baggage to carry, sacks of provisions heavier than we could manage—bread, sausage, sugar, fish, fat, and barley, the rations which we had not received. After walking a few more miles we reached this hill. As I let my eyes wander over the broad valley that lay open before us I wondered where we were. Vast potato fields stretched as far as the eye could see between autumn woods. Here and there a white church peeped out of the colored foliage of birches or the dark shadow of the fir trees. The smoke of the fires made by people roasting potatoes in the field rose straight as a candle into the bright autumn day. It might have been Silesia or southern Pomerania. But I tried not to think of that—homesickness can kill.

The leader of the convoy came toward us. He was wearing the blue cap of the NKVD brigade, which guards convoys of prisoners of war. "*Vot*—there it is," he said, pointing at one of the churches. "Camp, four miles; then eat, wash, shave, and sleep." He emphasized every word with appropriate gestures, so that we understood. Then he said something to the guards and we were given a meal such as we had not hoped for in our wildest dreams. But first we had to assure him that we held nothing against him, that he had treated us well, and that he was a good man.

The sacks soon disappeared into the nearby village. The guards who carried them there came back with bottles of vodka. Now we knew why we had had to go hungry. Mentally I prepared the complaint I would lay before the camp commander.

There was not a person to be seen on the road leading to the camp. The place, we had learned from a peasant boy, was the former Oranky monastery, somewhere in the neighborhood of Gorky, west of the Volga. Soon we reached the gates. We were led one by one through a small guardroom into the camp. The guards were furious because they could find nothing more on us to steal. The monastery church whose whiteness shone so invitingly at a distance now turned out to be a gloomy broken-down building which seemed to be used as a shed.

Prisoners brought wooden bowls, wooden spoons, two pots of soup and porridge. They spoke not a word to us. They moved automatically and wearily, like shadows in ragged uniforms, and looked around uneasily. Their presence made the sunlit street seem ghostly. We, the newcomers, remained silent and uncomfortable. After the meal was over a civilian came toward us. He was wearing a visored cap, and on his hooked nose was perched a pair of spectacles which had been mended with wire. In his crooked yellow teeth he held a grotesque-looking chewed and discolored pipe. The fellow wore a spotted black coat with a moth-eaten fur collar.

"All Italians?" he asked in German.

They pointed at me: "One German."

"Come with me," he ordered. "Your rank?"

"Lieutenant."

39

"Oh, an officer!" he said, and malicious pleasure rang in his voice. "You don't look so elegant. Where is your uniform? Why are you so filthy?"

At this I lost my temper. "How do you expect me to look when everything down to my handkerchief has been stolen? When we haven't washed for a month? When my hair's been shaved, and we've starved for three weeks because the guards wanted to buy vodka with our rations? They tried to shut our mouths with an end of sausage last night: I protest against this treatment."

"So you protest. What is your name?"

"Count Einsiedel."

"Oh, you're the fellow who wrote the leaflet near Stalingrad. Is that right?"

"How do you know?" I asked surprised.

"You'll soon learn how. Now go to the baths to be deloused and after that ask for me. I'm Commissar Wagner."

But I did not even get to see a bath. A guard came for me and took me into one the thick-walled buildings of the monastery. He led me to the cellar, unlocking and locking heavy iron doors, and finally pushed me into a dark cell. Thank God I was not alone. A corporal who had been given a job in the camp kitchen had been shut in here for ten days for exchanging a wooden bowl of porridge for tobacco. Now he was thanking his Creator for his punishment. It was warm in the cell, his friends in the kitchen did not forget him, he did not have to work, and here he had a newcomer to question.

"When will the war be over? Will we be home by Christmas? Will the Russians give up soon?" At first I thought the fellow must have gone mad.

"Home by Christmas? Where did you get that idea? The war will go on another few years, and who wins is anyone's guess; all that is sure is that Germany will lose it."

40

"You must be an antifascist," he said. "Where have you come from anyway?"

"What do you mean, antifascist? I am a fighter pilot, shot down over Stalingrad a month ago."

"Well, if German fighters are already over Stalingrad, the Russians are sure to be done for soon."

"Not only are German fighters over Stalingrad but the city may have fallen by now. When I was captured our tanks were outside the gates."

"There you are. So we shall be home for Christmas after all."

"All right," I said, "if you insist on believing it go on believing it, but congratulate yourself if you are home by Christmas, 1944. Tell me, though, what you mean by antifascist. And who was that with the cap and broken spectacles who speaks good German? What goes on in this camp and why didn't the others speak to us when we arrived?"

"Well, my dear man, antifascists are those who talk as you do. Those who say Hitler will lose the war, and who deal out propaganda in the camp, along with the Russians and the character with the nose. His name is Wagner, and they call him our political instructor, commissar for the prisoners. He gives out the jobs in the kitchen, and if the men say they are against Adolf then they are antifascists to him. That is why no one talks here. There are spies everywhere. If anyone spreads news of successful German offensives, he is a fascist. They also publish a paper here called *The Free Word*, but there's nothing free in it. It's all about German defeats, about another ten German divisions which have been destroyed after unsuccessful attacks. Pretty good 'unsuccessful attacks,' I call them, if they've got as far as the Volga! I think the Russians will fold up long before we die of hunger here."

"Die of hunger? Is there as little to eat here as there was on the road?"

41

"You'll see; 400 grams of bread, two bowls of watered soup, a half pint of kasha, and 20 grams of sugar. That is what you're to keep alive on."

"What's kasha?"

"Porridge made of oats or buckwheat, which is why the antifascists are called kashists here."

Of course I couldn't picture what 400 grams of bread amounted to. I had never eaten bread by weight before. The rest he had said wasn't very encouraging. So I was an antifascist because I believed a German defeat possible. At the same time I was a fascist because I had said we were outside Stalingrad. What sort of sense did that make? I couldn't figure Wagner out.

"Is Wagner a Russian?" I asked.

"No, he's a German Communist. He was in prison for murder and was rescued from Moabit prison by force."

"How do you know all this?"

"Oh, everybody talks about it."

"But why must all Communists be murderers?"

"Why try to defend them? You'll get to know what they're like soon enough. Wagner is a swine, you can tell him that from me. We'll hang him by the feet when we've won the war."

"I hope you'll have no other worries by then," I laughed.

"Who are you really and what is your rank?"

I introduced myself.

"Well, you see you are an antifascist after all."

"Why?"

"Wasn't it you who wrote a leaflet saying we're losing the war and that the Russians had treated you correctly? And you said that Bismarck was always against a war with Russia."

"How do you hear about this?"

"It was all in *The Free Word*."

OCTOBER 27, 1942. For six or seven days I was left in this cell. At night they sent for me for endless interrogations. I was told to disclose what military secrets I knew to prove my "not unfriendly" attitude toward the Soviet Union, or I would stay in that cell forever, as I had made seditious speeches in the camp. Wagner had reported my protest against the treatment during transit.

In the interrogations I continued to protest both the treatment during the move and imprisonment in the cell, though I had long since found out that it was much pleasanter to be in the cell than in the enormous, ice-cold, bug-ridden, quarantine room where the Italians had been put.

Finally I was given a room with a bed, a stove, and 200 grams of bread above the ration. Here I was to "rest" and to write down "everything I knew." To guard and serve me I had a German prisoner who was also orderly to Wagner. He was an antifascist, so he assured me. He had been deprived of his rank in the Wehrmacht for drunkenness and incivility toward a superior officer and had been assigned to a battalion made up of convicts. A Russian attack overran the battalion. Now he was passing himself off as a deserter. By profession he was a highway engineer. One day when he had forgotten to lock me in I discovered in the room next to mine plans showing German military targets which he was preparing for the Russians. They were based on information secured from prisoners.

One day this phase was over for me. As not even "friendly" persuasion had managed to extract military secrets from me, I was thrown out of my room and bed and into the quarantine room with the Italians. Three weeks later we were moved here to the general camp. Some four hundred officers are living here —Germans, Finns, Hungarians, Rumanians, Italians—in great unheated halls, painfully jammed together. Every few days somebody dies of weakness. The food borders on the minimum

43

required for survival. Hunger rules our life. Every step in the damp, cold Russian winter is an ordeal for the prisoners in their thin, ragged uniforms. Many had their boots stolen when they were captured, and have to use wooden shoes. There are almost no needles and thread to mend things that get torn during potato picking or wood chopping. Once we get wet in outdoor work our clothes may take weeks to dry again. To catch cold in this state means death. At night millions of bugs attack the sleeping men who are packed so close that most have to lie on their side.

Wagner has profited by these circumstances.* He invites

* Six years later in Germany I discovered who Wagner really was: Otto Braun, well known in the early 'twenties through a sensational lawsuit. At that time he had played a prominent part in the German Communist party and in the spy network of the Comintern. By taking advantage of the differences between the pro-German and the pro-French elements, he had managed with the aid of a few compositors of the newspaper *Rote Fahne* to undertake a house search in the home of a Russian colonel where valuable material on anti-Communist activity in Russia fell into his hands. He had stolen from the desk of the security officer of Berlin, a friend of his, the stamps for the search warrant. But he gave himself away by leaving his briefcase in a taxi. In the suit that followed he admitted he was an agent for ultra-rightist circles. The *Rote Fahne* feigned indignation. His helpers theatrically refused to sit next to him in the dock. But after serving a minimal term of imprisonment they all celebrated the success of this comedy.

Later on, Wagner was again arrested over an espionage affair, and since this time a great scandal threatened the German Communist party their men did in fact rescue him from Moabit prison and he was sent to the Soviet Union. The papers of course remained in the hands of the examining magistrate and were inaccessible to the public.

In the Soviet Union he was given various tasks to perform for the Far East but he fell into disfavor and disappeared. During the war he was brought out of oblivion again, but it was necessary for him to rehabilitate himself in some way. To do this he used corruption and oppression in order to be able to report as many "conversions" as possible.

44

everyone to discussion evenings, and those who come receive jobs in the kitchen or some other reward. When a man has got used to these favors, Wagner asks him if he would like to join the "antifascist" group in the camp. If the man refuses he is immediately deprived of his favored position. In this way one has in fact already capitulated merely by attending a single discussion evening. Near the camp there is an antifascist school where German refugees lecture on communism. From time to time we inmates of the camp are ordered to attend these lectures.

I attended one of them. It was exactly as I had imagined the soldier's councils of 1918 to be. The officer corps was represented as being one large criminal organization. The pretext for a disgusting baiting of the officers was a distorted generalizing and oversimplifying of conclusions (quite fair in themselves) about the moral corruption which the occupation of nearly the whole of Europe, race madness, and the war in general had produced.

The only result of these demonstrations is that no one who does not want to be identified with the Wagnerite antifascists would ever voice a word of criticism about the Third Reich.

NOVEMBER 4, 1942. I spent ten days in this atmosphere poisoned by espionage, envy, the luring away of friends, and the naked struggle for existence. One morning at four a Russian came and waked me.

"Get up, we're off! Transport!" he shouted. I had no preparations to make, as I was lying on my bunk in my thin leather jacket. I dragged myself to the camp gates through the ice-cold winter morning.

There were no farewells to make. It was true I had met several acquaintances from school, from the military academy,

45

and from my squadron. They had listened enthusiastically to my account of the summer offensive which made them dream of the fall of Stalingrad, of Baku, of early victory and release. But when I expressed my skepticism, and admitted I had written the leaflet without pressure, I was ostracized as a defeatist. So I parted from them without regret.

On November 3 we arrived at the Kursk station in Moscow, tired, worn, hungry, and yet eager to see the capital of the Soviet Union. Unfortunately we saw nothing but the front of the station where we spent several hours. Street urchins crowded around us and even the wrathful threats of the NKVD soldiers did not disperse them. The children stared at us with wide eyes as they chewed big crusts of dry bread. Finally a green van arrived to pick us up.

One of the men who had been here once before felt sure this meant we would be taken to a Moscow prison, either the Lubianka or the Butyrky, or possibly to a camp fifteen miles southwest of Moscow, in the industrial suburb of Krasnogorsk. When we had been on our way for some time and the prison possibilities were eliminated, we fell upon the provisions which the guards had incautiously put into our dark compartment. I got hold of the box meant for the guards, and remembered the saying "In a pinch eat sausage without bread."

When we were unloaded at the gates of the camp there was hell to pay. My nose was smeared with butter and the others were still chewing with their cheeks full. But we only laughed at the excitement of the Russians because even a prisoner cannot be deprived of what is already in his stomach.

NOVEMBER 25, 1942. Camp 27 is the transit camp for the central front and at the same time the interrogation center for the Moscow agencies. All the prisoners whom the Russians consider of any importance pass through this camp on the way to the famous Lubianka prison for thorough interrogation by representatives of the NKVD. Conditions here are scarcely better than at Oranky. But the commandant keeps corruption within bounds. There is no terrorism, no rousing the men against their officers, none of the bitter political animosity which exists in the officers' camps. The nearness of Moscow, with the occasional visit of a German Communist, the daily translations from *Pravda*, a large library, and the frequent arrival of new prisoners take our minds off daily worries.

There are some forty officers in the camp and some hundred others. There are the quarantine barracks, living barracks, hospital barracks, and mess—that is all.

Among the officers is a Captain Hadermann, organizer of the antifascist officers' group. He was an officer in the first World War and in this war was taken prisoner in July 1941, after being wounded out on patrol while in command of an artillery division. In peacetime he taught classics and German at a high school in Cassel.

The officers' group started in the spring, when it sent an appeal to the Wehrmacht urging the overthrow of Hitler and an end to the war. But only a few dozen officers joined it, although even his bitterest enemies cannot deny that Hadermann is a man of absolute personal integrity, honesty, and rectitude. I have spent many hours talking to him in the dim light of the passage in our barracks.

"The illusions most of our comrades have about the outcome of the war are terrifying," he said. "In 1941, when I was captured and we were moved farther east from Moscow, I was nearly beaten to death for expressing doubts that the Russians were taking us to meet the German army which had surrounded Moscow. Today the situation is not much better. When the day comes and our defeat is obvious to everyone, there will be

47

a painful awakening. The Nazis really knew how to convince the people that they are Germany and that Germany would perish with them. It is this that we must fight against, even as prisoners. We must try to give our comrades new purpose and new hope. Now we are laughed at and accused of being traitors. Our words and manifestoes and leaflets have no effect yet. But next year, or perhaps by 1944, the situation will be different, and then even here we will need people who will try to absorb the shock. Why shouldn't we cooperate with the Soviet Union like the greater part of the civilized world? No one can tell yet what will come of this. But the facts that we have to rely on ourselves and that our Fatherland is ruled by a criminal ready to do anything are so extraordinary that we too have the right to make extraordinary decisions."

I put forward my doubts hastily. "And what about Wagner and his kashists, his spies and deserters?"

"We shall have to guard ourselves against them as much as possible. We have no other choice. We cannot suddenly turn ourselves into Nazis and sing the "Horst Wessel Song" because of these people. The Wagners will do their work without us, but it is up to us to mobilize the decent elements and help them get the upper hand."

"A great many people have used these words to justify their capitulation to the Nazis," I replied.

"Yes, but today it is the only possible way, now that lawlessness rules. What are we to do? We can no longer appeal to international law with a clear conscience since Hitler violated it before hostilities against the Soviet. His criminal orders about the treatment of Soviet prisoners of war, civilians, Jews, commissars, and the fact that he has denied our existence here as prisoners all make for a situation which leaves us responsible only to our own conscience."

I cannot shut my ears to his arguments. I have nothing in common with the fanatical Nazis who see Germany's future irrevocably tied up with Hitler's, nor do I agree with the old and new Communists who, having lost all sense of proportion, know only one standard: the Soviet Union, wonderful; everything else, evil and bad. And yet we have to take some position, create some fellowship to make it possible to bear our imprisonment. The power which represents Germany today—and I am sure not for much longer—has already written us off. That in itself gives us the right to help ourselves. Moreover we are in the power of a state which, whether we like it or not, represents certain truths and forces that cannot in the future be brushed off with a Nazi phrase or an arrogant wave of the hand. These are the facts we have to face now that we are on our own.

If I had been killed instead of being taken prisoner, that would have been the price fate demanded for the experience of flying and fighting. I have never been afraid to pay that. But as it is, I am alive and life will continue even when the Third Reich is nothing but an unpleasant memory. Even convinced Nazis will not want to commit suicide then. So shouldn't one try to form a group that will attempt to work loyally with the Soviets, that will try to dispel the brain fog produced by the Nazis and to organize propaganda against Hitler on a broader basis, and so help the interests of the German prisoners of war in Russia? I have no hesitation about joining such an attempt. I see no "treason" in this. If anyone has betrayed Germany it is Hitler and his gang, and we have no alternative but to see things soberly and without illusion. I have therefore decided to join Hadermann's group.

DECEMBER 5, 1942. *Camp Meeting.* Subject: the reading of a special announcement by the Soviet Information Bureau. The speaker was the camp commandant, Colonel

Voronov, a broad-shouldered fellow from Siberia, a man with a "big heart" as the Russians say, a loud voice, and bearlike appearance. He pays attention to the complaints of his prisoners and keeps the corruption bearable in the camp. Some two hundred men thronged the hall expectantly, for this was the first time that a Russian army communiqué was to be read to the prisoners. The slogans for the celebration of the twenty-fifth anniversary of the October revolution still hung on the walls. "The Red Army is the most progressive army in the world!" "Death to the German invaders!"

At last Voronov entered the hall. His announcement was in fact sensational. Along the Don river and south of Stalingrad the Russians have gone over to the offensive and are reported to have encircled twenty-two German divisions near Stalingrad.

"We too will dance in the streets one of these days," Stalin said in his speech of November 6. If this communiqué is correct, his promise has come true very quickly.

But I am skeptical. When Voronov asked our opinion about the news I remarked:

"While I was being moved from camp to camp I saw something of the disposition of your armies, sir. The situation at Stalingrad called for such an operation. But twenty-two divisions surrounded sounds a little exaggerated. Perhaps they have taken prisoners from a number of different divisions and now they think that all of these have been surrounded. The Soviet communiqués about the strength of German units and their losses have always been very exaggerated."

The colonel smiled: "You are still half a fascist."

"What does that have to do with fascism?" I flared up. "I consider it simply unlikely that the German command would have failed to anticipate this danger. Any person of common sense would have seen what was coming and made plans accordingly. Surely the best attacking forces would not be left exposed to encirclement without their flanks being covered. This is not a political but a military question."

"All right," said the colonel, "we'll talk about this again in a couple of weeks."

Chapter Three / The National Committee

MARCH 4, 1943. For weeks I lay in the infirmary of Camp 27. I was brought there with maddening pains in my head and only half conscious. I lay feebly in my bunk among the other patients from Velikiye Luky, all of whom were reduced to skeletons like myself, after typhoid or malaria. The rooms were not heated. The watery cabbage soups and moldy bread froze as hard as stone. Most of the time the sick men got into bed in twos to keep each other warm and avoid freezing to death, although many a one woke up next to a corpse.

Now and again, in my lucid moments, I opened my eyes to find the white-haired woman doctor of the camp leaning over me, asking:

"How is, Einsiedel? I want you want to be well."

How kindly she cared for us, that Jewish woman whose only son had been killed in the first year of the war. With no medicines, no heat, and no means of making a proper medical examination and diagnosis, she saved many a life by kindness and encouragement.

The battle of Stalingrad was still the main subject of conversation in our sickroom. At the beginning of February Colonel Voronov had read out to us the news of the capitulation of the 6th Army near Stalingrad and had given the names of some twenty generals and several dozen colonels who were said to have been taken prisoner. As early as December about seventy Rumanian staff officers had arrived in the camp and had told us news which did not make the Russian successes sound so improbable after all. Later Hadermann had gone to the Stalingrad front, together with several German émigrés and two comrades, to give propaganda support to the Soviet proposals that the 6th Army capitulate. But in the camp we continued to have our doubts about the scale of this battle. Surely 300,000 men, twenty-two divisions, could have broken through any encirclement if they had only wished to? If Russian superiority had made this no longer possible, not all the generals would have survived the collapse of their divisions. Never before had this happened in a Prusso-German army.

"I would have to see the generals before I could believe it," I said to Voronov when he spoke to me after that meeting.

He merely laughed at me. "Their arrival has already been announced; they are coming here."

And so they did.

An orderly entered our room to report that the Stalingrad generals and three hundred officers of the 6th Army had arrived in the camp. I was too weak to get excited over something which only four weeks ago I had considered impossible.

One of my roommates was scraping almost half an inch of ice off the windowpane with a knife. With the help of some companions I was able to sit up and get a glimpse of the road leading to the camp. What I saw was a spectacle both weird and grotesque. With large, energetic gestures and radiant laughter the generals entered their quarters, glittering with medals

53

and monocles, fur coats and walking sticks, scarlet linings to their coats, and boots of felt and the best leather. Only here and there in this colorful and elegant picture could be seen a gray patch, the stooping figure of an old inmate of the camp, in a ragged Russian jacket and torn German uniform, rags tied with string on his feet instead of shoes, his face exhausted and lifeless as he gazed at the ground.

We learned that these generals had been brought from Stalingrad to Krasnogorsk in a special train with sleeping cars and white sheets on their berths. We old prisoners listened incredulously to the tales of abundant condensed milk, butter, caviar, and white bread during their transfer to the camp. Nevertheless several of the new arrivals were already infected with typhus.

I caught sight of a stack of huge pieces of luggage, among which were several trunks of the type used in the Mercedes cars made especially for the higher officers. The wretched prisoners nearly broke down carrying these trunks to the rooms of the generals. I fell back into my bunk. Another attack of fever relieved me of the trouble of thinking about what I had seen.

MAY 6, 1943 . During the past weeks, while I was slowly recovering from my illness, two things have happened which pointed to a new stage in the development of the antifascist groups in the camp. In the prisoners' paper, *The Free Word*, there appeared a report of an illegal peace conference in West Germany at which, it was rumored, representatives of all classes and all opposition groups decided on a program of joint action against Hitler. To judge by its tone, this report was written by German Communist émigrés in Moscow. It set off a wave of meetings in the prison camps during which the idea of a people's front against Hitler was for the first time put forward in concrete form as a subject of discussion.

Soon after that the Russian camp commissar, Major Stern, visited me in the infirmary. He asked me to make a declaration pledging myself to work sincerely with the Soviet Union in the fight against Hitler. I had no hesitation about giving such a written declaration, as under the circumstances there were no other means of fighting Hitler. Major Stern also advised me to do all I could to get into conversation with the Stalingrad officers. It was important, he said, to exploit the shock they had suffered in their defeat at Stalingrad, in order to win them over to political action against Hitler.

But there is no question of my doing this. I am the only officer already in the camp known to be a member of the antifascist group, so I am ostracized by the officers from Stalingrad. To return my greetings or to talk to me is considered a major offense against their esprit de corps. Even those officers who severely criticize Hitler's way of conducting the war, and in particular his treacherous behavior toward the Stalingrad army, never even consider discussing the possibility of an active rising against him. The extremely crude approach of some of the antifascist functionaries reinforces this attitude. But the teachers at the antifascist school, which has now been moved nearer to Camp 27, consider their "educational efforts" most successful when their scholars march past Paulus and his generals into the camp singing the "Internationale" and yelling wild abuse.

Meanwhile Moscow has obviously long intended to win over Paulus and his companions for political action against Hitler.

JUNE 2, 1943. The generals and nearly all the officers were moved from Camp 27 in the middle of May and transferred to the famous old Suzdal monastery, about 180 miles from Moscow. Up to now this had been reserved for Rumanian, Italian, and Hungarian prisoners. Only a small group of officers remains in Camp 27, though their number is continually enlarged by those whose interrogations at Lubianka prison are finished.

Winter, hunger, cold, disease and the danger of epidemics, together with the spiritual oppression which the silent treatment of the Stalingrad officers exercised on me, have become a nightmare of the past. The camp is quiet and peaceful again. The sun shines on the street. The other side of the fence there is a small lake, and on its beach the young people of Krasnogorsk frolic just as we used to do at home. I have nearly recovered from my illness and can do ten kneebends again without everything turning black before my eyes.

But anxiety about the future and about the fate of my country remains. It is clear that from now on defeat will approach with increasing speed. But what will the end be? Stalingrad showed the lengths to which Hitler's obstinacy will go. Is he really determined to fight with the remnants of the last German battalion on the ruins of the last German city?

On both sides hatred, bitterness, and the desire to destroy are bound to increase with every day of the war, and with them the sacrifices which war exacts. Is there really nobody in Germany who can put a stop to it, now that the madness is becoming apparent? There is only one group that is in a position to make such an attempt—the officer corps and the High Command. They control the armed forces and have an accurate view of the situation. They have the organization and the education which make it their duty to act. Or was Stalingrad, which was an example of unconditional surrender to the orders of Hitler no matter what the consequences, the final act of a drama that began with the murder of Schleicher, the drama of

56

the gradual capitulation of the Wehrmacht to the party?

Even here in camp very few have voiced indignation against the dictator, under the impact of their experience. Most of them consider the sacrifice of the 6th Army entirely justified morally and militarily. They even believe in Hitler's "star of destiny," in new victories and new German offensives. One day a Russian bomber making a trial flight from the nearby factory airfield left a trail of smoke behind as it circled. Some of the antiaircraft officers asserted that it was a German scout plane marking targets in industrial Krasnogorsk for the long-range German artillery. Nobody contradicted this utter nonsense. A major of the army personnel office assured me, amid the applause of those who were listening, that as yet Germany had touched Russia with only one finger but now after total mobilization she would strike with her whole fist. I would be surprised at how quickly I would find myself on the gallows.

If this sort of big talk is going on inside Germany too, there can probably be no hope of opposition on the part of the generals and officer corps.

I have found refuge from these dark thoughts in Marxist and Leninist books in our camp library. Last winter Hadermann prepared a kind of scheme for my studies so that I could find my way more easily. What impresses me most in this course of reading is the consistent way in which world history, in particular the history of the past hundred years, is strung on the red thread of technical and economic development. It is true that I lack the comprehensive knowledge of history which would enable me to judge whether all the factual material on which these theories are based is puncture-proof. But my knowledge is suddenly coming alive in this closed picture of history. I have been literally shaken by the analyses which Engels and Lenin make of their time, by their conclusions which often border on prophecy, and by the predictions they build on these foundations.

At last I have found an answer to the question which has figured in hundreds of talks, discussions, and arguments about the Nazis: was the war inevitable? Could Germany not have found some other way of overcoming the 1929–32 crisis instead of attempting to obtain the military and political power she wanted by force of arms?

Nobody was able to answer this. And the inability to give a clear and unambiguous reply to this question was the fundamental cause of our disastrous inconsistency in excoriating the Nazis while fighting their war with all our energy.

Whether or not the social experiment in the Soviet Union has been successful or will be, we Germans have lacked the Marxist concept of society needed in order to fight the Nazis effectively. We have also lacked such a positive aim as the Communists have, as well as a practical idea of how to master the problems of internal and external power politics and crises and mass unemployment. Moral indignation alone is no basis for fighting Nazism, especially if one has no better alternative to offer.

That is why I find the Communist ideas so convincing. To be honest, I have to admit I am completely defenseless against them. I see no force and no idea with a more positive, more realistic conception of the future. The church? Democracy? But have they been able to alter or prevent the catastrophes which have swept across the world? Is there any sign that they could do anything from now on? I see none.

The one fact that keeps troubling me is the terrible similarity in so many things of the Soviets to the Third Reich: their penetrating propaganda, which surpasses all the nationalistic banalities of the Nazis in tastelessness; the fanaticism with which they

58

too cling to their preconceived ideas, the indoctrination to which one is exposed, the leveling and pulling everything down to the primitive masses, the undue influence of party favorites, and the corruption which prevails everywhere.

Of course it is difficult to evaluate things from the perspective of a prison camp. I am inclined to look for excuses for all this. Even before I was taken prisoner I was upset by the hate and arrogance of the many officers who saw only the bad sides of the Soviet Union. Now they sometimes force me to the opposite extreme.

One can't overlook the fact that much of what we disapprove of here is to be ascribed to the earlier history of the social system in Russia, to the centuries-old stagnation of this vast land mass. It was bound to take time for the revolution to produce a new elite, a true class of leaders. The Soviets are changing greatly now during the war. They recognize the cultural values of the past and are abandoning the "revolutionary" leveling process. The restoration of shoulder insignia in the army, the invocation of Kutuzov, Suvorov, Peter the Great, and Ivan the Threatening (as the Soviet now interprets "Ivan the Terrible") are only a few signs of this change of attitude.

I believe that if the Soviet Union has a breathing space after the war to let her catch up with economic, technical, and cultural progress in the West without having to live in constant fear of being crushed by an overpowering capitalist coalition, she will herself become more liberal both intellectually and ideologically. It is surely the aim of communism to abolish the state entirely in the end, and with it the secret police, the party, the army, and the Ministry of Propaganda.

If the Communists and Social Democrats had come to power in Germany in 1933 instead of Hitler, their problems would have been much smaller than those that faced the Communists in Russia in 1919. A great deal depends on the extent to which

59

the intelligentsia support the revolution rather than bleed to death in a struggle against it. Maybe it is necessary to overcome one's natural aversion to the primitive, brutal, and uneducated masses in order to raise them to a higher level.

These thoughts torment me now. If only I had someone to talk to, someone who is above the battle.

JUNE 17, 1943. A few days ago two Communist émigrés, Walter Ulbricht and Erich Weinert, arrived in camp. They invited some of the officers to a meeting: Lieutenant Colonel Bredt, a former member of the Stahlhelm and official of the Pan-German Society; a Major Schulz who once went to America as a journalist; an export merchant, Major Büchler; the archeologist Dr. Greifenhagen; a former test pilot from the Luftwaffe testing ground in Rechlin; air staff officer Trenkmann; a Captain Dommaschk, a cavalry officer with a high decoration; myself, and a few others. They were mostly men who take a sober view of the situation in Germany and who, without being declared antifascists, have taken part in the political discussions and meetings organized by the teachers and pupils of the antifascist school at the camp.

The Communists put forward their plan for a national committee to unite people of all political persuasions, professions, and classes in common action against Hitler and to organize a resistance movement of all Hitler's opponents inside Germany by means of broadcasts, newspapers, leaflets, and sending men through the front.

Endless discussions have begun among the participants. Most of the officers think the proposals of the Communists much too far-reaching. Their idea is rather to foster common interests among the prisoners. They propose to reintroduce the salute in camp, make lists of officers killed (other ranks are not mentioned), arrange for mail to and from Germany; these are the points of their program. "Against Hitler and for a democratic republic!" sums up their political aim. The word "fight" is carefully avoided as anarchistic and an invitation to civil war. Ulbricht, who lacks all sensitiveness and skill in negotiation, nearly broke up the discussion several times with his monotonous repetition of Communist dictums. Finally Weinert, thanks to his greater powers of conciliation, succeeded in persuading the officers to draft a manifesto, which is to be the basis for this committee, and to call a meeting of prisoners. At this meeting we solemnly agreed to the text of the manifesto, which is to be published in *The Free Word*. But at this point most of the officers withdrew their signatures. All of a sudden they became terrified of so much high treason.

JULY 2, 1943. The proposal to found the committee has been published. It carries the signatures of Hadermann and several other antifascists, who, however, know nothing of their signatures appearing nor of the "historic initiative" which they have taken, for they are away visiting other camps to seek support for the committee.

When I asked one of the teachers at the antifascist school what the reason for the hurry was he replied that it was feared in Moscow the Western allies might anticipate the Soviet Union with such action.

A few days ago the first groups of antifascists from the camps arrived at the school to organize the committee. "Delegations," they call them. But who is to delegate? The officers' camps are against the committee and what the attitude is in the soldiers' camps nobody knows. Behind the delegates' ready consent to almost any political resolution and their signatures to anti-Hitlerite appeals lies mostly profound indifference or even despair resulting from the difficult conditions in the camps.

Hadermann is back from Suzdal. He visited me in Camp 27 and asked if I was prepared to accept possible election to the board of the committee. He said that he had proposed me and the Communists had no objection, but I was to consider whether I wanted to expose myself this way. Naturally I did not say no. At last something is happening. Whether we shall be able to achieve much through a committee the gods know, but at any rate it is an attempt to save what can still be saved.

JULY 6, 1943. Yesterday I was moved to the antifascist school where the other future members of the committee are. There are a few lieutenants who have already completed a course at the school and have become declared Communists, a number of delegates from the soldiers' camps—mostly former officers of workers' parties—and a few majors and captains from the three officers' camps: Heinrich Homann, artillery officer, son of the head of Rickmers Shipping Company, and a student corps man; two engineer majors, Karl Hetz and Herbert Stösslein; Captain Fleischer, an auditor from Brunswick; Fritz Rücker, a high-school teacher from Berlin; Major Krausneck, a bank officer and former member of the Stahlhelm; and finally an active young Captain Stolz.

They report from the officers' camps that after unbelievable hardships and hunger the 2,500 officers of the Stalingrad army have reached the Oranky and Yelabuga camps. Typhus raged for months in these camps and not over half their inmates survived the epidemics, the transports, and the starving. The death rate declined only when winter was over and camp rations were suddenly increased in April and May. The bread ration went up to 600 grams. The officers received up to 70 grams of butter and 60 of sugar per day, and here and there the other ranks got at least 20 grams. Condensed milk and powdered eggs were distributed to the sick. The quantity of other foods also went up. It is rumored that these measures were by direct order of Stalin, who after the fall of Stalingrad asked for a report on the conditions in prisoners' camps. Several NKVD officials are said to have been liquidated as scapegoats for the enormous death rate in the camps. Rumor has it that the entire administration of the Frolov camp was court-martialed and received draconic punishment. Out of 5,000 prisoners in that camp almost 4,000 died within a few weeks. The farther the camps are from Moscow the less living conditions supposedly have improved. When conditions got better the death rate among Stalingrad prisoners suddenly shot up, since the emaciated bodies could not stand the sudden increase of food.

According to accounts of survivors on which there is a good amount of agreement, out of 90,000 officers and men who were taken prisoner 60,000 now lie in mass graves at Stalingrad. Even the most favorable calculations count 15,000 survivors at most. With the exception of some higher staff officers, the prisoners were mostly so enfeebled and infected with every sort of disease when they were captured that they could not stand the hardships of the first few weeks. In addition, the entire Stalingrad area had been razed and there was no shelter. The nearest undamaged railway stations were over sixty miles away. In view of the German refusal to accept any invitation to capitulate and the order to fire on Soviet officers carrying flags of truce, the Soviet Supreme Command apparently felt justified in making no arrangements for caring for large numbers of prisoners. Conditions got a little better after the typhus epidemic declined, in May and June. The improvement in the food helped the men to regain some of their strength.

According to the reports of the officers from Oranky, the proposal to found the National Committee met with icy refusal. Wagner stirred up unquenchable hatred among the prisoners of 1941–42 with his terrorization and corruption, and their attitude naturally affected the Stalingrad officers much more quickly than the propaganda of the antifascists and the Russians.

In Camp 97, Yelabuga, which consists only of Stalingrad officers, an antifascist group has just been formed. So far only a few dozen officers out of eight hundred have joined it.

Captain Hadermann went personally to Camp Suzdal. But although—or perhaps because—the officers here, who are mostly staff officers, have been treated far the best by the Russians and can hardly complain of their living conditions, the proposal met with little response. The outbursts of anger against Hitler in the first weeks and months of captivity have long been forgotten. Summer and the higher sun have also raised hopes of further offensives by the Wehrmacht, which crystallize in crazy rumors. Some even hear at night the artillery fire of the approaching front.

A man who met with even less success at Suzdal than Hadermann was Professor Arnold, a secret official of the Comintern, about whose origin and past nobody knows anything. He is a little hunchback with a moist voice and queer-shaped, crooked head. His external appearance and the fact that he is a Jew were enough to make him ridiculous from the start in the eyes of the officers. His unquestionable knowledge of recent and present-day German history and his brilliant analyses of Adolf Hitler's politics and strategy did not help him. The overwhelming majority of the officers are far too convinced of their own glory to let themselves be involved in the intellectual effort of a serious political discussion. Those who possess more insight let themselves be led by the majority.

The presence of the generals in Suzdal contributed no little

64

to this sharp refusal, though they are by no means as united in their attitude as they pretend to be. The former president of the Supreme Military Court, Colonel General Heitz, has now become leader of a strong Hitlerite group; and the young divisional commander, Lattmann, who at the artillery school at Jüterbog was known to have been an emphatic National Socialist, is his righthand man. During a fierce argument with some of the generals who referred to Hitler in private conversation as a criminal amateur, Lattmann said: "Since we did not revolt before, we have no right to make accusations now that things have gone against us." They all unanimously reject the ideas of the committee. Quite apart from their objection, on principle, that to break their oath to Hitler is incompatible with an officer's honor, they subscribe to Field Marshal Paulus' view that it is impossible to have a clear picture of the situation from a prison camp. It is not beyond possibility that Hitler could bring about a draw or succeed in splitting up the alliance against him. But even if neither of these happened, action against Hitler should be left to the commanders inside Germany.

Our counterarguments that Hitler has betrayed the German people a hundred times over and that the oath taken in his name should no longer be binding were all useless. They also refused to listen to our argument that only a non-Nazi Germany might perhaps succeed in making capital out of the differences between the allies, and that it is utter nonsense to hope for a draw in view of the crushing superiority of England, America, and Russia. We tried in vain to show that the commanders inside Germany must be spurred on to action against Hitler and given psychological support in order to destroy the fatal Hitler myth and tell the German people the truth about the actual military situation. It is of supreme importance, we said, by our example to encourage all opponents of Hitler—of no matter what persuasion—to united action, if an attempt to overthrow Hitler is to be successful. But our arguments were dashed against the wall of illusions which the generals and officers have built around themselves, and against their fear of responsibility.

Who are these people who have suddenly found themselves at the antifascist school to take part in setting up the committee? I had not previously met the Communist lieutenants at the school. Charisius, a fighter pilot, and Reyher, an old sergeant of the Reichswehr who later commanded an engineer company, helped to start the antifascist officers' group. Berndt von Kügelgen, a journalist; Kehler, a postoffice employee; and a flight lieutenant, Willms, all passed through Wagner's hands.

Major Homann is a witty and charming talker. The Hamburg business circle from which he comes was never very keen on Hitler's economic autarchy and war politics. They knew they would have to foot the bill in any case. Moreover Homann belonged to a regiment where opposition to the party was particularly strong among the officers.

Captain Fleischer seems a skeptic and a pessimist by nature, besides being a walking encyclopedia of economic statistics. He is a member of the Democratic party and has long thought that Hitler's amateurishness would end in catastrophe.

Rücker and Krausneck I already know. They were commander and adjutant of a Landsturm battalion and were captured at Velikiye Luky in January.

"My wife always said I'd have to bleed for Hitler someday!" Rücker told us in his strong Berlin accent when he and Krausneck arrived in Camp 27. With boots far too big for him, fogged spectacles perched on a huge nose, visored cap and winter cloak, he looked like a little gnome. The sight of him both dismayed and amused us.

"They spat at me when I refused to hoist the swastika at

school," he continued, "because I was a 'November criminal' *
and a Social Democrat too. They spat at me and threw me out."

Although their battalion had not even been sufficiently
trained or equipped to defend the railway lines in France, it
was sent into action against a squadron of tanks. Before they
had time to realize what was happening or had recovered from
the first shock, these two World War I veterans found their
battalion overrun and the Russians in the middle of their units.
So it was an easy matter to win them over to the antifascist
group in Camp 27.

The two Communist deserters, Hans Zippel and Max Emmendörfer, and a young high-school teacher, Dr. Kertzscher,
are by far the most intelligent men in the ranks that the teachers
at the antifascist school have chosen for the committee.

The date fixed for the meeting to set up the committee is
July 12–13. In spite of this, no one is quite clear with what
political platform the committee is to step before the public.
The Communists brought a draft proposal with them from
Moscow, but its phrasing and slogans are more suitable for a
soldiers' council or a Communist party meeting than for a national committee for free Germany. Those officers who are not
declared Communists sharply rejected the draft. After vehe-
ment arguments between the representatives of the non-
Communist officers and the Communists, the text was finally
agreed on. As a result of the arguments, strong emphasis was
placed on the desire for national self-preservation, as against
Hitler's catastrophic politics and strategy; Stein, Clausewitz,
and Yorck were invoked; and an emphatic demand was made
to preserve the army, shun Weimar, and drop all the slogans

* A term used by the monarchists and extreme rightists at first for
the revolutionaries of 1918, as well as the Social Democrats and Communists, and later for all republicans. *Trans.*

of class war that are not connected with the punishment and disowning of war criminals.

Curiously enough, the Russians show much more understanding for these demands than the German Communist émigrés. In general the émigrés display an astonishing lack of feeling and comprehension of the situation in Germany. They are, for example, living under a complete illusion as to the strength of the illegal workers' parties in the Third Reich. I even read a statement of Dimitrov's in which he said that the civil war in Spain proved the fascist armies were not in a position to undertake large-scale military action because they would use their weapons to fight their own oppressors and exploiters. Such preconceived ideas are the origin of the completely false conception the Russians have of the relationship between officers and men in the German army. The émigrés greatly underestimate the changes of social views and problems which have taken place in Germany since 1918 or 1933. They cannot understand that the Third Reich brought with it a good deal of socialism, that the younger officers were not educated in select schools but in the Youth Movement and the Hitler Youth, and that the much-talked-of class consciousness of the workers has to a large extent disappeared. Thus in their judgment of the situation they have become victims of their own propaganda. Instead of analyzing the facts, as their eminent predecessors did, they project their preconceived tenets, which they imagine to be true Marxism, into these facts.

This is how it happened that at an officers' meeting in Oranky that old parliamentarian and public speaker, Ulbricht, was made fun of when he brought out in his Saxon dialect his eternal phrases about Thyssen, Pönsgen, and Zangen and "the watchdogs of monopolistic capitalism." He cannot understand that even with the best will in the world the officers can have no idea what he means by this catch phrase; it would take a knowledge of Marxist teaching that few possess. Furthermore, the refugees cannot understand that every reminder of the Weimar Republic produces an instant violent reaction in most Germans. Weimar is for most of them the symbol of a weak, aimless society, lacking in force and backbone, which justly came to an ignominious and inglorious end.

JULY 13, 1943. The National Committee has been founded. Yesterday and today three to four hundred people gathered in the hall of the local soviet in Krasnogorsk, which had been decorated with black, white, and red flags. The Communist émigrés from Moscow, the future members of the National Committee chosen among the prisoners, students from the antifascist school, the "delegations" from the camps, the Russian midwives of the committee—Professor Arnold, Lieutenant Colonel Janson (head of the antifascist school), Major Stern, and several other officers from the Politburo—were all present. There were also some "sympathizers" from Camp 27, remnants of the original group of officers which backed out so ignominiously, now reinforced by Colonel van Hooven, the communications officer of the 6th Army; Colonel Steidle, a member of Catholic Action; and Major von Frankenberg, one of the most experienced pilots in instrument flying in Germany.

After long speeches of greeting, the text of the manifesto of the National Committee was finally read out:

MANIFESTO:
OF THE NATIONAL COMMITTEE FOR FREE
GERMANY TO THE WEHRMACHT AND
THE GERMAN PEOPLE

Circumstances demand that we Germans make an immediate decision. The National Committee for Free Ger-

69

many has been formed in this hour of supreme danger to Germany's existence and Germany's future. Workers and writers, soldiers and officers, union men and politicians, men of all political and ideological views, who only a year ago would not have thought such an alliance possible, have today joined the National Committee. The National Committee expresses the thoughts and the will of millions of Germans at the front and at home to whom the fate of their Fatherland is of vital concern.

The National Committee feels itself justified and considers it its duty to speak clearly and unsparingly, as the situation demands, in the name of the German people in this hour of destiny.

Hitler is leading Germany to destruction.

At the fronts:

The defeats suffered in the past seven months are unparalleled in the history of Germany: Stalingrad, the Don, the Caucasus, Libya, Tunis. Hitler alone is responsible for these defeats and yet he continues to stand at the head of the Wehrmacht and of the German Reich. Scattered over thousands of miles of front, the German armies are far from home, supported by allies whose fighting capacity and reliability were dubious from the beginning, and exposed to the mighty blows of a coalition which is gaining in strength every week. The English and American armies are knocking on the gates of Europe. Soon Germany will have to fight on all fronts at the same time. Encircled by superpowerful opponents, the already weakened Wehrmacht will not and cannot resist much longer. The day of collapse is approaching!

At home:

Germany has today become a scene of battle. More and

70

more towns, industrial centers, and shipyards are being
destroyed. Our mothers, wives, and children are losing
their homes and belongings. The free peasants have been
deprived of their rights. Total mobilization is ruining the
artisan and the tradesman and sapping the working people's
health and strength.

Without consulting the people, Hitler has been preparing this war of conquest for years. Hitler has isolated Germany politically. He has not scrupled to provoke the three
greatest powers in the world and unite them in inexorable
war against the Hitler regime. He has made the whole of
Europe into an enemy of the German people and sullied
his nation's honor. He is responsible for the hatred which
surrounds Germany today.

No external enemy has ever brought as deep misfortune
upon Germany as Hitler.

The facts speak for themselves. The war is lost. Germany can drag it on only at the cost of irreparable sacrifices and deprivations. To continue a hopeless battle would
mean the end of the nation.

But Germany must not die! It is to be or not to be for
our Fatherland.

If the German people continue to let themselves be led
toward destruction without will and without resistance,
they will become not only weaker and more impotent
every day but also more and more guilty. Then it will be
possible to overthrow Hitler only with the help of foreign
arms. This would mean the end of our national freedom
and of our state. It would mean the breaking up of our
Fatherland. And we could blame nobody but ourselves.

If, on the other hand, the German people pull themselves
together in time and prove by their deeds that they really
want to be a free people and that they are resolved to

liberate Germany from Hitler, then they will have gained the right to decide their own fate and to be heard in the world. This is the only way to preserve the freedom and the honor of the German nation.

The German people need and want immediate peace. But nobody will make peace with Hitler. Nobody will even negotiate with him. It is therefore the urgent task of our people to form a truly German government. Only such a government will enjoy the confidence of the people and of their former enemies and it alone can bring about peace.

Such a government must be strong and must have the necessary power to render harmless the enemies of the people, Hitler and his backers and protégés; to put an end ruthlessly to the terror and corruption; to produce a stable government worthy to represent Germany abroad. This can be achieved only if all classes join in a struggle for freedom assisted by fighting groups who unite to over- throw Hitler. The patriotic forces in the army must play a leading part in this battle.

Such a government must break off the war immediately, must withdraw the German troops to the borders of the Reich, and enter into peace negotiations renouncing all conquered territory. In this way it will bring about peace and will lead Germany back into the society of nations having equal rights. Only then will the German people have the chance to prove their national will in peace and to reconstitute their sovereignty.

Our aim is a free Germany
This means:
A strong democratic state which has nothing in common with the impotent Weimar regime, a democracy which

will ruthlessly smother any attempt to revive conspiracies against the people's right to freedom or against the peace of Europe.

Complete elimination of all laws based on national and racial hatred and all institutions of the Hitler regime which dishonor our people, as well as abolition of all coercive laws of the Hitler era against freedom and human dignity.

The restoration and expansion of political rights and of social gains for all who work; freedom of speech, freedom of the press, freedom to organize, freedom of conscience and of religion.

Freedom of enterprise in commerce and industry; a guarantee of the right to work and to possess legitimately acquired property; the return to their rightful owners of property stolen by the National Socialist rulers; confiscation of the wealth of those responsible for the war and of war profiteers; the re-establishment of trade with other countries as the healthy basis of a secure national prosperity; immediate release and compensation for all victims of the Hitler regime; a fair, unsparing trial of all war criminals, war leaders, those behind the scenes and their helpers who have caused Germany's ruin, guilt, and disgrace. Amnesty, however, to all supporters of Hitler who have showed by their deeds that they broke with Hitler in time and joined the movement for a free Germany.

Forward, Germans, toward a battle for a free Germany!

We realize that sacrifices are inevitable. But the more determined the battle against Hitler the smaller they will be. The sacrifices in a battle for the liberation of Germany will be a thousand times smaller than the senseless sacrifices which a continuation of the war will demand.

German soldiers and officers on all fronts!

You have the weapons! Keep your weapons! Under

leaders conscious of their responsibility, who are united with you in the fight against Hitler, be brave and make your way toward home and toward peace.

Working men and women at home! You are the majority! Use this for organized action. Form battle groups in the factory, in the village, in the labor camp, in the universities, wherever you come together! Do not follow Hitler any longer! Do not allow yourselves to be exploited to help prolong the war. Fight with every means in your power, each in his own way, in his own place, in civic and economic life!

We have a great example in our history. One hundred and thirty years ago when German troops were fighting on Russian territory, the best of Germans, von Stein, Arndt, Clausewitz, Yorck, and others, called upon the conscience of the German people to fight for freedom, addressing them from Russia over the heads of treacherous leaders. Like them, we shall devote all our strength and even our lives to promote the struggle of our people for liberty and to hasten the fall of Hitler. The battle for a free Germany requires courage, action, and determination. Above all courage. Time is short. Quick action is required. Those who continue to follow Hitler out of fear, faintheartedness, or blind obedience are cowards and are helping to drive Germany toward national catastrophe. Those who place the requirements of the nation above the Führer's orders and who devote their lives and honor to their people will act courageously and help save their Fatherland from deepest shame.

For our people and our Fatherland! Against Hitler and his war! For immediate peace! For the salvation of the German people! For a free and independent Germany!

NATIONAL COMMITTEE FOR FREE GERMANY

Erich Weinert, whom the Communists intended as president of the National Committee, acted as chairman of the meeting. He is known as the author of political lyrics for cabarets, commissar of the Thälmann brigade in Spain, commentator for Radio Moscow, translator of Russian poetry from Lermontov to Maiakovsky, and author of crude pacifist leaflet poems. He combines a sort of lower middle-class bonhomie with fanatical devotion to the Soviet Union. This comes all the more easily to him since, as one can gather from one's first conversations with him, he is more at home in the sphere of "poetic" phantasy and Communist ideals than in the world of reality.

The two days of the conference were devoted to endless speech making.

Insofar as the speeches were not by the pupils of the antifascist school, who reeled off phrases they had learned by heart, but by experienced speakers such as Hadermann, Weinert, Willy Bredel, Homann, Fleischer, and Hetz, the conference was an impressive balancing of accounts with Hitler, his mad ideas and crimes, and the terrible disaster which he had brought upon Germany.

However full of contradiction, muddled, and ambiguous the early history of this meeting may have been, however cloudy and tinged with the motive of personal gain the intentions of those participating, and however much the Communists may regard the whole thing as a clever propaganda trick, hatred of the regime to which Germany has fallen a prey and hope of dealing it an effective blow permeated the conference and gave it a stirring quality which made me forget all my skepticism and doubts.

The sensation of the conference was the appearance of the first officer to have deserted on the Eastern front, only a few days before. He gave a moving account of the breakdown of the new German summer offensive near Kursk and of the Soviet counteroffensive. First Lieutenant Frankenfels had been

75

a party member and SA leader, and an infantry officer on the Eastern front since 1941. It could not have been cowardice but more likely a sudden short circuit under the shock of the complete destruction of his battalion that made him desert. In his report he analyzed briefly and clearly, from the point of view of the front-line officer, the unparalleled mistakes of the highest military command. He painted a picture of the inadequacy of German equipment and arms and the vast Russian superiority in material, especially the mass use of tanks and artillery, which demonstrated perfectly how baseless are the hopes of the generals for a draw. One can only wonder how it is possible for the military experts to have such a false picture of the situation.

I too spoke at the conference. My theme, as seemed appropriate, was the continuation of Bismarck's policy toward Russia. My talk was based on the following ideas.

Bismarck always desired political cooperation between Germany and Russia, but only with the presupposition that Russia must never be given a chance to play the part of extortioner toward Germany. It was this self-imposed condition in Bismarck's policy toward Russia that Hitler ignored when in 1939 he began a war leaning heavily on the Soviet-German Nonaggression Pact. Even if it were true that the Soviet Union had not dealt honestly with him in 1941, he alone must carry the full political responsibility for the present state of affairs.

But today when Germany is in such a hopeless position there is little time to choose. A Communist Germany at the side of a Communist Russia will always occupy an important place and be a decisive factor in Europe. Problems of finding markets and of unemployment would no longer exist, nor would any danger of a war on two fronts. Who in the world would make war against such an alliance? Orientation toward the West, on the other hand, would solve none of these problems and would only make Germany the buffer in all the conflicts between the capitalist and socialist worlds. Quite apart from this, is there any way out of the general crisis of the past thirty years but the socialist transformation of society? Is there any way of socialist transformation but the revolutionary way, the dictatorship of the proletariat? Has anything ever been achieved on these lines without revolutionary means, without resorting to force? Didn't the Nazis simply usurp the place which the Socialist party did not fill in 1918 but which in Russia the Bolsheviks conquered for themselves—the place of a revolutionary elite? It is certainly pleasanter, more comfortable and civilized to live in a democratic state than in one which like the Soviet Union no longer recognizes a man's personal sphere— provided one has money and work and provided this democratic state is capable of maintaining the normal conditions of economic life. But obviously for the past thirty years this has no longer been the case. Laissez faire may be quite pleasant so long as it does not leave humanity to the chaotic and destructive operation of blind economic forces, so long as it does not mean that absence of ideals and moral values which gives a free hand to pied pipers like the one from Braunau. Isn't it futile to be indignant about lack of freedom in the Soviet Union while the masses of people everywhere have no real freedom, are chained to their place of work, dominated by anxiety about their daily bread, ignorant and unable to decide their own fate? A Communist revolution in Germany would have had few victims compared with the victims and destruction of this war.

"Cooperation with a revolutionary socialist Russia," I concluded, "is bound to be a more productive arrangement for Germany than was Bismarck's friendship with the 'Gendarme of Europe.' "

When by noon on the second day of the conference the list of speakers was exhausted, Weinert rose to read the names of the candidates for the committee. There were thirty-two, of whom one-third were Communist émigrés, one-third officers, and one-third soldiers. Weinert put the list to the vote. "Those in favor of the list raise their hands." The election was unanimous. The newly elected members of the National Committee then signed the manifesto. Finally the committee elected its officers, Weinert, Major Hetz, and myself.

The conference wound up with dinner, a few sips of vodka, and a performance by a group from a Moscow theater. From now on we are to broadcast to Germany on several wave lengths. We have chosen as our theme song the first bars of Arndt's song of freedom. The newspaper, *A Free Germany*, with its black, white, and red masthead, is to replace *The Free Word* in the camps and is also to be dropped over the front as a leaflet. A representative of the National Committee is to be appointed to every Soviet division or so-called "front" in order to organize direct propaganda with the help of leaflets, loudspeakers, and men sent through the lines. These representatives are also to collect material for the committee. Whenever possible a student of the antifascist school is to assist the front representative in every division.

For the time being the National Committee is to meet in the lecture hall of the antifascist school, which is a large, low cellar. In some weeks it will move to a trade union building on the Leningrad highway thirty miles from Moscow. The émigrés remain in Moscow and are to come out only to meetings or to do their daily jobs on the radio and newspaper. They are to run an office of the committee in Moscow and to deal with the Soviets on any questions of organization that arise—the printing of the paper, running the radio broadcasts, trips of the representatives to the front and the camps, and things of that sort.

Chapter Four / Officers and Generals

JULY 28, 1943. I am sitting on deck of the river steamer *Rosa Luxemburg* and surrendering myself completely to the long-missed feeling of liberty which this journey on the vast Russian rivers gives me. I feel as if I were reborn. My hair is growing again. The thin flying shoes in which I was taken prisoner, and from which my toes were sticking out by the time the National Committee was founded, have been replaced by boots. We had been newly dressed out of captured German supplies, and received Russian clothes for this journey so that we would not be conspicuous when seen free and alone in the streets or in railway stations.

We have left the Volga and turned east into the Kama river. The journey will take two days upstream to Yelabuga, where officers' Camp 97 is located.

As far as Kazan we traveled in sleeping cars, and afterward until the ship left we spent several days in the government building of the Tatar People's Republic, where a people's commissar received us in the most hospitable fashion.

"We" are a delegation of the National Committee consisting of Friedrich Wolf, the doctor and German writer, known for his plays *Zyankali* and *Professor Mamlock* and for his fight against Paragraph 218 *; Major Homann, Captain Stolz, Lieutenant Colonel Baratov from the political headquarters administration of the Red Army, and me. In addition we have two German officers with us who want to prepare the way for starting a league of German officers. The idea for this came from Professor Arnold, that is from the Russians, and from the officers of the committee. It is clear that our propaganda will have a chance of success in the Wehrmacht only if Paulus and the majority of the higher Stalingrad officers back it. But along with their other scruples these gentlemen are unwilling to sit down with party politicians, especially Communists, to recognize a pacifist poet-agitator as president, or to sign anything like our appeal to found illegal fighting groups in preparation for the coup d'état against Hitler. But an officers' league would give them the opportunity of expressing themselves in the beginning in much more moderate and "officer-like" terms. They would be under the impression that they were playing an independent role and would gradually get used to our way of thinking. This is our means of making the decision to take part in our plan easier for them.

All these ruses would hardly have been necessary if the Communists were not so horribly clumsy and unacquainted with the German mentality. There are Communists like Bredel, Wolf, and Wilhelm Zaisser who are quite good at dealing with the officers. But party hacks such as Ulbricht with his wooden "dialectical" monologues are insufferable. Yet Ulbricht seems to have the most influence with the Communists. One of the students at the antifascist school compared him with a union

* Paragraph 218 of the German Criminal Code made abortion a penal offense. *Trans.*

80

big shot who is always arranging something behind the scenes and then presenting the workers with a fait accompli.

We had a pleasant impression of Moscow in summer and even of Kazan, as we drove through the streets. I felt though that to form any real judgment one would need to know what life was like inside the houses. But the people in the streets looked happy and contented. Friedrich Wolf told us an interesting story as we entered Kazan. In the winter of 1941 when the Germans were at the gates of Moscow, he was evacuated to Kazan with the Authors' League. Panic and defeatism reigned in Moscow. There were two or three days of complete chaos, and rumors went about that Stalin was dead. The German émigrés were in a desperate state of mind. Kazan is far from Moscow, but they were already anxiously discussing the best methods of suicide in case the Germans came. However, the government of the Tatar People's Republic had plans to send these eminent visitors from Moscow to the northern frontier in order to have a free hand in Kazan if the Soviet state broke up. It was only with difficulty that they were prevented from carrying out this order, which would have been a death sentence. In fact, a number of German émigrés died of starvation when a similar thing happened in Tashkent.

No, the Soviet system is not as unshakable as propaganda makes it out to be. Only a few days ago a Russian locomotive engineer argued with me that the government must be made up of criminals or it wouldn't have been possible for the Germans to break through in one push to Moscow, Leningrad, and Rostov.

"We've deprived ourselves of millions and millions for the sake of the army," he stormed, "but the money has gone into the pockets of our rapacious government."

I realize, of course, that this way of looking at things is

very elementary and unfair. It is true that the Soviets had at their disposal a colossal quantity of war material in 1941. But the superior German technology and much greater mental alertness and the war experience of the German soldiers and junior officers far outbalanced this in the first two years of the war.

I have become so much of a Marxist that I inquired at once what the class and background of this man were. He informed me that in 1928 his father had still owned over 120 hectares of land in the Ukraine. No sooner had he told me this than he began a violent tirade against the collective farms. He also expressed the bitterness of a Ukrainian nationalist. But I cannot help believing that the idea of modern industrialized agriculture on a collective basis has proved itself. Göring was right when he said that the Ukraine is a land flowing with milk and honey. Where would the Soviets be today if it were not for their mechanized large-scale agriculture which they were able to develop only by enforced collectivization? Without it they would have been completely overrun and would have starved during the war. It is true that enforced collectivization seems to have swallowed the revolutionary freedom of the 'twenties and created a new absolutism, followed by the great purges and strengthening of Stalinism. And yet the question remains whether a different, liberal method would have achieved its goal. It is impossible to prove this with certainty. Undoubtedly other methods would have required more time, and time is what the Soviets could not afford.

AUGUST 5, 1943. I found myself addressing a meeting of officers in the Yelabuga camp. It was a compulsory meeting called by the Soviet camp directors. Because, a little while before, a group of staff officers had stated that attendance at the

meetings of the National Committee of one's own free will was
in itself treason and would be punished accordingly after final
victory, we had asked the Russian camp authorities to make use
of their power by ordering the camp inmates to attend; this
would prevent the Nazis from coercing the other officers. Before me were gathered some eight hundred officers from the
Stalingrad army. About one-quarter of them ostentatiously
turned their backs on me. In the faces of most of the others I
read extreme reserve if not sneering hostility.

I began my lecture:

Gentlemen, comrades!

You will probably be surprised and even consider it
treason that the National Committee for Free Germany is
organizing a meeting in this camp under the black, white,
and red flag. I can assure you that it was a very careful
choice of colors. Under this flag the old dream of the
Germans of a unified Reich once came true, and the deep
longing of the German people for confederation was
realized. Today we fight for this Reich, which is threatened
by Hitler with destruction. By his hypocritical use of the
idea of the Reich Hitler has enticed us Germans to follow
him. But he has used the strength of the German people
and of their state immoderately and blindly, and now he
seems determined to endanger the very existence of this
Reich and to plunge it into the inevitable ruin for which
he himself is heading. That is why we are fighting against
Hitler. That is why we have chosen the flag under which
our Reich was founded as our symbol. Our decision does
not lose in value even though Communists play an important role on our committee. The Communists too require
the existence of a German state in order to put their ideas
into practice.

83

It was a great personal experience for me when I first saw the hall where the committee was founded decorated with the colors under which, seventy years ago, my great-grandfather completed his task of establishing the German Reich. I hold the profound conviction that if the great work begun by Bismarck is not to die we must take up the threads spun by him which have been so irresponsibly cut by his successors.

"I have helped the German people into the saddle, they will know how to ride by themselves," Bismarck once said, and these words seem very relevant to our present situation. The German people did not climb into the saddle by themselves nor have they taken the reins into their hands; since Bismarck they have allowed the reins to be held by increasingly incompetent successors of Bismarck, and today we must realize that the reins have got into the hands of a criminal. We must wrench them from him and show that we are determined to learn to ride by ourselves if we wish to avoid terrible suffering. Even in captivity we must not shut our eyes to the need of the hour. Wherever we may be, we too are responsible for the fate of our Fatherland. Although we failed to oppose the Hitler clique in the past, and the voice of reason can no longer be heard in Germany, we must now become the loud-speaker for that voice, in spite of the fact that our newspaper and our leaflets are printed in Moscow, our radio station is in Moscow, and evil and stupid people accuse us of treason. Why should it not be Moscow? Bismarck always regarded the relation of Germany to Russia as the key point of his foreign policy. Developments have proved him a thousand times right. It has been proved over and over again that Germany, in view of her position in the heart of Europe, cannot survive in the struggle for power unless her relations with Russia are on a basis of honest and equitable cooperation, which is bound to be fruitful in all areas through mutual supplementation. I cannot see why the radical change which the Russian state and social system have experienced since Bismarck's day should mean a fundamental change in German-Russian relations.

You will ask why this young man is addressing you on this subject and under these circumstances. I know too that many of you who are convinced National Socialists will despise me as a traitor, and others because of their higher rank will dismiss what I have to say as rubbish. Nevertheless I think I have a right to speak to you. I was brought up in an officer's family and am proud of the fact that my two grandfathers fought in the cavalry battle of Mars-la-Tour, when the German Empire was being forged in blood and iron. Hitler's national and social promises made a deep impression in the home of my parents also, even in the years of crisis before 1933. And the people of my circle saw with growing anxiety how, after 1933, the Nazis were heading more and more plainly toward war. They saw how Hitler, against the advice of the army and of experienced diplomats, continued with his increasingly adventurous policy of extortion and treaty breaking, a policy far worse than the escapades of William II and which was bound to set the world against Germany. The murders of June 30, 1934, when several good friends of my parents were among the victims, produced violent indignation. The increasingly insolent attacks of the party and the SS on the army and deserving patriots such as Baron von Fritsch, to mention only one example, caused them to turn more and more against the system. I myself had my first serious encounter with the system as an enthusiastic supporter of the Youth Movement which believed in free development of the spirit and body of the individual and encouraged comradeship and love of nature. This movement was opposed to the Hitler Youth with its uniforms, its ridiculous playing at soldiers, and its misuse of the word "comradeship." My hatred of the system began when my friends and leaders in this movement were exposed to the arbitrariness of the Gestapo and sent to concentration camps and I myself was released only because of my name and the "consideration" the Gestapo still felt it had to give in 1938. It seemed to me that the English system of government was an ideal to be aimed at and I regretted that we entered into a war against England in 1939, allied with the Soviet Union, instead of the other way about. Nevertheless, for Germany this alliance seemed the only way out of a hopelessly mismanaged situation. But as early as the autumn of 1940 I heard from one of Himmler's adjutants that there was to be no attack on England as we intended to march against the Soviet Union the following year. The air attacks on the British Isles were merely to "prepare" the English for an alliance.

Force an alliance with bombs! To throw away irresponsibly the only chance of avoiding a war on two fronts! To gamble on the hope that England and the rest of the world would sit back and watch Germany take the Ukraine in order to be able later to fling herself at the others' throats! This seemed and still seems to me the height of political madness. In spite of all this, I was an enthusiastic fighter pilot and by no means a pacifist. I have only now, through my work with the National Committee, accepted the consequences of my horror of the Nazi system. But I prefer to accept the consequences late rather than not at all. You look upon this as treason. I believe it to be correcting an excusable sin of omission, an understandable mistake. Hitler has betrayed everything of value, all his promises and oaths. We owe him no loyalty such as the Nibelungen showed. But if you insist on your officers' conception of honor, if you berate and insult us as traitors, I should like to remind you very definitely of the way your officers' honor has been trampled underfoot by Hitler's Wehrmacht. If you are honest with yourselves, you will recognize how much we have all, without exception, been exposed to the disintegrating influence of National Socialist morality.

Which of us was immune to all the temptations that the campaigns in Europe—which were so successful at first—brought with them? Which of us did not participate in the bargain sales, of France for example, about which Sperrle and Göring said: "Buy all you can, even if you collapse on the other side of the frontier"? Which of us really believed that he was defending the Fatherland? Was it not clear to all of us that it was a war to subjugate Europe —at least Europe?

How different this makes today's army with its swastika on its chest from the army of 1914–18, even allowing for a false glamorizing of the first World War. "To be rather than to seem" was the motto of the old army. In the Hitler army a wild chase after decorations, from the Reichsmarshal on down, has driven out all feeling for achievement, care of the troops, and real comradeship. Which of you will deny that things have gone so far that when a new commander arrives without a Knight's Cross the soldiers often have bitter words, fearing from experience a new period of reckless gambling? I was told by a commander of mine who was one of the wildest daredevils along the Channel coast that after this war he would like to become commandant of an airdrome and a landowner along the Black Sea, so that he could rule "those serfs" with a whip. Here in prison I learned that a commander of my fighter squadron had left the squadron in the middle of the Stalingrad disaster to take the leave granted him on the award of a decoration. I heard that a few hours after receiving the Knight's Cross a pilot asked to be transferred home, which was granted, and that another avoided taking part in any further attacks after getting the same decoration. These are not isolated cases but examples which go to prove what sort of things happen in a war of conquest as opposed to a war of legitimate self-defense.

You will probably think one should not wash one's dirty linen while prisoner of a foreign power which is at war with Germany. But if you accuse the supporters of the Free Germany movement of damaging accepted standards of honor, then you must also be prepared to let them remind you that there are cogent reasons for fighting the Hitler system in order to defend the honor of our nation. You must let us ask you not to identify serving a system which is run by traitors with service to the German people. I will not pretend that I saw all these things clearly before I became a prisoner. But being a prisoner and seeing the inability of each of us to defend with conviction the justice of the cause for which we were fighting; and not least, witnessing the drama of Stalingrad, of which you were the victims—all this developed my views in this direction. I never gave up hope that the heads of the army would sooner or later put an end to the activities of the Brown Shirts. It was the greatest shock to me when twenty-four generals carried out Hitler's order to continue a battle which was completely senseless from a military point of view and could result only in the 6th Army's destruction—and let themselves be taken prisoner, complete with fur coats, trucks, and walking sticks, when two-thirds of their army of 300,000 men had been destroyed and the rest were on the point of death from starvation and disease.

I have often cursed my imprisonment, and its consequences have been difficult to bear—for like you I have known endless hunger marches, long weeks of dangerous fever and disease without proper medical care, and I too have slept on bare bunks in ice-cold barracks. In spite of this, I know today that it is my payment for the fatal inconsistency of rejecting Hitler and yet fighting his war. And this applies not to me alone but to us all. If today you tell me of the dead among the Stalingrad prisoners and demand that the Russians treat us in a manner more becoming to officers before we discuss cooperation with them, I should like to reply that in my opinion we cannot ask a foreign government (especially not in our present circumstances) for something we never even demanded of our own government.

I am even grateful in some ways to fate for leading me into captivity. For a young man like myself it may have been the best way out of the dilemma of not believing in Hitler and yet fighting for him, of flying with enthusiasm and doubting the sense of the attack. I am thankful to fate also for wresting me out of an intellectual immaturity in which I could never have reached any real power of judgment and forcing me into an encounter with ideas which we in Germany were called upon to destroy without even understanding. I have also learned to realize that nothing can be more pernicious than lack of understanding, underestimation, and contempt of your enemy—or, generally speaking, of foreign nations. I know that many of you regard with suspicion anyone who takes up a Marxist book and occupies himself with the ideas on which the Soviet state is based, though this is merely a justified desire to catch up with something that my generation, at least, of necessity missed. I cannot share this attitude and I admit that I can see some truth in socialist and Communist ideas. Germany would have saved herself something by taking this into consideration. I also do not mind admitting that I have found among the Communist émigrés in Moscow who work with us on this committee people whose clear-sighted political judgments have made a great impression on me. These people in no way correspond to the picture which the Nazis have drawn of them. They have answered various questions to which I had consciously or unconsciously sought answers before my imprisonment. As long as I have no convincing counterproof I shall not let myself be persuaded that cooperation with the Russians is out of the question and that an attempt to save Germany from Hitler's claws with their help is impossible.

I hope I have succeeded in making you see why I belong to the committee and why I am speaking to you here. I hope that you will feel it is not personal advantage but sincere concern for our Fatherland and our nation which prompts me. I hope that you will not reject our request that you take up, along with the National Committee, the fight against Hitler and his henchmen, who are determined to let the whole of Germany suffer the fate of the Stalingrad army.

When I finished there was isolated applause here and there. The majority of the officers remained silent. But not quite as many backs were turned on me. Friedrich Wolf and Major Homann spoke next. At the close of the meeting our camp was like a disturbed beehive. Before it the antifascist group was something not to be taken seriously, but now views for and against it are being exchanged heatedly. Immediately after the meeting over fifty officers decided to join our group, and the others have stopped not speaking to us. The road seems open for a serious and friendly discussion of our plans of action.

AUGUST 10, 1943. Our hope for a friendly discussion was an illusion. By the next day the countermovement of the fanatical Nazis among the officers had begun. The leaders of this movement are officers of the General Staff and young front-line commanders who had quick promotion for distinguished service at the front. "Fight on to final victory" is their slogan, and terrorization of their comrades their method. From the start they have tried to make any discussion with us quite impossible by every kind of insult and provocation. On the one hand they claim that we are all opportunists and on the other they demand that the Russians treat them in a way more "appropriate to officers" if they are to work with them. At the same time, long before the founding of the National Committee they signed a declaration about their treatment in the camp. In this, 840 German officers affirmed that they were being treated humanely and according to the principles of international law. The Russians dropped this declaration in leaflet form over the German lines in order to dispel the soldiers' fear of Soviet captivity. Yet these same officers who signed this declaration of their own free will are now accusing us of treason against the tens of thousands who died during the first few weeks and months of imprisonment after Stalingrad. These men are well aware that in similar cases the same thing happened in Germany. They themselves tell how, during the first year of the war, some 500,000 Russian prisoners died of hunger on the German side. In any case the 90,000 captured at Stalingrad were already semistarved and infected with every conceivable disease before they were taken prisoner. In a temperature of —22°F. the lice clustered in thick gray layers on the men's collars. This was resistance to the last shot. "Hold on, the Führer will get us out!"

But they do not hold Hitler accountable for the dead. On the contrary. One day when we had arranged a Heine evening and one of the officers sang "The Three Grenadiers" as set by Schubert, the applause at the words "Then my Emperor will ride over my grave" turned into a demonstration of loyalty for the man from Braunau.

Of course there are a number of things our side has done which are grist to the mill of the Nazis and which strengthen the officers in their attitude. The Russians and the German political instructor are continually being taken in by the most blatant opportunists, people one can tell a mile off are Nazis, and giving them special jobs in the camp. Our camp commandant is a drunken hero of the civil war whose whole education consists in having learned the history of the party by heart and who is corrupt to his very marrow.

Besides, Yelabuga is a singularly depressing hole. It was once a famous place of pilgrimage with two large monasteries and many churches, and an important unloading point on the Kama river. Today most of the traffic is by rail, and in the winter when the river is frozen the town is virtually cut off from the outer world. The real nightmare in the place is the prison. Next to the broken-down churches and monastery buildings, it is the largest building, like a house of death in Dostoevsky. Before our camp was ready, a number of the officers went there several times to be deloused, but they saw only stupid Russian trusties. Recently, however, the Russians released a German officer who was taken from our camp in 1941 for alleged instigations to riot and mass demonstrations. Since then he had been in solitary confinement in the prison, without any news whatsoever about the war. The authorities had either completely forgotten him or been too lazy to transfer him to Oranky, where the camp was moved in 1942. When we ask the Russians how such a thing can happen they shrug their shoulders. *Nichevo*. For them this is nothing unusual. They have no imagination about such things.

One of the questions we are constantly being asked in the camp is what sense there is in joining the camp group of the National Committee. "Surely, while we're here, we can't change the course of events," the officers say. It is true that our propaganda can have an effect in Germany and on the army only if the whole body of prisoners, especially the officers, are behind it. So long as we make no headway inside the camp the Russians are not likely to give the committee much opportunity to function. So far the edition of our newspaper and leaflets is ridiculously small and does not compare even with the number of leaflets we German pilots dropped over the Kharkov basin in May 1942. In addition, the front propagandists from the antifascist school are on the whole incapable of drafting a sensible leaflet and use only clichés and abusive language. The whole purpose of the National Committee is to avoid having only Communists and Communist proselytes doing the propaganda. But most people fight shy of such activities. Many fear that reprisal will be taken on their relatives, a thought which never occurred to me. But the officers here do not draw conclusions of any kind about the character of a system which they consider capable of such things.

SEPTEMBER 5, 1943. The house of the National Committee is a comparatively modern and intact rest home, with central heat, running water, and pleasantly furnished rooms.

It is situated in a little wood, more like a park, on the steep bank of the Kliasma, a small tributary of the Moskva. This is the farthest place the German troops reached in their advance on Moscow from the northwest in December 1941. There are still mines lying about, and the damage caused by hand grenades can be seen on the buildings.

About one hundred officers have arrived from the various prison camps, among them quite a number of staff officers who want to join our officers' league. Outstanding among them are Colonel Steidle, Colonel van Hooven, Major Bechler, Major von Frankenberg, Colonel Czimatis, Colonel Pickel, Major Büchler; there are several military lawyers and doctors, as well as some lieutenants of the reserve, a high-school teacher named Gerlach, Dr. Greifenhagen, Dr. Arras, Dr. Wilimzig, schoolmasters and lawyers.

In addition a fleet of cars suddenly arrived yesterday bringing a group of six generals. At their head was the large upright figure of white-haired Walter von Seydlitz, commanding general of the 1st Corps. Then followed the divisional commanders, Edler von Daniels, Martin Lattmann, Korfes, Hellmuth Schlömer, and von Drebber. The Russians have brought them here from the generals' camp near Ivanovo, although they don't want to have anything to do with us. They do not return our greetings when we meet them, and associate only with the officers they know personally and on whose advice they were selected by the Russians from the rest of the generals. Although the newcomers regard our activities as "treason," the officers who know them think they can perhaps be won over in time.

Seydlitz used to be considered a decided favorite of Hitler's. The relief of the Demiansk pocket took place under his command and he received the Oak Leaves for it. Later, when it became clear that the army before Stalingrad was encircled, he handed a memorandum drafted by his chief of staff to Paulus,

Count Einsiedel as first ensign in Paris

Count Einsiedel after his return to Germany

Colonel Sergei Tulpanov

Alfred Kurella

Begrüßung an das Nationalkomitee

Erich Weinert, Präsident des Nationalkomitees „Freies Deutschland"

MOSKAU

Der Rat der „Bundesgenossen innerhalb Deutschlands", eine überparteiliche Organisation von Massencharakter, die das Ziel verfolgt, die Antinaziopposition innerhalb Deutschlands zu unterstützen, sendet dem Nationalkomitee „Freies Deutschland" wärmste Grüße und bewillkommnet seine Schaffung als das bedeutendste Ereignis in der Entwicklung der deutschen Antinazibewegung. Der Rat erblickt im Nationalkomitee die Verkörperung der Bestrebungen aller jener Deutschen, die den Nazismus als den Todfeind ihres Landes und der Menschheit betrachten und die bereit sind, sich aktiv seiner Vernichtung sowie der Befreiung Deutschlands aus der Schande und Degradation zu widmen, in die es die Verbrechen der Nazi gestürzt haben. Der überparteiliche und interkonfessionelle Charakter des Nationalkomitees sowie seine breiten demokratischen Ziele zeigen deutlich, daß es eine Basis bildet, auf der alle Kräfte innerhalb Deutschlands gesammelt werden können, die wirkliche und wirksame Gegner des Nazisystems und alles dessen sind, was es bezweckt.

Im Auftrage des Rates der „Bundesgenossen innerhalb Deutschlands":

Bischof von Bradford, Frau Elisabeth Cadbury, Marjory Corbett-Ashby, Lord Faringdon, Ruth Fry, Dr. G. P. Good, Arthur L. Horner, John Horner, Dr. Julian Huxley, J. B. Priestley, Gordon Schaffer, Jack Tanner.

London, 36 Upper Park Road NW 3

A message from the West to the National Committee for Free Germany. The Soviet Government did not allow the committee to get in touch with the West.

WIE BEHANDELN UNS DIE RUSSEN?

Die Gestaltung des Lagerlebens ist weitgehendst uns selbst überlassen. Das heißt: Ordnung und Disziplin, die Tages- und Arbeitseinteilung liegt in den Händen der deutschen Lagerältesten. Zur Arbeit werden Offiziere nur mit ihrem eigenen Einverständnis herangezogen (Lazarettarbeit, Gartenarbeit, Instandhalten der Sportanlage, Küche, Essenausgabe).

Die russische Lagerleitung achtet die Ehre des deutschen Wehrmachtsangehörigen, behandelt uns höflich, korrekt und zuvorkommend. Dies kommt schon darin zum Ausdruck, daß wir unsere Uniformen, Rangabzeichen, Orden und Ehrenzeichen tragen. Unserem Interesse, die Heimat über unser Wohlergehen zu benachrichtigen, kommt die Lagerleitung dadurch entgegen, daß sie uns Rote Kreuz-Karten zur Verfügung stellt und für ihre Beförderung sorgt.

Das Bild oben zeigt die Eröffnung einer Ausstellung künstlerischer Arbeiten von Offizieren. Rechts: Deutsche und russische Offiziere unterhalten sich an Hand der Karte über die Lage an den Fronten.

A page from the Soviet Illustrated News of the Front. *The pictures are of Camp Suzdal.*

The front page of the first issue of the newspaper Free Germany

Walter von Seydlitz, Erich Weinert, and Luitpold Steidle

The founding meeting of the League of German Officers in the house of the National Committee

General Lattmann speaking in Camp 97, Yelabuga, in January 1944

Ninety-six participants in a conference of clergy in Lunovo, June 1944
1. Arndt, 2. Schröder, 3. Krummacher, 4. Klein, 5. Sönnichsen,
6. Kaiser, 7. Mohr, 8. Ludwig

German prisoners from the Cherkassy pocket, February 1944

Wilhelm Pieck and General Paulus in Lunovo, August 22, 1944

An die

Kriegsgefangenen deutschen Offiziere und Soldaten

in der U. d. S. S. R. und an das deutsche Volk.

Bei Stalingrad hat die 6. Armee unter meiner Fuehrung, dem Befehl Adolf Hitlers folgend, bis zum äussersten gekämpft in der Hoffnung, durch ihr Opfer der Obersten Fuehrung die Möglichkeit zu schaffen, den Krieg zum einem fuer Deutschland nicht allzu unguenstigen Ende zu 'fuehren. Diese Hoffnung hat sich nicht erfuellt.

Die Erkenntnisse der letzten Zeit haben die Fortsetzung des Krieges fuer Deutschland zu einem sinnlosen Opfer gemacht. Die Rote Armee geht auf breiter Front vor und hat die Reichsgrenze in Ostpreussen erreicht. Am besten haben Amerikaner und Engländer die deutsche Abwehr am Westflügel durchbrochen und gehen in den offenen französischen Raum vor. weder im Osten noch im Westen verfuegt Deutschland über Reserven, die die Lage wieder herstellen könnten. Die feindliche Ueberlegenheit in der Luft und zur See ist so eradrueckend, dass die Lage dadurch noch aussichtsloser wird. Der Krieg ist fuer Deutschland verloren.

In diese Lage ist Deutschland trotz des Heldentums seiner Wehrmacht und des ganzen Volkes durch die Staats- und Kriegsfuehrung Adolf Hitlers geraten.

Dazu kommt, dass die Art, wie ein Teil seiner Beauftragten im besetzten Gebiet gegen die Bevölkerung vorgegangen ist, jeden wirklichen Soldaten und jeden wirklichen Deutschen mit Abscheu erfuellt und uns in der ganzen Welt schwerste Vorwuerfe zuziehen muss. Wenn sich das deutsche Volk nicht selbst von diesen Handlungen lossagt, wird es die volle Verantwortung fuer sie tragen muessen.

Unter diesen Umständen halte ich es fuer meine Pflicht, vor meinen Kriegsgefangenen zu sagen und vor dem ganzen deutschen Volk zu erklären:

Deutschland muss sich von Adolf Hitler lossagen und sich eine neue Staatsfuehrung geben, die den Krieg beendet und Verhältnisse herbeifuehrt, die es unserem Volk ermöglichen, weiter zu leben und mit unseren jetzigen Gegnern in friedliche, ja freundschaftliche Beziehungen zu treten.

Moskau, 8.August 1944

Paulus

Generalfeldmarschall

General Paulus' appeal of August 8, 1944

Major Heinrich Homann came to
be vice president of the People's
Chamber in the Soviet Zone even
without attending the antifascist
school.

General Arno von Lensky, now
leading National Democrat in
the Eastern zone, while a pupil
in the antifascist school

State Security Minister Wilhelm
Zaisser, once a keen opponent of
Walter Ulbricht, now his
collaborator

Friedrich Wolf at Melitopol in
1943; now East German representative in Warsaw

Der Befehlshaber der Ordnungspolizei   O.U., den 4.Sept. 1942
        für die Ukraine
    -Ia-

Betr.: Kennzeichnung der sowjetischen Kriegsgefangenen
       durch ein Merkmal.

   Nachstehende auszugsweise Abschrift geht den Dienststellen zur
Kenntnis zu.
                          Für den Befehlshaber:
                          Der Chef des Stabes:
Beglaubigt: gez. Müller-Brunckhorst.
gez. Unterschrift
Oberwachtm.d.Schp.
Verteiler
Alle Kdr.d.Orpo.....je 1-9
pp-
         Abschrift von Abschrift!

Oberkommando der Wehrmacht
Az.2.f 2482 hChef Kriegsgef./Ben./Allg.(Ia /org.(IVe.Nr 3142/42
                Berlin-Schöneberg, den 20.7.1942
                Badensche Str. 51
   Betr.: Kennzeichnung der sowjetischen Kriegsgefangenen durch
       ein Merkmal.
   1) Die sowj.Kr.Gef. sind durch ein besonderes und dauerhaftes
      Merkmal zu kennzeichnen.
   2) Das Merkmal besteht in einem nach unten geöffneten spitzen Win-
      kel v. etwa 45°u. 1 cm Schenkellänge auf der linken Gesäßhälfte
      etwa handbreit von der Afterspalte entfernt.   (∧)
   3) Die Kennzeichnung ist keine ärztliche Maßnahme. Deutsches Sanität-
      personal darf deshalb und wegen des Mangels an San.-Pers. mit
      ihrer Durchführung nicht beauftragt werden.
   4) pp.
   5) Die Kennzeichnung hat zu erfolgen:
      a) bei künftig neu anfallenden sowj.Kr.Gef. in den Bereichen der
        Wehrmachtbefehlshaber Ostland und Ukraine u.d.Mil.Befh.im.Gen.
        Gouv. nach Körperreinigung bei der ersten Entlausung.
      b) Bei allen übrigen Kr.Gef.im OKW-Bereich bis 30.Sept. 42 Voll
      zugsmeldung bis 15.Okt.42 an OKW.
   6) der Arbeitseinsatz darf durch diese Maßnahme nicht gestört werden
   7) Die erfolgte erste Kennzeichnung ist sofort auf der Personalkar-
      te I in der Spalte " Besonder Kennzeichen" mit
      "∧ am 1942
      zu vermerken.
   8) pp.
                  Der Chef des Oberkommandos der Wehrm.
                  Im Auftrage :
Der -u.Pol.Führer in Stalino   gez. Unterschrift
-Der Kommandeur der Ordnungspolizei-
    -Sch-

   Abschriftlich den im Verteiler genannten Dienststellen.

Verteiler.
Kdr.d.Orpo. 38.Kdeur d.Gend. m.Neb. 10, B/u. Pol-Standortfhr.26
20/-u. Pol.-Gebietsf. Nebabdr. 80, Res. 6. 160
Beglaubigt: I.V.
                  gez. Loose
Rev.-Ltn.d.SchP.

*Facsimile of the German order to brand Soviet prisoners of war. This
document fell into the hands of the Red Army in Stalino.*

Walter Ulbricht as special agent of the Soviet secret police, the most powerful man in the East zone

. . . and Bernhard Deuter, one of his most willing collaborators

Max Emmendörfer and Vincenz Müller. Emmendörfer was arrested by the NKVD in Berlin in 1945 and taken to Russia. In 1950 he was again removed from a home-bound transport and held in the Soviet Union.

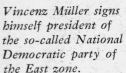

Vincenz Müller signs himself president of the so-called National Democratic party of the East zone.

General Seydlitz broadcasts to the German staffs.

General von Daniels talks with new German prisoners at a Soviet staff headquarters.

A Christmas party in the house of the National Committee. Left to right: W. Pieck, Seydlitz, E. Weinert

in which he urged an immediate break-through, "if necessary against Hitler's orders." Seydlitz had experience of encirclement which may have led him to this impulsive action. Now there is a kind of rivalry between Seydlitz and Paulus, because Seydlitz claims to have taken the more definite stand. Paulus claims that Seydlitz as a result of his memorandum was made directly responsible to Hitler as commander of the northern flank of the pocket and that he obeyed Hitler's orders; that by this action Paulus' own hands were now tied. A suggestion for a break-through in January on all fronts, including east across the Volga, is said to have come from the 1st Corps; it would have meant suicide for the entire army.

The truth of these things will probably never be known. Seydlitz was certainly not mentioned in the honor roll of the 6th Army. This meant that his démarche met with disapproval.

Lattmann is a general who is continually boasting of being a National Socialist. At the artillery school at Jüterbog he used to rebuke the officers in his classes if they had not read *Mein Kampf*. Everyone considered this presumption on his part. His lieutenants called him "the peacock" on account of his vanity.

Schlömer was one of the most respected and popular divisional commanders in the Stalingrad army. We know next to nothing about Drebber except that he was a police officer in Oldenburg.

The most controversial figure among the generals is Edler von Daniels. There are wild rumors about the conditions in his divisional staff owing to his addiction to wine and women.

SEPTEMBER 7, 1943. This morning I nearly fell out of bed when Seydlitz suddenly shouted in the room opposite and banged his fist on the table so the windowpanes rattled:

"As long as Zippel and Gold are around there can be no question of my participating," he roared.

Zippel, a German Communist who deserted to the enemy in June 1941, has now been made secretary of the National Committee. Gold, also a Communist and a deserter, helped the Russians, dressed in German uniforms, to blow up the commander's headquarters at Velikiye Luky. For this he received a Soviet decoration. This distinction was furthermore mentioned in flamboyant style in the prisoners' newspaper. The Russians presumably thought this would convince the prisoners of the internationalism of the Red Army. To make a pact with deserters, even though they are deserters by political conviction, is inconceivable to the generals. But to everyone's great surprise (the news spread by lunch time) Generals von Seydlitz, Lattman, Schlömer, Korfes, and Edler von Daniels have decided to take part in starting an officers' league. The details of what decided Seydlitz and his fellows to swing round so suddenly are not known. The most difficult point during the negotiations with them was the question of the armed forces disintegrating. The generals did not wish to be party to propaganda of disintegration. Under this heading they included every call to disregard the orders of higher commands, the appeal in our manifesto to form illegal groups (which reminded them disagreeably of the soldiers' councils of 1917–18), and the desire to fight a way back to the Fatherland under responsible leaders, which they regarded as incitement to civil war and anarchy. The most the generals will do is request the commanding officers of the Wehrmacht to "ask that Hitler resign" in order to make way for armistice negotiations. They do not want a popular revolution but at most a palace revolution of the top men. The argument which probably convinced them in the end is the fact that no one is disintegrating the German army more quickly than Hitler himself, and that they would lose all influence in the reconstruction unless they took part in overthrowing the regime. Stalin's speech immediately before the battle of Stalingrad must also have had its effect. He said that no one had any intention of disarming Germany or annihilating the German army. These words are now interpreted by the Communists as an invitation to the German generals to cooperate with the Red Army, to drop Hitler, and to orient themselves toward the East.

In any case, the road is now open to found the officers' league. Seydlitz and several officers together with Wilhelm Pieck are to go to the generals' camp in order to persuade Paulus and the rest of the generals to follow their example.

SEPTEMBER 11, 1943. Major von Frankenberg told us the results of the trip to the generals' camp. Seydlitz and his friends arrived in the camp late at night when all the generals were in their beds. They rushed to the corridors in their nightshirts and pyjamas and pressed around him full of curiosity. Seydlitz was so excited that all he could shout was "Tauroggen, Tauroggen!" But the spirit of Yorck could not be conjured up among the generals in their nightshirts.* Nor did they get anywhere on the next day when they tried again somewhat more systematically to convince Paulus and his comrades of the necessity to act. Paulus stuck to his position that it was impossible to judge the situation rightly and that one should not endanger a possible military action by premature activity. They paid no attention to Pieck, who invoked against the generals his mandate in the last legitimate Reichstag election. And so tomorrow the founding of the league of German officers will take place without Paulus and his group.

* Count Yorck von Wartenburg was one of the generals commanding the auxiliary corps Prussia sent into Russia in support of Napoleon in 1812. Believing the French army doomed, he neutralized the Prussian army by the Convention of Tauroggen. *Trans.*

SEPTEMBER 12, 1943. We were standing in the large hall of the National Committee building. The colors of imperial Germany were shimmering on the walls. Hundreds of captured German officers were seated at the tables set out in long rows, covered with white tablecloths, and decorated with flowers. The hall was crowded and it was almost impossible to push one's way among the tables.

The first speeches rang out. Staff officers and generals boldly and critically discussed the situation and the aims of the league which they were deciding to found. Their speeches were a merciless condemnation of Hitler. One thought involuntarily of the radios tuned to a whisper at the front and in German towns, at which we hoped Germans might be listening to these appeals and might think and feel along with us. The league of German officers was in the making!

The sober analysis of the situation given by Colonel van Hooven, former information officer of the 6th Army, received universal praise. He said:

> It must be a unique event in history when officers who are prisoners of war are able to come together from different camps, air their views freely, and found a league. Efforts of this sort appear to be contradictory to the aims of an enemy who has slowly but surely won superiority in this long and bloody war and sees final victory approaching.
>
> The world situation, however, and especially conditions in the Soviet Union, which we have learned to know and appreciate only as prisoners, show common interests of both countries on many decisive matters. A great many officers, at first quite independently of each other, have carefully analyzed the general situation for themselves and have recognized the positive factors necessary for the

life of nations. They have reached the conclusion that the time and circumstances have come for action to end the war quickly. They realize also that the political and economic interdependence of all nations would give a strong guarantee—quite apart from emotional and moral considerations—of attaining an honorable peace which will insure Germany's right to existence and exclude the possibility of future wars . . .

Total war has become totally useless. To continue it would therefore be both mad and immoral. It could end only in complete destruction, slaughter, the war of every man against every man, a blood bath, the division of Germany, destruction of industry and commerce, hunger, misery, and slavery. Reason and humanity demand imperatively that this war end and peace be made before it is too late. Comparison with 1918 forces itself upon us. But history does not repeat itself. This time the end will be very much worse after the Wehrmacht has been defeated, because this war is being fought not only for the political and economic issues of power politics but also, according to Nazi party doctrine, for beliefs, like the religious wars of the Middle Ages, and because the hatred of all the world is directed against Germany.

This time there is no Reichstag in Germany, there are no political parties, no organizations as there were in 1918. There is no factor which could prevent the worst from happening and guarantee order and security after the Wehrmacht is destroyed. Such an event would leave Germany an object without weight of its own.

Only an early peace can alter the foreseeable fate, because it will preserve the one instrument that can safeguard order and prevent chaos: the German Wehrmacht. Again the first World War offers us a comparison. In 1916 Germany could have concluded a just peace when Wilson published his Fourteen Points and threw the weight of America into the scales for this. At that time Germany was still very strong, the United States had not yet entered the war, and the world was inclined toward peace. We had another great opportunity in 1917. Russia had dropped out as an enemy, France was nearly at the end of her strength, England in the midst of a crisis, and the United States not yet actively in the war, whereas Germany was unbeaten on all fronts. At that time foolish blindness thwarted the peace resolutions of the Reichstag. And on August 8, 1918 Ludendorff had to announce that the war could no longer be won; now the diplomats must act. It was much too late. The German army had been defeated on all fronts and the country was in a state of revolution. As there was no strong democratic regime to deal with the situation, we got the dictated peace of Versailles, which resulted in the complete exploitation of Germany from without and within. . . .

Today the situation is similar to that in 1917. The German Wehrmacht is still a force. But just as then the very last moment to make peace has come, for the rafters of the German house are shaking and the foundations are beginning to crack . . . To end the war now would guarantee that Germany would receive an honorable peace, insuring the continued existence of the nation. I am convinced that it is not in the interest of the USSR or of England or of any other power to see Germany destroyed as the heart of Europe. Her ruin would bring about a political vacuum and reduce the European economy to disorder for a long time to come. It would also carry with it the seeds of future conflicts.

We have a further guarantee in the solemn declaration of Marshal Stalin delivered before all the world on November 6, 1942. His declaration, which is to be the basis for the work of the league of German officers, runs:

"The English-Soviet-American coalition has as its program the abolition of racial exclusiveness, equality of all nations and the inviolability of their territories; the liberation of oppressed nations and restoration of their rights of sovereignty; respect for the right of all nations to govern themselves as they wish; economic aid to all nations that have suffered damage, and support in their attempt to reach material prosperity; the restoration of democratic freedoms, and the annihilation of the Hitler regime."

In spite of all the bitterness of recent years, the Russian people have not forgotten the centuries of peaceful cooperation. The cultural achievements of Germany, her language, her music, her classics, her work in all branches of learning, are unalterably alive today in the Soviet Union and are objects of public respect and admiration. The continuation of the war would undoubtedly increase hatred among the nations and their desire for destruction. This is why early peace and friendship with the Soviet Union and all other nations are essential for the survival of Germany. General von Seeçkt, with his great political intelligence, always stressed this point.

If a timely end is put to the war, on the basis laid down above, the shaping of the postwar era will have great advantages for Germany too. By close cooperation with all the nations of the world and mutual trade especially with the USSR, her industries will have unlimited markets; at the same time Germany would be a grateful customer for rich excess produce of Russia. Only such a peaceful order of things can solve the question of "living space," which has been so mishandled by propaganda and directed into false courses, and which has already caused so much blood to flow senselessly and uselessly. Friendship with the Soviet Union and all other nations would bring to Germany too the lasting peace which she needs so desperately.

Friendly relations with the Soviet Union would mean work for everyone and the means of livelihood, instead of unemployment, hunger, and misery. Again the parallel with 1918 and the years that followed forces itself upon one. It is true that an immediate conclusion of peace will place heavy penalties on us. We have the courage to say so openly. In any event we shall have to make amends for what we have done wrong, and many lean years of deprivation are bound to follow. But at least we shall have the certain prospect of prosperity and of being treated with respect in the great family of nations, whereas in the opposite case ruins and permanent subjection will be the only result. We cannot count on the voluntary resignation of Hitler's government, as the bosses in this system fear for their lives. Their consciences and their hands are unclean. They will prefer a desperate battle with the whole nation to the bitter end to facing the fate which awaits them if the German people and those the world over who have suffered loss of life and property sit in judgment on them. They have no other course. The appointment of Himmler as minister of the interior in Prussia and the whole Reich, assisted by the police force of the entire country, and as chief commander of all SS units, shows clearly that Hitler has no intention of ever letting the executive power fall into the hands of the Wehrmacht. Both the government and the system intend to protect and support themselves against the people through the police and the SS.

Germany has an enormously difficult choice: either war under Hitler to complete destruction or the overthrow of the regime and the formation of a new, strong, national people's government, which must give three guarantees: 1) that it has the confidence of the entire German nation; 2) that it will rely on the people and the Wehrmacht to uphold order and represent the interests of Germany; 3) that it is willing and able to negotiate for the immediate ending of the war and creation of the conditions for an honorable and lasting peace.

This is why, comrades, we German officers consider it our urgent duty to raise our voices over against our people and demand the resignation of Hitler and his regime. The war must stop immediately, an armistice must be signed, and German troops withdrawn to the frontiers of Germany. A government supported by the confidence of the entire nation and with sufficient power behind it must give peace back to our sorely tried people and to the world. It must prevent any partition of Germany, must reinstate freedom of religion, freedom of conscience, and the right to free expression of opinion, must guarantee all lawfully acquired property, and must preserve friendship with the Soviet Union and all other nations of the world.

Stalingrad was the flaming signal of the catastrophe which threatens our people. The 6th Army, the Stalingrad army, was declared dead. Today those who were declared dead rise and call upon the people to reflect and save the Fatherland in the last hour. No one has more right to do this than they. Long live free, independent, and peaceful Germany!

After Colonel van Hooven, it was Colonel Steidle's turn to speak. As a devout Roman Catholic he analyzed the Nazi system's attacks on the church, on the family, on right and law. He concluded with the demand that the captive officers above all should raise their voices to save Germany, even though at home they had already been written off or been declared dead.

Finally Major General Lattmann stepped onto the speaker's platform. He discussed the meaning and value in our present situation of the military oath given to Hitler:

We have taken our oath to the person of Adolf Hitler, there is no getting away from that; and we vowed it solemnly before God. The question is therefore serious, very serious: May we break this oath? Are there reasons that can justify this step before our conscience, before our God, and—less important—before the world? Let us ignore the questions which start with the fact that many did not give this oath of their own free will; there are examples in history where the breaking of an oath has subsequently proved to be a great and saving act.

The most profound Christian conception can derive the right to break an oath from the commandment to obey God rather than man. The ethical concept of loyalty depends in the last analysis upon the relationship between the leader and the follower whose loyalty he has made sure of through the oath. The truly honest generals and officers at Stalingrad told their troops clearly and openly what the position was. I should like to remind you of the order given by one of the commanding generals long before the battles were over. It ran as follows: "The Führer has ordered us to fight to the end. That order, men, is sacred." Such generals and officers demanded from themselves and from their soldiers the fulfillment of the military oath to the last, that is to say in a situation where death, as compared with the spiritual and physical terrors, had lost its sting. How far knowledge of the need for peace must have progressed if men like this could be prevented from acting only by their military oath. If one carries such loyalty to its logical end, one comes to the conclusion: Let Germany be annihilated if only the military oath is not broken. This extreme provides the justification for regarding further adherence to the oath as unethical. Since we believe that to continue the war will bring about the annihilation of the German people, we consider the oath given to Adolf Hitler under very different conditions now to be invalid. Because he knew that our oath bound us to him he was able to devise plans which were to make him the "greatest of all Germans." For this idea, and no longer for Germany, the precious blood of our comrades was sacrificed. Is this not misuse of our loyalty? Is it not insistence upon a right which he made bold to derive from our ethical conception of the wording of an oath? But we never gave our oath to make Hitler or ourselves the "Lord of Europe"! We swear before God that we shall be most loyal if it means fighting for Germany. But he to whom we have sworn this loyalty has made a lie of this oath. Today we consider ourselves all the more obligated to our nation, and from this inner obligation we take the right to act, yes, we feel the compulsion to act. In view of our circumstances we can at present act only with words. But with these words we call the generals, officers, and soldiers of the German Wehrmacht to join us against the war! Help preserve the men of the Wehrmacht for the German people! Our Fatherland needs them. Recognize the summons of the hour! Create the basis for an armistice and peace! Lead the Wehrmacht back to our frontiers! Help prevent the disintegration, the collapse of the army and of the Reich. Preserve the Wehrmacht for the new Germany as an instrument of peace . . .

Loud applause greeted his words. Solemnly over one hundred delegates from various officers' camps put their signatures to the declaration of the Officers' League; and the vice president of the National Committee, Major Hetz, stated at the same time that the officers of the National Committee would also like to sign the declaration and become members of the league. To this he added his request that the league appoint its officers and several other members delegates to the National Committee. Seydlitz was completely carried away by his new role and so intoxicated that, forgetting his resentment against the officers who had founded the National Committee, he agreed to the suggestion with tears in his eyes. For several minutes he demonstratively shook the hand of the deserter Zippel and addressed him as Mr. Corporal. Seydlitz and his comrades do not suspect that with their entry into the National Committee the Officers' League has fulfilled its purpose and its further existence has little meaning.

SEPTEMBER 21, 1943. In a plenary session today the formal election to the National Committee of nine members of the Officers' League took place. During this election the first violent collision occurred in the committee. At the last moment the generals seemed to realize after all that by joining the National Committee they have buried their dreams of the league. Perhaps they consoled themselves with the idea that the National Committee is bound from the very start to be of greater political significance, since the Officers' League comprises only people of a certain rank. But they obviously wanted to assure themselves of a little more influence and with the committee already in session they raised the condition that another general besides Seydlitz be elected to the board of the committee. For this role they selected von Daniels. After a sign from the Russians Weinert agreed to their suggestion so that the whole project should not founder on this single minor point. However fourteen members of the committee, including myself, were so shocked at this intrigue on the part of the generals that we voted against the choice, emphasizing von Daniels' dubious character.

Chapter Five / The Front

OCTOBER 15, 1943. A few days after the Officers' League was organized the National Committee sent Friedrich Wolf, Lieutenant Colonel Baratov, and me to the south Ukrainian front. With us went five students of the antifascist school. The journey to Rostov took us through Voronezh, Millerovo, Kamenskaia, and so on—all places over which, barely fourteen months ago, I had heavy air battles with the Russians. It was with very mixed feelings that I saw from the window of a Russian sleeper the place where my Messerschmitt squadron had been stationed near Millerovo.

From Rostov we were taken by truck to the headquarters of Marshal Tolbukhin, commander of the 4th Ukrainian Front. There I met again the same Colonel Tulpanov who interrogated me at Stalingrad and at whose request I wrote the letter for the leaflet. He is chief of Department 7 of the Red Army political staff, attached to the 4th Ukrainian Front. His department is responsible for propaganda among enemy troops. In peacetime he was an instructor at the Leningrad War Academy. He showed me the leaflet which was printed on the basis of my letter. With my shorn hair and face swollen with eczema from the tetanus injection, I am unrecognizable in the photograph on it. In addition, Tulpanov felt it impossible to leave on a leaflet intended for German soldiers the statement that a German flier had shot down thirty-five enemy planes. So he simply had the figure "five" erased, leaving "three," but prefaced my letter with a statement that I was a well-known pilot decorated with the Knight's Cross. By so doing he made certain that every German soldier would believe the whole letter to be a forgery.

The day after our arrival in the area of the Mius position we were received by Marshal Tolbukhin and his chief of staff. Friedrich Wolf and I explained the status of the National Committee fully to the marshal, who promised us all support in our work. Our task is to concentrate chiefly on strengthening and improving our propaganda at the front, organizing illegal groups of the Free Germany movement within the German units, and collecting information about the situation inside Germany and in the German army. The propaganda is relayed to the front by means of leaflets, cars with loudspeakers, and secret transmitters. Only a few leaflets, explaining the fundamental ideas of the National Committee which are of significance to the entire Eastern front, are sent out from Moscow. All the others are drafted by the representatives of the committee in the Russian army groups, and by their assistants in the armies and divisions, and printed by the Red Army frontline printing presses. Our most urgent task therefore is to draw up leaflets and prepare broadcasts for the front loudspeakers. We also hold courses for antifascist students and new prisoners of war, who come of their own free will to be instructed. Our work meets with lack of understanding on the part of the Russians and with great organizational difficulties. Infinite harm to our propaganda is done by the Red Army leaflets, which are full of clumsy lies and exaggerations. Moreover, unlimited paper is at the disposal of the Red Army, whereas we have difficulty in getting permission to print a single leaflet of the National Committee in even such a small edition as ten thousand copies. Ten thousand leaflets dropped at night disappear on the thinly manned German lines like needles in a haystack. It is mere illusion to expect the German soldier to differentiate clearly between the leaflets of the Red Army, which aim at demoralizing the soldier and inviting him to desert, and those of the National Committee which try to persuade him to organize in illegal groups and to take definite political action against the Hitler regime. On the contrary the German soldiers transfer the negative prestige which the propaganda of the Red Army has acquired in two years to the leaflets of the National Committee. The only thing that merits the designation of truth in the Red Army leaflets is the conclusion that Hitler is losing the war and that the Nazis are leading Germany to catastrophe.

But worst of all is the unwieldiness of the Russian organization, the Russian bureaucracy. Before an idea reaches execution it is usually lost in a forest of red tape. To this are added indescribable stupidity and lack of independence among the lower ranking Russian soldiers who are responsible for the propaganda work in each unit up to the division. Without their support we can accomplish nothing, but they fear every independent decision as they would fire and are interminably worrying about what their superiors may think. They also believe it sacrilege not to sprinkle every leaflet with Marxist slogans and hymns in praise of the invincible Red Army and the wonderful "Great Socialist October Revolution."

All these difficulties mounted up as we set to work to organize illegal groups inside the Wehrmacht. For this task we brought the five antifascist students from Moscow with us.

Armed with German papers and dressed in German uniforms, they are to cross the lines and establish themselves in some base town behind the front from which they will carry out their illegal work. But just to provide these five men with the requisite German uniforms, papers, pay books, leave passes, service travel vouchers, and so forth, and above all with German arms, will take us two months. The most difficult part is acquiring the particulars for drawing up these documents: accurate information concerning the units opposite us is essential.

The Russians underestimate the hazards connected with this kind of work because their people can rely on the support of the population behind the German lines, whereas for us everyone, whether Russian or German, is at first an enemy. The Russians are really interested only in being able to report to their superiors that so many German antifascists have been sent behind the lines for illegal work. They are indifferent to the fate of these men who are undertaking this enormously dangerous work inspired only by their love for Germany and their hatred of Hitler. Because of this attitude several of our best people who were equipped not by us but by the Russians have fallen into the hands of the German Secret Field Police.

Furthermore, our activities at the front are made more difficult because many Russians inevitably reply to all our criticism and suggestions for improvement that it is the Red Army which is winning the war and therefore they understand everything better than we. Matters become even more difficult when we try to intervene on behalf of the German prisoners and antifascists working at the front with the Russians. The Russians answer by pointing out the tremendous sacrifice in lives they are suffering in the war or the destruction and devastation which the retreating German troops and special demolition commandos have left behind as a result of the scorched earth policy of the High Command. We can only be silent when, on the way to the front, we pass through villages deliberately burned down, where the corpses of shot civilians and the carcasses of shot cattle poison the air. Towns like Mariupol and Stalino were systematically burned to the last house by the German commandos, who were ordered to destroy everything before pulling out without fighting. Often enough charred bodies can be seen lying among the ruins.

I once stood with several Russian officers in front of a well which was filled to the top with the bodies of civilians shot by the Germans. After that I never dared to criticize Russian stubbornness and lack of feeling if we met a column of German prisoners of war and a sergeant refused to take into our car the wounded men who were obviously unable to go on marching. I was too ashamed.

OCTOBER 20, 1943. Among the captured documents I found the diary of Wolfgang Heinz of Nürnberg, a young German officer cadet. He arrived at the front in August and has presumably been killed or taken prisoner. I could discover no more about the origin of the diary, but I have copied it:

Aug. 30, 1943. I am right in the front line and have got to know it well, not with shouts of victory and hurrahs but in retreat. There have been examples of the best sort of comradeship, though gross examples of the opposite too. I can't write down my experiences. They were too much and too terrible.

Sept. 1. Today begins the fifth year of war. Here everyone hopes for an attack on England, and if that succeeds everything may yet be all right. If only the air attacks would stop. They worry us out here more than our own problems.

Sept. 3. The Mius tragedy of 1943. The characters: German soldiers, hungry, tired, wet to the skin. The place: plowed fields. The opponents: four hundred yards apart. Time: day.

I. Sunrise. Germans are preparing to retreat. It has been raining, everyone is wet, dirty, and tired. The men are in tolerable spirits. Suddenly the order is given: Halt! Dig in! We are staying here. Long faces.

II. Sudden noise of engines. For once these are not Russian but German cruiser tanks. And now it begins: The second battalion rises and rushes to attack, our own artillery fires, tanks fire and carry us with them, Russians retreat. Rejoicing. But then comes the counterbarrage. Antitank, antiaircraft fire, hand grenades, rockets, tanks like mad! Casualties! Attack over. Dig in; the end!

III. The sun which shone just for the attack has gone. The men are painfully digging in under enemy fire. A violent storm is raging from the sea, becoming a cloud-burst. Everybody wet to the skin. The Russians fire. Men lie in their foxholes as if in graves. Our tanks have vanished. Our artillery has stopped shooting. Finis! It has been one of the most eventful and difficult days of my life, this first attack. One knows no fear although comrades fall beside one; only the one word Forward!!! One must have lived through this once. The greatness of the moment in indescribable.

Sept. 8. Now I have been at the front for fourteen days and it seems like fourteen months. I have lived through so much and I am so tired, physically and spiritually. If only one knew what it is all for. One day we are told "Hold the position to the last man," and the next morning battalion headquarters has gone and we follow at night! I am certain the front will not be held here either. How I long for

113

the end of the war! And I would like to be around when everything is peaceful again and everyone can work, think, and live as he likes. Nobody can take that personal freedom from you. If everything should go, I am still young and still have the courage to begin a new life. But I shall work for myself and never again for "lofty goals," ideals like "Führer," "nation," and so forth.

If peace should surprise us while we are still here in Russia it will be difficult for us to get back to Germany, for everything will become chaos and no one will give a thought to the people at the front.

Sept. 9. We run into so many people here, one gradually gets a view of many areas of life and learns to look at things differently. I can't write freely about all this yet. The end of the war will clear up everything. But one thing is plain to me now: one of the reasons for the great defeats which our army has suffered is the false official communiqués. Everything is lied about, embellished, improved on, touched up, so that a tank division which had say twenty tanks still at its disposal suddenly has two hundred again. I wonder whether headquarters realizes what the troops are going through in the Mius retreat; that they have no blankets to cover them at night in zero temperatures; not a tent, nor a spade to dig in with; nor clean underclothes nor sweater nor socks, since everything has been burned during the retreat!

Sept. 10. It is often terribly difficult to carry out some of the orders. We have had to burn down a village today. The poor people who had so laboriously built it all were in despair. "But you are a civilized people," one woman said to me, and one can only shrug one's shoulders. They went down on their knees to plead with us, offered us all their money and held up icons to us. But what could we do? Orders! And while the women wept, we burned the village down. "C'est la guerre!"

Sept. 11. 4 P.M. Now it is beginning to rain slowly. "Lasciate ogni speranza," said the captain when we started out. What crimes have we committed to be punished like this at the age of twenty? And whom is it all for? Isn't the war just a swindle? Is it only for material things after all and not for ideals? I almost believe so.

Sept. 12. Why does one stand all this? Is it for the Führer, the Fatherland, and one's people? No, no, a thousand times no. It is only because one's comrades are in the same boat and one mustn't forsake them. That is the reason, nothing else! Out here we want a quick end to all this mess where our comrades get killed while the high and mighty at home grow fat. And we want to get home!!! Why give one's bones for a regime which isn't worth it? This war has proved its unfitness for life. We should put an end to this murder of young people now while there may still be time. But the gentlemen at the top have no conscience. They are afraid to stand up for their actions. I must stop. The Russians have begun to attack. Goodby. No doubt it will soon be over.

And here by contrast are a few letters which were also found at the front.

From Professor Wilhelm W———

> *Berlin-Lichterfelde-West*
> *July 18, 1943*

My dear Wolfgang:

. . . One who like yourself is of one mind with his dear ones can succeed. I thank God that by holding your men to comradeship through life and death you have held high and realized the only principle of the old soldiery. Of this I am especially proud.

By the time this letter reaches you the Russian attacks will be weakening and perhaps the insanity of their bloody sacrifices will have had the necessary repercussions on the Russian masses. Think of 1917 when almost overnight, unsuspected by us or by anyone in the world, the collapse came in Russia and freed us from pressure in the east. What madness it is, too, that that devil Churchill is free to act the way he does and encourages the hope that he will get us down as in 1918. You have to clutch your head to discover the meaning of it. . . . Let's drop this! When things are quieter I will write in greater detail, and maybe send you a copy of the lecture I am to deliver during the first part of August at 18th Army headquarters (Colonel General Lindemann) up in the northeast. On August 3 or 4 I will be flying to Reval and from there to army headquarters. But I shall stop at various military camps to lecture and will get to know the towns and countryside of that region which are as yet unknown to me. Imagine the bait they have held out to me: that I shall see the great city of Peter through a telescope!!! . . .

At the end of August I shall be speaking to the young officers of the Germanic Legions and those of the SS officer candidate school at Tölz. We'll see what happens there! On September 1 there is a "refresher course" starting for the wounded and for servicemen—no one has any idea how that will turn out. And so it goes without a moment's pause all through the winter. Such fun! Goodby for now, my dear eldest boy—you make us happy and proud of you in every way. Affectionate greetings to you from all of us.

YOUR FATHER

Aug. 2, 1943

My dear Wolfgang:

You can imagine how eagerly we listen to every word of the communiqué. Things are going well. That is all that matters. Today for the first time the name [of Orel] was not mentioned—which means that you had a quiet day yesterday—how well you deserve it! Perhaps things are going to happen soon. When once our "clever Hans" [Field Marshal von Kluge] has his right hand free to attack, there may be such a haul as we've never had yet. Then it will soon be all up with the Russians. But add things up for yourself: they have five million men in reserve for this year. The second half of the winter offensive has cost them horribly. In the north, at Lake Ladoga alone, an army of one million men was utterly destroyed. Judging by your area (and there can't be fewer elsewhere) one can add another two million to the number of men killed along the entire front since July 5. A blow such as that I have suggested above would dispose of yet another million. After that the 55–60 age group won't be enough. According to what people say here—based on English reports of the period before the summer offensive—Russia has so far lost thirty million men, including those who have died of hunger. Today the figure would have to be much increased. And one should add the fifty million people in the area occupied by us, which leaves Stalin only eighty or at most one hundred million at his disposal, and even that figure must be smaller by now. But Stalin has to garrison his entire southern frontier and that includes Iran and Turkestan. And even if he keeps only a few troops in Siberia, so few that one day the Japanese will be able to reach Lake Baikal without firing a shot, his gigantic organization requires a larger percentage of men than we need.

Hence the shrinking of his armed forces so that he will accomplish no more this winter—if at all. . . .

. . . The air attacks on the cities of the West are annihilating. Cologne and other cities, and now Hamburg too, have "ceased to exist." This is what people say who have seen them. Also heavy losses in lives. And much excitement, bitterness, panic.

All Churchill's plans. This man whom German propaganda has riduculed instead of taking as seriously as possible is the devil in human form. He is destroying Europe in order to make himself ruler of the world. He has Roosevelt in his pocket.

In this connection something puzzling happened yesterday. For some time people have been whispering that Berlin is to be destroyed! Last night leaflets signed by Goebbels were distributed from house to house: "It is urgently desired and it is in their own interest that everyone who is not obliged professionally or for other reasons to remain in Berlin should move to an area less liable to air attack"!!

I was horrified and shocked. The effect of this announcement? Panic, overcrowded National Socialist Union offices, ticket windows, railway stations, and so forth. But I don't believe these threats. At least not the threat that "the whole of Berlin will become a heap of rubble," as the ministry official said to my colleague!!! That would take several million tons of explosives which means several tens of thousands of airplanes coming over several times. How could that be? How could they attack Berlin at all except as a demonstration? They would need at least five thousand planes to produce an effect on Berlin as great in proportion and impressive as that on Hamburg.

Even then it would mean risking two to three thousand planes. Utter madness!!!

Aug. 14, 1943

My dear Wolfgang:

. . . You ask why I am still here, when I had written that I was on my way to the 18thArmy? The reason is a simple one. Official propaganda has painted Churchill in such a different light that I run the risk of criticism from those to whom I would like to present my view. Since the decree about the "fliers' court" * I have no alternative but to protect everybody from doing anything stupid.

We have therefore postponed our lecture tour for a month "owing to the general situation, especially in Italy." Whether it will take place then or not remains to be seen. But I shall write out my lecture in the next few days and shall send it for approval to the Censorship Office. If they agree to it, they will then take the responsibility. In that case I and my listeners are covered.

Be assured that I will stand or fall with the front. As ever, I still believe in our victory and wish it for you, as you have deserved it a thousand times over. Ignore those wretches who waver and run away. Remain steadfast and be men. You will know how to deal with the others later. I am happy and proud of every word in your letters. I can only say to you: I believe in what you are doing.

Affectionately,

YOUR FATHER

This is a father of those officers who force people like Wolfgang Heinz into "comradeship" through life and death.

* A circuit court empowered to pass sentences, including the death sentence, and have them executed. *Trans.*

The professor, the typical example of pan-German megalomania, for whom war is still an opportunity for pleasure trips and study tours: "I shall see the great city of Peter through a telescope!!!" That is what drew him! This man who puts on airs about wanting to fight the fatal official ridicule of the enemy proves in the same breath, by fantastic calculations, that Churchill cannot bomb Berlin, and by even more grotesque figures that the Russians, in August 1943, are at "their last gasp." While he is wondering how to make the war appear more palatable to the misled young officers of the Germanic Legions, he certainly does not say "Lasciate ogni speranza"— he has already got one eye on the authorities to make sure that he is saying the right thing. He wants to be certain that someone will take the responsibility from him when he presents Churchill to the German people as the devil rather than an insignificant bugbear, as his "commander in chief" is doing. This man is not even clear about the meaning of his own words when he writes in another place that he hopes the storm of "disenchantment" produced by Goebbels' instructions to evacuate Berlin will soon pass over. He has not the courage to admit to himself that he is living in a state of intoxication because this intoxication is the last hope of this "100 per cent German."

Is further proof needed that our work is necessary and vindicated in spite of its ambiguous nature? Must we not try everything to show a way out to these boys in uniform who only sense instinctively that something is not quite right—to give them a road along which they can move with conviction? Must we not give them more enduring values than those vague, undefined, meaningless, topsy-turvy conceptions which the professor throws around? When it is too late, old gentlemen like this will be the first to make wise speeches about the cynicism and nihilism of the young, and turn up their noses at us in Russia: One just does not do that sort of thing! And if one has become a Communist as well, then their horror will know no bounds.

OCTOBER 28, 1943. The position of the German troops is catastrophic. Overwhelming Russian superiority in artillery, tanks, and aircraft. At the same time, the front is becoming longer and longer, instead of shorter, since Hitler has forbidden all tactical and strategic retreat. The Russians are outside Kiev, and the battle for the hamlet of Melitopol still continues.

I have just returned from the front. For hours we drove alongside continual battery and rocket fire. The German artillery hardly replied. I saw German aircraft only once: eight JU-88's bombing field positions from a height of twenty thousand feet, which is of course quite senseless.

During the hours of darkness when we maneuvered our heavy car, fitted with loudspeaker, as near the front line as possible, we were filled with tension. Our trumpet signal boomed across the steppes and reached the combatants of both armies sheltering in their dugouts and foxholes: "Attention! Attention! This is the National Committee for Free Germany speaking!"

Usually a commentator gave the military and political news first and then announced a talk by Friedrich Wolf or me. We tried in the most matter-of-fact way possible to explain the war situation to the German soldiers and rouse them from their resignation and lethargy.

German officers and men! The destiny of the nation lies in your hands. You must reckon with the fact that every day the war lasts Hitler is dragging Germany deeper into disaster. Do not let irresponsible adventurers put you off with empty promises. The fate of the Hitler regime cannot be altered by continuing the war. To continue the war means the destruction of our Fatherland. Comrades! You know the situation, but you wonder what the individual can do to change it. Comrades, you individuals are an army of millions! You cannot beat the three greatest powers in the world. But you are a powerful force if you organize yourselves against Germany's real enemy— Hitler. Organize the men at the front! Organize all ranks and all the units in the Wehrmacht against Hitler. Against Hitler! Clear-sighted and courageous comrades from a great many divisions have already formed illegal groups in the Free Germany movement and established contact with us. Follow their example! Organize yourselves into small groups and fight for our goals: The removal of Hitler by the army! Orderly retreat to the frontiers of the Reich! An immediate armistice! One word is sometimes enough; a skillful criticism may open the eyes of a comrade. Work illegally until you have won your unit. From the individual to the group. From the group to the division. That is the way to prepare for the rising against Hitler. You can rest assured that there are enough determined men among the generals to act when they know that the troops at the front are on their side. Each individual can and must act today!

Comrades! Forward toward a free and peaceful Germany!

The reactions to these speeches were extremely varied. In many places the front sank into deep silence, listening. We had suggested the soldiers fire three shots into the air in token of agreement—they did it. On the other hand, in certain units angry machine gun and hand grenade fire was the reply, and

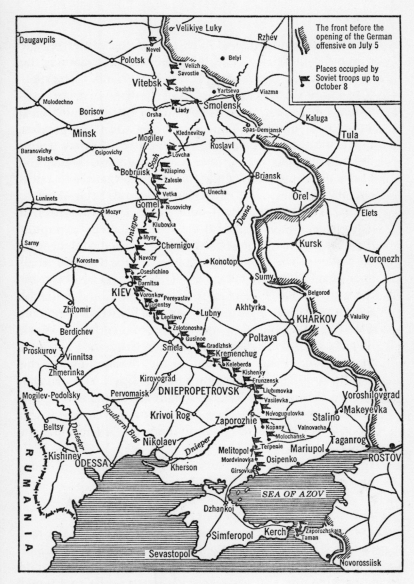

The legend in the upper right of the map reads:

The front before the opening of the German offensive on July 5

Places occupied by Soviet troops up to October 8

The front on July 5 and October 8, 1943

sometimes even the artillery took part in these attempts to silence us. Occasionally assault groups were sent out to wipe us out.

It is interesting to see the reaction of the Russian front commanders. Some of them give us their full support, emphasizing their friendly feelings and sympathy for us German antifascists. Others are bitter because of the additional burden we are to their troops. "Hand grenades, rocket launchers, tanks, and bombers will win the war. One must kill the German fascists. That is the only propaganda they understand." Argument is useless. It has no effect even if we quote Lenin, who said that war for the common soldier is merely a state of continued self-defense which he himself can hardly alter. And yet this quotation hits the nail on the head here on the Eastern front. Illegal activity inside the Wehrmacht means far greater risks than fighting at the front. There is no incentive to surrender, for when the Germans counterattack the Russians, they have too often found prisoners murdered. Only recently one of our propaganda officers at the front saw three German soldiers, who had crossed over to the other side after hearing our speaker through the microphone, shot down by a drunken Russian. Every prisoner I have spoken to has witnessed extreme cases of maltreatment of prisoners. The organized mass murders of the Nazis are certainly without precedent; but the brutality of the Russians and their cruel excesses at the front are equally terrible. If this war is not over before the Russians set foot on German soil, if they invade Germany, God have mercy on us!

NOVEMBER 8, 1943. Together with Colonel Tulpanov, Friedrich Wolf, Lieutenant Colonel Baratov, and a certain Colonel Maltopol, the organizer of a Rumanian prisoners' legion, I am sitting listening to the radio. In a moment Hitler is to address the old party guard in the Bürgerbräu in Munich on the twentieth anniversary of the march on the Feldherrn-halle.

Yesterday we were invited to the celebration of the twenty-sixth anniversary of the October revolution. Kiev had just fallen, and the Russians were glowing with the joy of victory.

All it takes on occasions like this to put me in a rage is one of the Communists or Russians telling me how superior the Soviet system of government is and that the successes of the Red Army clearly prove it.

Their enormous superiority in men and material is crushing us. And they use these with a slowness and caution which are positively provoking. With such superiority in material, the German army would chase the Russians beyond the Urals without letting them get their breath once. But there are twice as many supply troops as fighting forces. Orders can be given only by messenger or radio. Not even Tolbukhin has a tele-phone connection with Moscow or with the other armies. When I told him that as a lieutenant in Kalach I was able to speak to a private number in Berlin as often as I cared to (al-though of course it was officially forbidden) he simply would not believe me.

If the Soviet propaganda line is right that the morale of an army depends on the progressiveness and social justice of the society it defends, then the Third Reich is a model state com-pared with the Soviet Union. Down to Stalingrad, more Russians went over to the German side than Germans to the Russian. They were astonished to hear from the Germans the same story that had been put out by their own propaganda— that the Germany army was encircled. They have that little faith in their leaders. Tulpanov told me recently that Red Army men continue to go over to the enemy.

Friedrich Wolf considers this "fascist nonsense," racial arrogance, and "nationalism"! He feels it his duty to defend the state dogma about the superiority of the Soviet man, and if one pushes him *ad absurdum* he gets so furious that discussion becomes impossible. All Communists react in that way. In this they resemble the Nazis.

I cannot see the need of all this. Surely the Bolsheviks are not to blame if the Russians are far behind the West in civilization, technology, and organization. It would be impossible to look at Russian achievements at all objectively if one denied these difficulties. Are the Russian people really mentally so slow and utterly lacking in self-confidence that they have to be continually urged on by this sort of propaganda? It seems to me that this only brings on a pronounced inferiority complex, prevents the recognition and removal of weaknesses, and leads to a quite false estimate of the situation. Outside this strait jacket of propaganda theses and dogma the Russians are magnificent—earthy and genuine, high spirited, good natured, and hospitable—and they can lose themselves gloriously in the moment. Even their *nichevo* has wonderful moments.

During the celebrations yesterday I was sitting rather mournfully at a table reserved for "dignitaries," sunk in gloomy thoughts, when a Russian suddenly spoke to me. I was a little taken aback, because it would not have been the first time that a drunk had insulted me or Germans in general in the most vulgar way. The colonel who had approached me was the Red Army's specialist in hate propaganda and had never made a secret of his enmity for me. To my surprise he apologized. When I arrived at the front, he said, he had regarded me with great suspicion. The Germans had murdered his family. He could understand it when his son was shot as a partisan, but he could never forgive the fact that his wife and eleven-year-old daughter had been shot as hostages, and so he hated all Germans. He had never thought I was sincere. But now he had watched me for six weeks and made inquiries about my work and what I had to say about Germany. This had made him revise his judgment. "I want to apologize for the low opinion I have had of you. When I heard that you passionately defended your Fatherland against unjust accusations, that in spite of everything you were proud of being a German, you gained my highest respect."

This conversation was like a signal. All at once the Russians went out of their way to receive me into their circle. Suddenly everybody had something good to say about Germany. They asked me to dance and join in their fun and they assured me they were convinced Germany would have a wonderful rebirth after the overthrow of Hitler.

The colonel slapped me on the back: "What is the use of so much thinking? Nichevo! Everything passes. Today is a holiday. Enjoy yourself, dance and drink with us."

That was yesterday—and now Hitler is speaking.

The "Badenweiler March" came over the air. Hitler entered the Bürgerbräu. We could hear his hoarse, hard voice. He spoke to icy silence. When he paused, clearly awaiting the audience's applause and appreciation, one could hear only sparse, lonely clapping from the front rows which no one took up. He got more and more excited, shouted more and more wildly, but did not succeed in carrying the crowd with him. "What does it matter if we withdraw a few kilometers in the east?" he screamed. "Or even a few hundred kilometers," he added in a confused stutter. "If this test were enough to break the German people I would not shed a tear for them."

This is the end, I thought to myself with a flash of hope. Surely he would never say anything so unheard of if he did not realize that his own end is near. Not even the old party members responded. But again my hopes were shattered. Wild howls of exultation beat against him as he announced revenge against England and the destruction of the island in a fortnight. Could this be the mood in Germany? Were all the feelings of hate stored up for the outside world? Or was it only party members who were present and who reacted in this way?

When he had finished I turned the radio off and looked at the faces of the Russians around me. This was the first time they had heard a Hitler speech. What a wide abyss there is between this hysterical shouting and the sober speeches of their statesmen, who calculate accurately every exaggeration of their propaganda.

Tulpanov smiled. "The war will go on for a long time," he said at last.

We contradicted him: Germany is bound to see through this declaration of bankruptcy; the Wehrmacht will act now.

But Tulpanov remained skeptical.

"You can see for yourselves. Barely a fifth of the Stalingrad generals have broken with Hitler, and the officers at the head of the fighting divisions are always inclined to see things more optimistically than one does in a prison camp."

I hope he is wrong.

NOVEMBER 22, 1943. A small village immediately behind the front line near Perekop, the approach to the Crimea. The Russian commander led us to a house where we met a first lieutenant and battalion adjutant who had been captured only a few hours before.

The tall, thin student from Dresden looked at us disconcertedly from behind his spectacles. In a faltering voice he told us how he had been taken.

The battalion counted just thirty men when we took up our position two days ago on the edge of this village. . . . We had had no rest and no reinforcements for weeks; we had retreated, fighting all the way, suffering heavy casualties. Ten, twenty, thirty times we received the order to hold our position at any price. Each time we were promised reinforcements, artillery support, and God knows what else. But that same evening the Russians filtered in on our left flank in battalion strength, and the T-34's fired from almost behind us. Our commander asked the regiment and the division for permission to retreat into the hills beyond the marshy valley. We would have had contact again on both flanks there and some security from tanks. But the reply was a categorical refusal to give up even a hundred yards of ground. Our commander insisted.

"This is plain murder," he roared into the radio.

The division commander came to us that night and suddenly was very friendly.

"You're absolutely right," he encouraged us. "But you know the Führer's order. It's only a matter of a few more hours: two batteries are already moving up to give you support. At noon you will have four tanks at your disposal and a field regiment of the Luftwaffe will get here in the evening. With this help you'll be able to throw the Russians back."

What choice did we have? In the early morning a lieutenant of the artillery regiment arrived. When he tried to contact headquarters he was told the battery had not started on its way since the neighboring regiment had refused to let it leave. As it was, it had only five rounds left per gun. And two hours later hell broke loose. Half an hour's barrage from guns of every caliber, and in the middle of the firing an attack by three battalions and twenty tanks. Our only antitank gun had been knocked out. In ten minutes we were overrun. We were able to hold our command post a little while; then the tanks shot it to bits. The last four men of the battalion and three officers, the commander, the artillery man, and I, were sitting in a deep dugout. The Russians blew the entrance open and told us to come out. Then they threw hand grenades in. We squeezed ourselves against the walls. In a quiet moment while I was burning papers and cards a sergeant major suggested we give ourselves up. The two other officers didn't want to. A Russian shouted: "Two more minutes and you're dead." A private jumped toward the entrance shaft and tried to climb out. There was a shot. I turned round and saw the lieutenant staring at the private who was collapsed and moaning. Before I could move, he put his pistol to his head and shot himself. The other soldiers climbed out of the dugout. I looked at the commander. He just nodded. So I went to the entrance too. A private gave me a hand to pull me up. Another shot. The commander had killed himself.

I found myself standing among the Russians. One of them pointed at the dugout:

"Any more in there?"

"Three dead," I said and put my hand to my head as if shooting myself.

"Dead—why dead?" he asked. "No good. You live, go home. German soldiers live in Russia. Hitler dead—good. Germans live—good."

The prisoner had finished. After a while I asked if he had ever heard about the committee in Moscow.

"Yes," he said, "there was something about some officers'

committee in a news release to the officer corps, but of course that's all nonsense."

He considered the existence of the committee impossible. We handed him the newspaper with the account of the founding meeting of the Officers' League and left him alone to read it. An hour later we came back.

"Well, what do you say to that?"

He shrugged his shoulders. "The speeches don't sound improbable, but I'd have to talk to one of those men myself to be sure it isn't a forgery."

At this I took off my Russian fur coat and stood before the lieutenant in my German uniform. I introduced myself. He was speechless with astonishment. While I was telling him about the committee and the Officers' League, his eyes filled with tears.

"If only we had known of it sooner," he said.

"Would you or your commander have acted differently?"

"I don't know. We were always hoping the war would take a turn for the better and we would get through unhurt."

"Well," I said, "we'll talk about it some more. If you agree, I'll arrange to have you taken to committee headquarters at the front. We have a small group of German prisoners there who had the sort of experience you did. You said you wished you had heard about the committee earlier; perhaps you'll help us see that our comrades over there hear of it in time. Of course it would mean the war isn't over for you; you'd have to go on crouching in ditches, dugouts, minefields, and under artillery fire. If you're not convinced that our way is the right one all you have to do is say so, and we'll send you to the officers' camp without penalizing you.

After a few moments' thought the lieutenant agreed to my suggestion.

Chapter Six / "Politics"

JANUARY 15, 1944. During our return journey to Moscow in the middle of December Friedrich Wolf and I prepared for the committee a detailed account of our experiences at the front. We pointed out first of all that our propaganda was being conducted on far too small a scale ever to give the Wehrmacht concrete knowledge of our existence, and that it was altogether inadequate to convince our comrades on the other side of its honesty and accuracy. So far just a fraction of the troops had even heard of us. If we were to achieve anything our editions of printed leaflets and number of loudspeakers and transmitters would have to be greatly increased; we would also need many more people for front propaganda. At the same time the compromising propaganda of the Red Army would have to be throttled down if we were to succeed. It was especially important to redouble our efforts to smuggle letters from prisoners through the army mail. With Tulpanov's help we succeeded in getting a few hundred such letters through. And our radio station is broadcasting hundreds of messages each day from prisoners to their families. If we could organize the smuggling of letters on a really large scale, that is supply several thousand families in Germany with letters from their missing relatives, it would be an effective counterblow to the interception of the official prisoners' mail by German postal authorities.*

In addition to many practical ideas for organizing our propaganda we also gave the committee new suggestions about the content.

Our appeal to overthrow Hitler and withdraw the army to the Reich frontiers is, practically speaking, directed only at the generals, and we assume that they—unlike the troops—have enough information about us from their intelligence officers. An appeal like this means very little to the soldier at the front. What are encircled troops to do who are about to be sacrificed like the battalion at the approaches to the Crimea? They are actually between two fires. The only advice we can give them is to make an orderly surrender, not only in order to avoid the senseless sacrifice of life but as a positive political gesture against the regime. If such surrenders became a mass phenomenon in even one army, the generals would have to act. Our advice to the soldiers must be to organize so that in the decisive moment they can assert themselves by force and against their generals if need be.

The so-called right wing of the committee, the members of the Officers' League around Seydlitz, were of course horrified at these suggestions for "disruptive" propaganda. Seydlitz put large red exclamation marks and angry comments in the margin of our report, in an attempt to copy Frederick the Great's laconic methods and show his indignation. The opposition of the generals to these suggestions was so strong that

* Goebbels noted in his diary that he had suggested that mail from prisoners in the USSR should not be delivered. The suggestion was carried out.

even the Moscow émigrés refrained from discussing them at this point. Presumably they were afraid the National Committee might break up over this. Only yesterday, after interminable discussion and disagreement, a plenary session was called to consider our front propaganda. After a violent verbal exchange with some of the generals it was agreed to alter it. The generals always come out badly at these discussions, as they have no solidarity. On this occasion Lattmann suddenly set himself up as spokesman for the "radicals."

One of the main objections to our call for capitulation, which all members of the committee share, is concern for the fate of the prisoners of war during transport and in the camps. Can we take the responsibility of assuring our comrades at the front that their lives will be spared and that they will eventually return home if they give themselves up as prisoners? I have answered this in the affirmative. There is no doubt that captivity brings with it considerable privations and demands numerous sacrifices. But is there any alternative? Surely the casualties will be greater still if the hopeless defense Hitler conducts so clumsily continues. If the army at Stalingrad had accepted the Russian proposal for capitulation while the soldiers were still healthy and had some resistance left, would not the death rate among the prisoners have been far lower than it was?

Our only choice is between greater and lesser evils. Even though Lattmann got up suddenly and grandly announced his conviction that if necessary the Red Army would cut down its own rations to feed the prisoners, he knew quite well that was the opposite of what he and all of us thought possible. Things are not as simple and ideal as that. "Put an end to a hopeless defense! Go over to the side of the National Committee!" This is the leitmotiv of our propaganda to the front. Yet as long as the scale of our propaganda is not increased tenfold our arguments over these slogans are just academic.

134

In the course of the arguing I have incurred the lasting hatred of the generals on the committee. In an article in our paper *Free Germany* addressed to the young officer corps I accused the German leaders of lack of civic courage and of making obeisance to the party. In another article I declared that the generals who pursue the scorched earth tactics merely further Goebbels' thesis that the Germans have burned their bridges behind them. If General Dietmar were to recommend these tactics as a military solution in his weekly analyses it would draw down a storm of anger which would burst like the last judgment upon Germany.

The generals, especially Seydlitz, accused me of insulting the Wehrmacht and of fouling my own nest.* The same accusations were leveled at Major Bechler, who had so far been considered one of the most faithful supporters of Seydlitz. In his position as adjutant to General Eugen Müller he had gained an insight into the origin of various orders of Hitler—the assassination of commissars, the branding of Soviet prisoners of war, shooting of women in uniform, and so on. But when he had dared to prophesy in an article that not even Germany's enemies would believe the figures of the victims of Hitler's extermination policy when they one day became known, his position of trust with Seydlitz was over. The generals seem to believe that it is still possible to hush up the gas trucks, the extermination camps, the mass shootings and deportations. With innocent faces they declare they have never heard anything about them. Lattmann told me proudly that he had immediately asked every person who spoke of such things where his information came from, as he had to make an official report in order to prevent those "wicked fairy tales" from spreading. He did

* Neither Seydlitz nor I could foresee then that Goebbels himself in his diary would deem me worthy, because of this article, of being placed next to Seydlitz as "one of the worst agitators of the clique of nobles."

not even realize he was admitting both that he had heard of these things and that he had even threatened to denounce those who were concerned about them.

The position of the generals in the committee is on the whole just as insincere as in this particular. They have not the courage to answer for the consequences of their own actions. They always want to be regarded as gentlemen conspirators. Their ideal is to sit in Moscow and compose documents full of patriotic fervor—now that they have been brought here against their will and dragged by the hair into the committee.

It seems to be beyond the generals' comprehension that in order to distribute the leaflets at and behind the front it is necessary to acquire knowledge of the troops on the opposite side, by methods which are indistinguishable from espionage; that it is impossible during this illegal work not to sacrifice a few innocent lives before being taken prisoner oneself; that in order to bring about the overthrow of Hitler which they demand it may be necessary to have a veritable civil war with the SS and even to kill several of its very pro-Hitler people. At the same time, they continually approve a point one day which only the day before they considered to be the acme of depravity, unworthiness, and dishonor. The cases of Zippel and Gold and the discussion of front propaganda and of the fate of the prisoners are examples of this.

The generals have allowed themselves to be taken in tow before in exactly the same way, from the time of Schleicher's murder, of the Fritsch and Beck affairs, to the SS massacres in Poland. They fear responsibility as much as they are concerned with saving face, and do not care what the actual facts are. The case of Daniels is typical of this. The generals insisted by ultimatum on his election as an officer of the committee, and out of their esprit de corps thought it right to ignore the objections raised against him. They expected Daniels would represent them on the committee in the same spirit. But they miscalculated completely. Daniels says yes to everything the left wing of the committee proposes. He signs articles which Seydlitz and Lattmann would never approve and which he himself does not even read. He is interested only in the privileges he enjoys as a general and member of the committee. Thse facts confirm the rumors which circulated about him.

MARCH 15, 1944. I again spent several weeks in the officers' camp at Yelabuga, with Lattman and Schlömer. The officers from Oranky are now there too. But I did not enjoy the journey, interesting as it was, in the Russian winter, in trains stuffed full of refugees and over a hundred miles by sleigh through snow-covered forests with wolves howling in the distance.

The conditions in the Yelabuga camp have again deteriorated and are almost as bad as they were in November 1942. The political disagreement between the supporters of our committee —at most one-third of the officers—and their opponents has turned into fanatical hatred. The Nazis use every method of provocation. The corruption of the camp administration, in which many adherents of the committee who have functions in the camp allow themselves to be involved; the spy system which the NKVD has fostered, the reappearance of Wagner as camp instructor—these have put all the trumps in their hands. Even so their political arguments cannot be taken seriously. "Assi" Hahn, the commander from my old squadron who was such a daring pilot on the Channel coast, embraced me heartily, in spite of all political differences, when we met again, slapped me on the back, and said: "You may be right with all your political arguments, but I'd like to fly with you against the Tommies again!" It was he who once gave us at

Cherbourg his idea of life after the war: "Why not live in Russia? I should like to command an airdrome in peacetime, somewhere on the shore of the Black Sea, say, and run a large estate nearby—then those Russian serfs would see . . ." and he made the motion of lashing with a whip. Another time in Oranky prison he jumped up in the middle of a speech by Walter Ulbricht and shouted amid thundering applause from the officers: "Even if there are only twelve million of us left, we will fight on till final victory!"

My own commander, who was present when I was shot down and with whom I had flown in maybe a hundred engagements during which we more than once saved each other's life, refused to speak to me at all. He even refused to let me know through a third person what he told my relatives when I did not return from the attack.

A captain of a Stalingrad tank division, a nephew of Rundstedt, said in a discussion with Lattmann and me: "We Germans want to see the sunny side of life for once. We want to live like Dutch colonials, whose villas in the Hague make the most beautiful houses in Berlin-Dahlem look like dog kennels. If we can't succeed in this, Germany might as well perish." When Lattmann asked whether one could sacrifice millions of lives for such an aim, expose millions of women and children to air attacks, he replied loftily: "My wife is the wife of a soldier— she must die as I do." But he was unable to answer when asked why he had given himself up at Stalingrad against Hitler's orders.

However, there are some splendid fellows among our opponents who call themselves National Socialists with a steadfastness and disregard of the consequences which one can only admire. If these men were on our side we would be able to prepare first-rate propaganda for the front and should really obtain help for the prisoners from the Russians. As it is, all of our energy goes into a battle among Germans.

In the circumstances one hardly dares to think of the soldiers' camps. In Yelabuga at any rate death is no longer a daily companion of the prisoners. But not even this can be said of the soldiers' camps. A thousand signatures to resolutions and glowing reports of the Communist delegations fool nobody.

And yet the Russians cannot be blamed too much. Their own population lives and works on rations which would mean death to us. The occupation of the Ukraine deprived them of their larder. If it had not been for the tinned meat from Chicago, millions would probably have died of hunger. It is precisely this misery among the population which has immeasurably increased the corruption at the expense of the prisoners. When we speak to the Russian administration of the prison camps about these matters they always take the view that the war must be won first before major efforts can be made to relieve the situation. As long as the German army continues to fight fanatically for Hitler the prisoners too must carry the burden which this battle imposes on the Russian people.

"You can see," a Russian colonel said to me, speaking of conditions in Yelabuga, "that the German officers are fanatical supporters of Hitler, and all this talk of opposition to the regime is based on illusion. Your committee has so far given us no proof of its thesis. We simply dare not tell our people the amount of food which has gone to the camps in the past year. It was much more than they themselves were receiving. The officers were given nearly three times as much. And what is the result? They remain arrogant. They sing Nazi songs and declare that not nearly enough 'inferior races' have been exterminated. We have proof that during the first winter of the war at least 400,000 prisoners died of hunger in German hands. And

these gentlemen here complain when they are bitten by bugs."
What could I say? What can one do?

The encirclement of the Cherkassy pocket has proved once
again that there is no solution for a surrounded army but
timely capitulation. On February 3 the Red Army succeeded
in encircling nine infantry divisions, one SS tank division, and

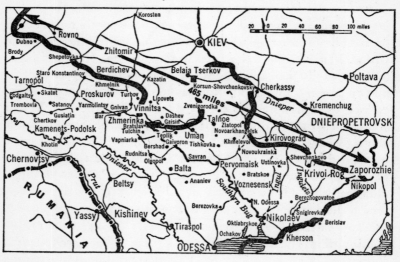

*The front in the Ukraine before the
encirclement of ten German divisions*

an SS brigade, between Cherkassy and Belaia Tserkov. Those
encircled units, like the others at Stalingrad, Hitler handed
to the Soviets on a platter when he refused, no matter what
the price, to evacuate this sector of the front, which was nearly
sixty miles long and only twelve to eighteen miles wide.

The Russians generally maneuver very ponderously and
cautiously. They appear to be still afraid of a recurrence of the
terrible encirclements of 1941. Perhaps also, for lack of leaders
in the junior and middle ranks, they do not wish to take the

risks which are involved in extensive strategic exploitation of their armored penetrations. To this must be added their extremely careless use of radio, which enables the resourceful and adaptable German leadership to anticipate the Russians' intentions wherever Hitler's insanity and the hopeless inferiority of German troops in manpower and material allow.

But now Hitler has achieved his masterpiece. The eastern

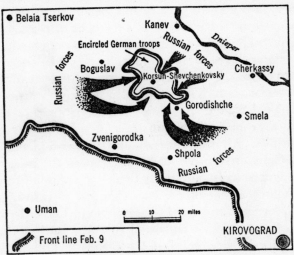

Soviet version of the encirclement of ten German divisions at Cherkassy

Ukrainian front has grown into a northern front over 450 miles long. The already ridiculously weak German forces are even more extended and thin. The Red Army had weeks to regroup so as to be able to cut off the Germans' narrow escape route in the bulge on the Dnieper. This is a unique opportunity for us to score a decisive success. If the commanding officers of the encircled armies were to decide to capitulate and to join the committee in a protest against Hitler, it would no longer be possible to hush up our existence in Germany. A definite step would have been made toward the rebellion of the Wehrmacht against the system. At the same time the position of the committee with respect to the Russians would be infinitely strengthened; we would automatically carry much more weight which could be used to the advantage of the prisoners.

A visit to Seydlitz by Colonel General Shcherbakov, Manuilsky's successor as head of the political administration of the Red Army, showed how greatly this idea interests the Russian Government too. Shcherbakov is a member of the Council of Five, the actual Soviet war cabinet, in which even Stalin figures only as *primus inter pares*. Seydlitz, Korfes, Hadermann, and Major Lewerenz left for the front in the saloon car of Shcherbakov's special train. They arrived at Vatutin's army group where Colonel Steidle and Major Büchler were already busy preparing a propaganda action on a grand scale for the encircled armies. All the generals and higher officers of the National Committee had addressed letters to the commanders they know personally, imploring their comrades not to make a second Stalingrad out of the encirclement; to refuse to obey Hitler; by orderly and timely capitulation to save the lives of 75,000 German soldiers entrusted to them, and at the same time strike a decisive political blow against Hitler. Seydlitz and Korfes addressed the encircled staff directly over the radio and received confirmation that they had been heard. Germans and Russians waited expectantly to see whether the commanders of the encircled armies would decide to open negotiations with the committee. But no reply came from the pocket.

Both armies were impeded in their operations by a sudden wet period which turned the ground to mud. Stubborn battles continued for the narrow strip that separated the pocket from the main front. Hitler had ordered the encircled troops to commit suicide if they could not be relieved. Finally, when they were concentrated in the narrowest possible space, a shock troop made up of all the units still fit for battle succeeded in hammering their way through at night, leaving all the wounded and equipment behind. Eighteen thousand prisoners remained in Soviet hands. On the battlefield lay tens of thousands of German soldiers. Among the dead was the commanding general of the 11th Corps, Stemmermann, the commander inside the pocket.

The battle was another big military success for the Russians, but for the committee it is a definite defeat. It is true that for the first time several hundred soldiers and officers appealed to the National Committee when they were captured, but without any real idea or knowledge of our propaganda. The generals ignored us, either because they continue to believe in Hitler and in the possibility of a favorable peace or because they refuse to work with us and the Russians. The fact that Paulus and the majority of the Stalingrad generals kept silent must have made our propaganda appear very unconvincing in their eyes.

MARCH 28, 1944. On March 27 General Melnikov, the Russian liaison officer with the National Committee, appeared and invited Seydlitz, Lattmann, and several members of the committee including me to a discussion. This discussion had a story behind it.

At the beginning of January *Tass* published an official statement on Soviet-Polish relations. Although the Soviet Government maintained no diplomatic relations with the Polish Government in Exile in London, on account of its attitude to the Katyn murders, it now invited these Poles to join in the Soviet-Czechoslovak pact of friendship, making it clear at the same time that the eastern frontier of Poland must follow the Curzon line. This line, which was decided upon by the Supreme Allied Council in 1919 and which gave the western Ukraine

and western White Russia to the Soviet Union, corresponded
with the demarcation line worked out between Germany and
the Soviet Union in 1939. The Poles naturally insisted on the
frontiers they had forced the Soviet Union to agree to in the
Treaty of Riga in 1921. The Soviet Union on its part promised
Poland, more or less as compensation in the West, the annexation of territory which had been taken by Germany but was
originally Polish, without which the entire Polish people could
not be united in one state, and which moreover would provide
Poland with the necessary outlet to the sea. Soviet press comments left no doubt that this elastic formula referred to large
sections of Silesia, Pomerania, and East Prussia. In addition to
this, Churchill made a declaration in which he demanded 250
miles of Baltic coast for Poland west of Königsberg.

All this of course profoundly shocked the committee. Even
the Moscow émigrés were speechless. Pomerania, Silesia, and
East Prussia had been used by Hitler as jumping-off points
against Poland; therefore they said Poland had a right to these
territories in the interest of security. This was their incredibly
stupid comment on this plan for a peace settlement. In reality
they know of course that it is no longer primarily a question of
Germany but that a power struggle for Europe has begun
here between Soviet Russia and the capitalist countries; that it
is a race run for the favor of the Poles over the body of Germany. Poland would be able to hold these territories only if
she were protected by Soviet Russia from the rear—that is if
she were pro-Soviet in outlook.

It is easier for the Communists on the committee to resign
themselves to this solution. The power and security of the
Soviet Union as the backbone of the Communist world movement is their first principle. National interests must be subordinate to the interests of the revolution is the way they put it.
If one is convinced of this the situation does not look so

desperate. The only solution to the problem of the German-Polish frontier is in fact an approach to a real federation such as should be possible among socialist states. The frontier question would be no problem between a socialist Poland and a socialist Germany. Molotov declared in the autumn of 1939 that the Poland of Pilsudski, which lived by oppressing other nations, and which had been designed in the imperialistic system of Versailles as part of the *cordon sanitaire* against the Soviet Union as well as a pistol at Germany's back, must not be allowed to rise again. If the Soviet Union is taking a different line today it is for tactical considerations of the moment and is not necessarily a grave matter. There is still time, and a great deal depends on when and under what conditions the Third Reich breathes its last.

The right-wing members of the committee refused even to discuss such "dialectical" constructions. They merely declared that this attitude was a relapse to imperialistic methods and a flagrant violation of all Marxist and international principles. The Communist "sympathizers," on the other hand, did not fail to point out to their comrades of the right that Churchill's proposal was a violation of the Atlantic Charter.

All this was too much for the generals: first the discussions of the propaganda at the front, then the disaster of Cherkassy, and finally this! In their Sunday villa to which the Russians always used to drive them for week-ends, they decided to send a memorandum to the Soviet suggesting a reorganization of the committee. Only generals and members of the Reichstag were to be represented on its board, which would thus acquire the character of a government-in-exile to which the Russians should give a guarantee regarding German frontiers. It looked as if the vodka they consumed in their week-end villa in the company of prominent émigrés and Russian officers had gone to their heads.

But they did in fact have such a document drafted by First Lieutenant Huber of the Reserve Corps, an SS officer and section chief at the German Ministry of Education. Behind the back of the committee they handed it to Melnikov's personal adviser, Colonel Schwetz. After a week he gave it back to them with the ironical comment that, in the interest of the ten undersigned members of the executive committee of the Officers' League, he considered it best not to pass it on to his superiors. Think of it: a handful of generals, prisoners of war, with not even a following worth speaking of in the camps, who had no significance save as a propaganda façade, demanding a political guarantee for postwar developments from one of the most powerful countries engaged in the war! Their lack of judgment had made them believe that they could play politics while sitting in their villa drinking vodka and wine from the Crimea, and not only remove from the committee the officers and soldiers they disliked but outsmart the Moscow émigrés. When they received Schwetz' rebuff, the "company of the upright ten" * broke up immediately. Seydlitz had to apologize to the committee for "violating the democratic principle" and he received a real dressing down from Melnikov.

When we were all assembled, Melnikov asked Seydlitz to get the manifesto and read it aloud. I wanted to spare him this humiliation at least, and offered to do both these things for him. But Melnikov insisted that Seydlitz do them personally—just like a naughty schoolboy being punished. He even made Seydlitz repeat the following sentences:

> If the German people continue to let themselves be led toward destruction without raising a hand they will become not only weaker every day but also guiltier. Then

* A reference to Gottfried Keller's novel, *The Company of the Upright Seven*, about a group of Zurich citizens who dabbled in politics. *Trans.*

Hitler will be overthrown only by the arms of the coalition. This would mean the end of our national independence; it would mean the breaking up of our Fatherland. And we could blame nobody but ourselves. If, on the other hand, the German people pull themselves together in time and prove by their actions that they want to be a free people and that they are resolved to liberate Germany from Hitler, they will have gained the right to decide their own future and to be heard in the world. This is the only way to preserve the existence, the freedom, and the honor of the German nation.

When Seydlitz had finished this reading exercise, Melnikov put these questions to him:

"Have you signed this manifesto? Do you believe that this political judgment of the situation is right?"

Seydlitz said yes. Melnikov continued somewhat as follows:

"Then you will also understand that the fate of Germany and therefore of its frontiers lies exclusively in the hands of the German people and so in your hands too. Do all that is in your power to encourage the German people to overthrow Hitler. The sooner this happens the more advantageous the peace negotiations will be for Germany. Strengthen the National Committee and refrain from anything which may prejudice its political significance." With these words Melnikov left the room.

MAY 7, 1944. During the night Lieutenant Huber was arrested by the NKVD and taken away. In the morning the people in the house bustled about like a disturbed swarm of bees. Gradually it became known what it was all about. Huber was not only an SS officer but also a fanatical Nazi who cooperated with the Gestapo and had joined the committee only in order to work against it from within. He had cleverly suggested the idea of the memorandum to Seydlitz, hoping that once the generals had gone as far as that they would be too proud to retreat from their position and that it would cause the break-up of the committee. When this plan failed he tried to persuade some of the officers who were to be sent to the front to escape to the German army in order to give information about the committee, disclose its place of operation, and propose that it be kidnapped by parachute troops. But he had taken too many people into his confidence. The plan was betrayed to the NKVD and his accomplices were arrested in the Moscow station.

Chapter Seven / The Antifascist School

JULY 5, 1944. A few weeks after the Huber affair the Communist émigrés asked Major Bechler and me whether we would be interested in taking a course at the antifascist school. I gladly agreed to this proposal, as life in the house of the National Committee had gone stale and was extremely unsatisfactory. Though nobody wants to admit it to himself, we are all becoming increasingly aware that our work with the newspaper and the radio and our discussions about the text of the leaflets and manifestoes go on in a vacuum and that we are in fact separated from Germany and the German army by an unbridgeable abyss.

I already feel myself fundamentally a Communist. I have continued my Marxist reading eagerly and I can only say that this well-knit, clear religion which so closely adheres to tangible reality has a magical attraction for me. Here is a plan—based on a merciless criticism of existing society, or rather of a society going to pieces—for a new order which promises to solve and overcome all the conflicts and contradictions in social living that appear in world wars and economic catastrophes, need, misery, and despair. Here is no empty talk about the inevitable accompaniments of politics and power politics, with pretty declarations about human rights, love of peace, and honesty. Terror, force, deceit, and lies, however, acquire a new meaning: the end sanctifies the means. This courage to carry things to their ultimate conclusion in thought and action fascinates me.

It is not only the comparison between the liberal and humanitarian aim of this theory and the hazy blood-and-race myth of the Nazis which makes it appear so fascinating; it also compares well with an order called democracy, which in a time of economic and political chaos is helplessly driven into bankruptcy and allows Hitler and his accomplices to mobilize the tremendous powers dormant in the German people and misuse them for their ends.

There seems no reason to doubt that one can trace back a significant part of the tensions and conflicts in modern society —especially the terrible conflict between the individual and the group—to the grotesque malrelationship between the ownership of the means of production and the actual productive organization, to the deep conflict between capital and labor, between private ownership and steadily increasing collective production. If this is so, nothing can be more natural and obvious than to adjust these conditions of ownership to the collective character of modern production—even by force if necessary.

Marxism shows me in a new light the events in which we have become involved. The same thing is happening to many of the young officers and soldiers who were picked from the camps and have come to the antifascist school. All the terrible, meaningless, and inexplicable things we have experienced receive an explanation and a new meaning: the agony of a world which has lost its right to existence, the birth throes of a new epoch.

Where before we were unable to distinguish between good and evil, between truth and falsehood, right and wrong; whereas all concepts of bravery, honor, Fatherland, justice, freedom, and duty had become empty of meaning and been degraded to misused phrases—we now find a new standard of judgment, a new aim: socialism, the free brotherly community of all men, all nations.

It is true that life in the Soviet Union does not correspond at all to the Marxist ideal. There is first of all our own personal fate as prisoners. We have not really got to know the best side of the Soviet Union. Not even the most fanatical Communists can argue away the inhuman suffering and hardships we have had to bear and which caused the death of so many of our comrades. But we are prepared to draw a line across the past. Colonel Tulpanov was right, after all, when he said to me, on September 4, 1942 that we did not come into this country as guests. No, we came as an army bringing death and destruction to the land, as soldiers of a regime which was indisputably guilty of terrible crimes against the population and against its war prisoners and which is now repudiating us captives. It is clear that these facts were bound to have painful results for us. But the sufferings we underwent in prison were due less to ill will than to incapacity, lack of imagination, and a corruption which was almost oriental in character. We do not want to be unfair to the Soviet Union because of these things.

Furthermore, the material standard of living of the Soviet population is far and away below the standard in the capitalist countries, and not even the terrible ravages of this war suffice to explain this gulf—in food, housing conditions, clothing, articles of daily use such as sewing needles, light bulbs, cooking pots, radios, motorcycles, or cars. I am prepared to recognize that the young Soviet regime took over a wretched inheritance here: it was a country, which in its technical development was fifty to a hundred years behind the rest of Europe; which, owing to war, revolution, and civil war—the latter partly stirred up from without—had been completely laid waste; where 75 per cent of the population was illiterate and had no contacts with the modern world. One cannot deny that, judged in this light, much has been achieved in barely twenty years of peace.

But have people become better in the new system? Has the principle of the war of every man against every man, the right of the stronger, been replaced by a new social consciousness? Are the people more helpful, more just, more honest, less envious, more brotherly in their relations with one another? Has harmony between the individual and society become a reality? Does the individual have a sense of responsibility toward society? And does society in turn secure right and freedom to the individual?

No, the answer to these questions is certainly negative. On the contrary, instead of a sense of duty taken for granted by us, and a customary regard for norms of right and decency, instead of tradition, the revolution in Russia has apparently created a vacuum which cannot be filled despite the daily uninterrupted hammering in of instruction, manifestoes, and slogans. In Western Europe there exists a tradition dating back to the early Middle Ages of burgher industry and peasant pride, and each independent entrepreneur and intellectual as well as artisan and worker has self-evident pride in a piece of work well done; in Western Europe over centuries there has come to be an increasing desire for a minimum standard of internal and external orderliness and cleanliness even among the masses, and in spite of all the existing social injustices there can be found everywhere sympathy for misfortune and suffering. In the Soviet Union, on the other hand, there is still an attitude of indifference and indolence which has something chaotic about it. There is a kind of insensitivity about one's own and other people's sufferings which is frightening because too often it is the cause of inhumanity. The prisoners of war can certainly speak of this.

The revolution may have removed innumerable bonds and barriers which under tsarism retarded the development of man. But at the same time it destroyed many existing traditions of European culture which so far it has not been able to replace with anything new. The short intoxication with freedom and the revolutionary élan of the 'twenties—during which innumerable experiments were made to reform social life between one day and the next according to the most modern and liberal theories, and allow the individual the utmost possible freedom and responsibility—have now given way to an unequaled degree of interference by authority in the life of society and of the individual. But although the past thirty years can show enormous technical and economic achievements, they have also subjected man to the demoralizing effect of misery, deprivation, hunger, and struggles for power. In view of that can one expect a new and better generation to have grown up already? Could envy, hate, and the lust for power already have disappeared from the heart of man? No, it is not to be expected or demanded. One can expect it even less of the vast illiterate peasant population, which has had to be driven with an iron fist along the path the Bolsheviks are determined to take and probably must take if they want to avoid the dangers Gorky once foresaw. Gorky said that the peasant masses with their animal individualism, their anarchism, and their complete lack of social stirrings were in danger of swamping the entire Russian revolutionary intelligentsia. Yes! It is impossible to ignore the fact that the Soviet Union is governed by an iron hand, by a "dictatorship of the proletariat" exercised by a power apparatus

which centralizes everything to the last degree. No "achievement of the Soviet system," no constitution, no declaration
about a universal, equal, and secret vote can hide the fact that
this dictatorship of the proletariat is fundamentally (as Lenin
said) the dictatorship of an elite party built upon the strictest
discipline and subordination, if it is not the dictatorship of a
small leading group within the party. If the dictatorship of the
proletariat is "power based directly on violence," if the heads
of such a state are fused with the heads of the party, if "not a
single important decision is arrived at by the mass organizations
of the proletariat without directions from the Party" *—then
there is no longer any real difference between the dictatorship
of the masses and the dictatorship of the leaders.

To prove the supposed existence of this difference Stalin
wrote an article entitled "The Party and the Working Class
within the System of the Dictatorship of the Proletariat." His
argument is as follows:

1. The dictatorship of the proletariat does not consist only
of control by the party but of seeing that its directions are
carried out by the masses.

2. The party must never forget the political maturity of the
masses, their awareness, and capacity or lack of it.

3. The party cannot replace the state organs. The authority
of the party can be based only on the confidence of the working class; confidence is not to be gained by force.

4. The party members are merely a drop in the ocean of the
masses; they can govern only if they know how to interpret the
will of the people correctly.

All these proofs become meaningless once the leaders of the
party have the power to decide exactly on what lines the people
and the party members may think. If opposition or the attempt

* Quotations from Stalin's *Problems of Leninism* (New York, International Publishers, 1934), pp. 36–37, 40, 51. *Trans.*

154

to correct the party line means suicide, because the party can and should "force the minority to submit to the will of the majority" *—if therefore even an inner-party democracy no longer exists and party leadership once in power can no longer be made to resign—then what Stalin himself predicted is bound to happen: the party will no longer try to convince but will command, saying to the people, "Do not dare to object, for the party is all-powerful."

To express such views in the antifascist school would of course be considered highly heretical and bring immediate expulsion. Yet each of us knows basically what is meant when "actual Soviet democracy" is referred to—with a wink—as against "bourgeois, formal democracy." But perhaps, although these things must be regarded as evil and accompanied by most regrettable results which resemble the practices of the Gestapo, they should also be regarded as inevitable. An army involved in a battle for life or death has no time for democratic discussion. And what are the Communists but a fighting troop based on the poorest, the most wretched, and most ignorant of people, fighting an enemy who has all imaginable advantages: money, power, education, experience in government, administration, and the conduct of war, tradition, and a long-recognized authority? Surely the Communists must win the confidence of these wretches in order to come to power in the first place. But can they give them the right to self-determination overnight? Would the masses understand that the seizure of power in one country is only the first step toward building a new and better order of society, that unending sacrifices and deprivations must be made before it is proved that the new order is higher not only in theory but also in practice? Has it not been the tragic fate of many revolutions to rejoice in victory too soon, to be

* Stalin is referring not to a minority of exploiters but to possible opposition within the party.

overconfident and to underestimate the unscrupulousness and toughness of their opponents, and therefore suffer decisive defeats after initial successes? Perhaps nobody has described this conflict better than Gorky again, when he reported a comment of Lenin's made while listening to the "Appassionata."

> I know nothing which is greater than the Appassionata; I would like to listen to it every day. It is marvelous superhuman music. I always think with pride—perhaps it is naïve of me—what marvelous things human beings can do! But I can't listen to music too often. It affects your nerves, makes you want to say stupid, nice things, and stroke the heads of people who could create such beauty while living in this vile hell. And now you mustn't stroke any one's head—you might get your hand bitten off. You have to hit them on the head, without any mercy, although our ideal is not to use force against any one. H'm, h'm, our duty is infernally hard!

Gorky himself said:

> The duty of true-hearted leaders of the people is superhumanly difficult. A leader who is not in some degree a tyrant, is impossible. More people, probably, were killed under Lenin than under Thomas Münzer; but without this, resistance to the revolution of which Lenin was the leader would have been more widely and more powerfully organized. In addition to this we must take into account the fact that with the development of civilization the value of human life manifestly depreciates, a fact which is clearly proved by the growth in contemporary Europe of the technique of annihilating people, and the taste for doing so.
>
> I challenge any one to say frankly how far he approves of, and how far he is revolted by, the hypocrisy of the

moralists who talk about the bloodthirstiness of the Russian Revolution when they not only showed no pity for the people who were exterminated during the four years of the infamous Pan-European War, but by all possible means fanned the flame of this abominable war to "the victorious end." *

Yes, this hypocrisy is all the more uncalled for since today the world has again been plunged into an infinitely more horrible and destructive war and there is no indication that a third and perhaps final catastrophe of mankind can be avoided except by the socialist revolution. Such a revolution is in full swing in the whole world, and it is not over in Russia. As is the case in all political wars in history, it is a process of using power and applying force, of lying, blackmail, and exploiting the baser instincts of men, with all the demoralizing effects that are bound to be produced even on the revolutionaries. However much this battle may degrade men and foster the dark, revengeful strivings of the undeveloped masses, who want to destroy and disfigure what is more highly developed and noble, the ideal for which the war is waged must win in the end, must awaken the consciousness of human dignity, and must curb the lower instincts and lead to the inner perfection of its protagonists.

My teacher at the antifascist school is Zaisser, a former officer of the German Imperial Army who, during the battles in the Ruhr area, fought on the side of the insurgent workers against the Free Corps. Later he was head of the military side of the Communist party in West Germany, a Comintern agent in Germany and China, commander of the International Brigade base in Spain, and inmate of a Soviet concentration camp. He is one of those Communists who make an impression, who still

* *Days with Lenin* (New York, International Publishers, 1932), pp. 52, 34.

have some idea of how people in the rest of the world live and think, who have not grown rigid in dogmatism, and with whom one can talk critically and openly without having the feeling that at the slightest deviation one will be considered an "enemy" or reported to the NKVD.

Lindau is in charge of the German section, a pre-1914 Social Democrat and later a Spartacist, the barricade agitator type. Behind a repulsive exterior and fanatical revolutionary hatred he is in fact a man full of kindness, the faculty of understanding, and empathy. Compared with these two, the other teachers are unimportant.

There are about four hundred men at this school, among them Germans, Austrians, Hungarians, Rumanians, and Italians. Of these, the two hundred Germans are divided into groups of thirty, like the units at a military college. For the first time half the students are officers. We have ten hours of instruction per day, of which four to six are devoted to lectures and seminars. The remaining hours we can spend reading what we please. Lectures are delivered on dialectical and historical materialism, German and Russian history, economics, the history of the labor movement, and imperialism.

I keep wondering how many of the students are sincerely interested in all this and may later become active Communists. Among the ranks there are a great many who have swum with the tide, joined the movement in their camps, and were then picked for the school. A number are even writing reports for the NKVD. Many lack the mental capacity and the education necessary to comprehend and digest the subject matter.

Among the officers, however, the situation is different. They had to swim against the stream. There are fewer conscious opportunists among them, though there are many who as yet have no civilian occupation and are now looking for an opportunity to establish themselves through politics and the party.

JULY 22, 1944. The news of the attempt on Hitler's life and the failure of the generals' revolt has just been announced. When we first heard the news of the attempt there was no end to our rejoicings. I was hardly able to control myself for excitement and joy. But slowly it became clear that Hitler was still alive, that several of the conspirators had already been murdered, and that the Gestapo continued to rule the country. I cannot describe my feelings. All our hopes of the Fatherland's freeing itself by its own strength are now buried!

The Communists are very downcast too. They are all homesick though no one admits it. Only the hundred percenters find the Fatherland of Socialism so wonderful that they don't wish to return to Germany, and even in their cases it is clear they are deluding themselves.

JULY 26, 1944. Herrnstadt arrived from Moscow for a visit. He is one of those ice-cold theoreticians, though his intelligence makes him more tolerable than Ulbricht's type. But his cynicism is baffling. As he analyzed the Twentieth of July, the Putsch was nothing but an attempt by the ruling classes in Germany to free themselves from their Praetorian Guard. To avoid the revolution which was imminent, they had once called in these men and then became their prisoners. Now, under the orders of heavy industry, the generals were to overthrow Hitler and so clear the path for an orientation toward a capitalist democracy. The proofs: The influential positions in industry held by Witzleben's relatives and the attempts of the conspirators to get in touch with the Western allies.

Herrnstadt is further of the opinion that the failure of the Putsch has given Hitler an opportunity to continue the war, and in it he will pull down with him all the forces which can hold back the advance of communism in Europe. The Western powers had speculated on Germany and Russia destroying one another while they would come out of the war the gainers. Churchill in particular had over and over again sabotaged the formation of a second front in Europe. The Western powers' offensive was opened in Africa and Italy in 1943 instead of in France, in the hope of being able to gain a footing in the Balkans and keep the Soviet Union out. But this only had the opposite effect. It made it easier for Hitler to defend Europe and prolong the war, and thus gave the Red Army time to come closer to Central Europe. It was not until it became clear that the Soviet Union would reach the German frontiers this year that the West determined on the decisive blow in France, although the German forces there were now stronger than they had been the previous year. If the Putsch of July 20 had been successful, it would have deprived this miscalculation of its consequences and would have been a gift to the Western allies. Its failure on the other hand will speed the advance of communism into Europe.

Perhaps this analysis of Herrnstadt's is correct. I have never been able to understand why the second front did not start long ago. As early as the spring of 1942 the staffs in France were daily and anxiously expecting a landing, so weak were our defenses. By 1944 they had of course been strengthened, and as far as one can tell from the reports of prisoners it is very likely we have a much stronger army there now than we had in 1943.

However to rejoice at the failure of the Putsch because it helps the Communist party is really going too far.

I asked Herrnstadt how he could be certain that the conspirators had not included many men from the old Reichswehr circle who had always believed in working with Russia. He assumed an air of secrecy and said nothing. Then I asked what his attitude was toward our National Committee, since in the last analysis it had called for just such action as that of July 20.

"That is something different," he said. "The committee is controlled by us, and in case of a successful German opposition movement it would have insured our influence. We had to be prepared for such a possibility and could not isolate ourselves."

This is not the first time that Herrnstadt has so candidly disclosed the intentions of the Central Committee of the party. He told von Frankenberg several months ago that men such as he are only temporary allies. When Frankenberg complained about this to the Communists and the Russians, they replied that Herrnstadt's opinion was not authoritative but only a left-wing deviation. The Communists were "democrats" with a right to their own opinions. Maybe the reason for the definite lack of interest on the part of the Communists in really activating our propaganda at the front can be found in Herrnstadt's statement. Perhaps they are not at all interested in the success of the committee but merely regard it as a Trojan horse to be used in the event of a non-Communist opposition movement getting the upper hand.

This may be a rather daring conjecture. But the Communists would hardly refrain on moral grounds from common action with the most fanatical Nazis. "The end justifies the means" is their highest principle. They have only one concept of honor: devotion to the party. They consider it honorable to behave dishonorably whenever it serves the party. All ethical ideas are measured by the ultimate aim and thereby become relative. Or is it just then that they become absolute?

At all events a great deal of self-respect, honesty, and "prejudice" has to be sacrificed if their demands are to be satisfied. The human being as a personality counts for nothing; he is only a tool, a means to an end. But the end, the final aim, is the liberation of personality. The party still prefers to find a student from the antifascist school who is a Communist by conviction rather than someone who became a Communist under pressure from the NKVD. But this means only that the party too still has "prejudices." According to its logic it should make no difference since it is usefulness which is decisive.

"We of the party . . ." Herrnstadt said. So I am included in this—a tool, with reservations. Too weak, too much sentiment, too much emotion, too little discipline will be the verdict. Though Zaisser told me that in giving his opinion of me to the Central Committee he had said I might one day become a useful party member. Owing to my heretical views on some questions, the antifascist students have christened me the "feudal bourgeois."

If, in spite of everything, they do not count me as an enemy, it is only because they feel that I am frank. It has been clear to me from the very beginning that there was no sense in my pretending to hold views which I did not share.

Major Homann is an example of the opposite type. He thinks that he is being especially clever if he carefully weighs every word he says, if he agrees calculatingly with the Communists; and he always waits for the official Communist opinion on all tricky questions before committing himself. One cannot help but admire the self-control with which he plays his role. But the two or three times he has acted his part badly weigh double against him. The Communists know how ambitious he is; but he is too clever, too diplomatic for them, and wins no friends by it, though they are pleasant to him.

If I were to gamble, I should prefer to stake my future on fairness, honesty, and decency rather than on political astuteness. Some days ago, during a discussion in Zaisser's group, a comparison was drawn between the Red Army and the Wehrmacht. The points for debate were fighting morale, fairness, humanity, excesses against prisoners. Everybody talked around the point in order to give as favorable a mark as possible to the Red Army. I felt that a man like Zaisser was bound to sense the

falseness of these statements and I made no secret of the opinion
I had formed in the Ukraine. Zaisser turned on me sharply:
"This is racism, an insult to Soviet man!" Of course he can't
react any other way.

AUGUST 14, 1944

I, a son of the German nation, out of fervent love for
my people, for my Fatherland, and for my family, swear
to fight until my people are free and happy, until the
shame and disgrace of fascist barbarism has been expunged
and Hitler's fascism exterminated.

I swear to take merciless measures against anyone who
breaks this oath.

If I should break this oath and thereby become a traitor
to my people, my family, and my Fatherland my life shall
be forfeited. May the hatred and scorn of all honest men
fall on me and may my comrades in battle judge me as
befits a traitor and enemy of his people.

Two hundred new-made antifascists were gathered in the
cellar of the antifascist school, which had been draped with red
flags, in order to repeat this bombastic oath solemnly after one
of the teachers, with raised right hands.

I could have laughed aloud at this performance, which was
more like a conspiratorial scene in a third-rate melodrama than
a solemn plighting. But I kept silent with shame.

Zaisser assured me that this form of oath is necessary, as many
of the students will be sent out for illegal work behind the
front and inside Germany. The memory of it may help one or
another of them to remain steadfast in critical moments of moral
doubt. One sentence devoted to the oath and three threatening
punishment and retribution! An oath taken in an atmosphere

which is anything but free! I felt physical disgust and violent hatred of myself for taking part. If only I had had enough courage I would have refused to repeat the sentences. It was not because I had anything to fear in solemnly pledging myself to fight against Hitler. Except for the fact that I have no high opinion of my powers of resistance in the event of physical torture, I have no reason to be afraid that I would ever break it. Yet never in the whole period of imprisonment have I been so embarrassed for myself as while taking this oath. We are all in a position where it takes too much courage to refuse. It would mean immediate expulsion from the school, which would bring unpredictable consequences.

How humiliating this all-permeating distrust is which manifests itself in the wording of the oath. And yet how understandable. Basically, there is no certainty that any man says what he really thinks, from the Russian director of the school through the teachers to the humblest student. It is not enough to recognize the principles of communism and be determined to act as a Communist. No, every single word from Stalin's mouth, every propaganda line of *Pravda*, every party directive on any question whatsoever has to be regarded as the last word of wisdom, an almost divine revelation. Criticism and an independent opinion are sacrilege, crime, treason. An unprecedented system of control is watching to see that every sin against this monolithic spirit is recorded, as if by the good Lord who sees all little children's secret nibbling.

In the National Committee it is still possible to avoid obeying the NKVD's degrading demand to report on one's comrades. (According to the NKVD, this is one of the obligations of working loyally with the Soviet Union, and Major Stern made me agree to this in Camp 27. It was only after I had several times given him my opinion of the secret agents on the National Committee that he left me in peace.) An antifascist who is not prepared to report his student comrades might succeed in convincing his teachers that he is nevertheless a true Communist, but the NKVD will certainly consider him at any rate a potential enemy. I am convinced that at least 90 per cent of the students are involved in giving information of this kind in one form or another and that a large percentage, out of fear, produce at least a little evidence against their comrades during these interrogations in order not to become suspect themselves.

A short while ago, for example, I had a quarrel with a comrade about a photograph in *Pravda* of two Russian prisoners, worn to skeletons, who had been liberated by the Red Army from a German extermination camp. "So what?" said the lieutenant. "We looked exactly the same when we were in Yelabuga." He was right, of course. Almost every prisoner of 1942 and 1943 had once looked like this. But I disagreed with him that one could compare the two things: the systematic extermination which went on in the SS concentration camps had nothing in common with the hunger and hardships we had suffered. The latter had been a result of negligent corruption and a general state of deprivation, and was not organized and desired by the government, like the murders of the Nazis.

Our entire group joined in this quarrel, and after a lively argument for and against we finally put the question to Zaisser. He is a man with whom one can talk about these things and who possesses a great deal of weight with us. The result was the immediate removal of the lieutenant from the school. It was said that many such "unfriendly remarks" about the Soviet Union had already been reported against him by his comrades to the school management and the NKVD. As I felt myself to blame since I had started the discussion, I asked Zaisser to intervene on behalf of the young man, who was one of the most honest and sincere men among us. Zaisser assured me he had already done this but that he was powerless since the NKVD itself had ordered the expulsion.

These are the circumstances under which we are expected to exercise criticism and self-criticism. Every one of us has to tell his life story and examine his social and political attitude in front of his comrades. The others are supposed to criticize what is said in order to help one "discover one's weaknesses." In some cases gross impostors were unmasked. Alleged former members of the Red Front League turned out, under cross-examination by their comrades, to have been high-ranking SA leaders; or supposed officers were found to be noncommissioned officers downgraded for criminal offenses; alleged intellectuals persecuted by the Nazis turned out to have been working with the Security Service. In one such case the culprit was not expelled from the school. Dr. Kröger, a tall, lanky, anemic lawyer, who had been forced to admit that he had worked for the Security Service, was allowed to remain at the school and was even appointed assistant teacher for the next course. The NKVD wanted him and the teachers had to submit.

But do these revelations justify the forced public confessions, during which one's entire life, including its most private details, has to be disclosed, and in which a great deal of self-accusation is necessary if one does not want to be exposed to annihilating indictments from one's "comrades"? Lucky is the man who need say no more than that, as a person not interested in politics, he failed to take part in shaping the political fate of his country and so helped the Nazis indirectly.

Those who cannot conceal the fact that they do not belong to the indifferent middle class, but on the contrary have held convictions and taken a stand, have to be prepared to undergo inexorable cross-examination and are not left in peace until they admit how wrong and sinful their life has been so far. It is almost impossible to escape this inquisition: "Did you eat sweets secretly when you were a child? Did you masturbate? Did you seduce working-class girls? Was your father socially active? Did your mother read the *Grüne Post?* Do you play cards?" These questions continue until the victim gets tied up in contradictions and nervous and begins to look for excuses for any "immoral adventure" he once mentioned lightheartedly in the circle of his comrades. He becomes more and more entangled until he is crushed, and finally to avoid further questions makes a confession, saying he is guilty of all possible offenses against the party's moral code, the code that alone leads to salvation, and promises to repent and change his ways.

An amusing interlude occurred at one of these public confessions. One of the most active and intelligent students, and a proven anti-Nazi, took it into his head to admit that he was a homosexual, remembering the old socialist demand for the abolition of Paragraph 175.* Great dismay in the school. Homosexuality was a typical sign of the degeneracy of the parasitical ruling classes, the teachers remarked, with raised index finger. And with that a persecution of the incautious confessor began, though he belonged not to the ruling class but to the artisan middle class. The persecution was increased by the more or less unconscious jealousy of some of the comrades, who had already watched with disapproving eye the friendship of this man with an attractive young Rhinelander.

Then the head of the German section, Comrade Lindau, intervened—this was for once a bright spot—and said he would not permit these Nazi methods of defamation against a proven antifascist: he himself delighted in being with our youngest comrades, and it was like a degenerate bourgeois to suspect only

* Paragraph 175 of the German Criminal Code made homosexuality a penal offense. *Trans.*

sexual perversion in every attachment of an older person to a young man.

And so the public persecution in this case was stopped. Sexual irregularities were considered less serious than political deviation. It soon got around the school, amid much meaningful laughter, that the NKVD had discovered a new field. The commissars shook their heads in astonishment and asked what the word "homosexuality" really meant. Evidently they have never heard anything of this subject before. In the Soviet Union, following the slogan "What must not be cannot be," they believe that one can get rid of this phenomenon, which fits into their dogma so badly, simply by hushing it up, even though it may have played a fundamental role in the last three thousand years of cultural history.

Behind a curtain of thirty pairs of inescapable eyes and ears sits the real inquisitor, the commissar of the NKVD, mechanically registering everything, making petty, mechanical, detailed notes, often without any idea as to the meaning of what he is putting down, for his horizon is blocked with Soviet stars. He knows nothing of the world beyond the frontiers of the Soviet Union. This world is an abstract construction built on party dogma and propaganda theses which he has learned by heart, as we once learned our catechism or the ballads of Uhland. In order to come out of the cross-examination undamaged when making one's confessions, it is important to find the balance between voluntary self-debasement and artful hypocrisy. In any case, the self-esteem and personality of the individual are undermined, and his past at least partly destroyed. The more thoroughly this happens the greater the value attached to criticism and self-criticism. Those who are made to feel completely at a loss will cling all the more firmly to the lifesaver graciously held out to them, the party dogma. Those who become so confused that they can no longer tell guilt from error will be all the more grateful for having the party make the decision between good and evil for them. Compulsion of conscience and distrust are to whip each other up to the point where there can no longer be any question of independent Marxist thinking and of having an objective interpretation of reality. The hope that one day—when the Soviet Union has caught up with the economic and technical advance of the rest of the world, and through revolutions in other countries has shed her "splendid isolation," so that she no longer has anything to fear—these conditions will at last become liberalized is poor consolation for those who now live in this anxious atmosphere poisoned by suspicion, hypocrisy, and Byzantine intrigues.

When I made it a condition of my attendance at the school that we be excused from classes for all the meetings of the committee, that we have a room to ourselves, and that we be let off all work assignments and other special duties which were not directly connected with the purpose of the school, the Communist proselytes of the committee were horrified. I was not willing to let myself be subjected once more without protest to the socialism of the recruits' barracks which is extensively practiced here at the school too. Also I wanted to avoid giving Seydlitz and Lattmann any further pretext for such everlasting remarks as "Einsiedel wears long hair to prove he is a Communist" or "Einsiedel agrees with everything the émigrés say."

But our special position brought upon us the hostility and envy of the egalitarians at the school. Moreover we refused to address everybody in the obligatory, familiar second person singular. "Why should we say *du* to people we don't know at all?" I declared when, a few days after we entered the school, a complaint was brought to Zaisser. "We used it in the SA cafés and in the barracks without any real comradeship growing out of it." As a precaution I also pointed out that, unlike the German Communist party, the Communist party in the Soviet Union never used the familiar address. Zaisser approved our point of view, and we would have had peace from any further attacks if it had not been for Bechler. Bechler capitulated to the general hostility with the gesture of participating of his free will in one of the Sunday work assignments (behind my back, I may say).

My life confession would certainly become a battle to the death, but Zaisser has spared both Bechler and me this. He is well aware with what hatred they would pounce on us, the privileged members of the committee, especially on me, who owing to my name, my youth, and my heretical point of view have acted as a considerable irritant.

Why does he do this? Out of personal sympathy? Or does the party consider it inopportune at this moment to subject the first representatives of the National Committee to attend the school to all these humiliations, because by this action the authority of the committee would also be affected? Or perhaps his attitude merely conforms to the general turn against egalitarianism which is taking place in the Soviet Union?

The majority of the teachers certainly share the hostility of most of the students for anyone who shows any signs of resistance to becoming collectivized. (The word "collective" creates an entirely false impression if translated by our word "community." If what we have at the school is a community, then bricks in a wall also form a community.) Privileges and favors have to be accepted here as gifts and recognition from the authorities—as recognition that the only privilege which really matters, that of preserving one's own personality and convictions, has as far as possible been surrendered.

But what does this mean? Haven't the Bolsheviks claimed for themselves the highest imaginable privilege—to overthrow a century-old order, destroy all traditions and laws, arrange the

world according to their conceptions, and impose on the anarchistic, formless masses their thinking and political principles?
Here at the school obedient subjects and a group of drilled
receivers of orders, narrow-minded doctrinaires, and heresy
hunters are being trained, but no revolutionaries. What was
born of the hardship and difficulties against which the party in
Russia had to fight in the making of a new society—an iron
party discipline, enforced at the cost of personality, initiative,
and creative thought; total compulsion of conscience and general mutual spying—all this is now to be raised to the rank of a
virtue and imposed on the Communist parties outside the Soviet
Union.

This attempt, thank heaven, is sure to fail of itself, or it must
mean the death of communism. The émigrés too, once they
get abroad again, will be forced to find their way back to thinking for themselves and to showing tolerance for opposed opinions. Among the students at the school only those who have
preserved their integrity will be able to stay the pace; the others
will be blown away like chaff by the keen winds of the revolutionary struggle, at the latest when for the first time the order
fails to reach them according to plan.

AUGUST 22, 1944. Plenary session of the committee, and
Seydlitz' birthday. Bechler and I were driven to Lunovo by car.
It seemed to me we had come to a madhouse.

I was still feeling the shock of July 20, but the generals were
living in euphoria. Seydlitz when he saw me forgot all his hatred,
rushed toward me, and took me into his room.

"In four weeks we shall be in Germany!" he shouted. "That
was only the beginning—but now things are going to happen!
You will see!"

He showed me the draft of an appeal to the Northern Army

Group, which had been cut off for several days in the Baltic. In this appeal, which the Russians had already released for printing, a guarantee was given to the army group that if it capitulated and went over to the side of the National Committee its units would be preserved and the soldiers would be allowed to keep their small arms.

"You see, the Soviets don't want any disintegration either," Seydlitz said, unable to resist throwing this in my face. "They want to keep the troops intact to preserve peace and order just as we do."

It would have been useless to reply. But the appeal was never sent out as the German command succeeded in re-establishing contact with the Northern Army Group. In any case I had no chance to answer because I had to admire the enormous marzipan cake which the Russians had given him for his birthday. Four red roses made of marzipan symbolized his four daughters. "Isn't that lovely?" he exclaimed over and over. "A work of art!"

The "father of his people"—as he was called since his attempt to form a government—was no longer in his right mind. I muttered something polite and withdrew. Our doctors always maintained that Seydlitz was a manic-depressive. Now I think so too. The reason for his present manic phase is the presence of von Paulus, Strecker, and twenty other generals who were recently taken prisoner on the central front. On August 8 Paulus made a pronouncement against Hitler over our radio. All the generals of the central front have signed the Russian leaflets appealing to the German people to stop the war. After this "victory" over the field marshal and the influx of generals, Seydlitz is now rid of the worry that the military caste would one day expel him as an outsider, a traitor, and a renegade. This worry had been tormenting him. It was the same fear which prompted Colonel General Strecker—in order not to be outdone by Paulus, who supposedly went down fighting—to continue his defense of the northern flank of the encircled army at Stalingrad for two more terrible, bloody days, although the commanders of two regiments implored him on their knees to capitulate. It was the fear of other people's judgment, the fear of making a decision, the desire to save face. But now Seydlitz feels himself no longer isolated. Now he feels himself justified. Now all his problems are forgotten and with them all sense of reality.

The plenary session was a kind of staged performance in which the "broad popular front" of the committee was to be demonstrated to Paulus and the generals of the central front. Seydlitz made a speech on the political and military situation. After a tearful introduction, during which he spoke at length of his three friends—an officer, his horse, and his groom—he described, amid general laughter, how he had happened to take part in founding the Officers' League. "I was 100 per cent against it," he assured us. "But after five minutes' conversation with Weinert and Pieck I was won over. Korfes has always written my speeches for me, but I select the quotations." And then followed a declaration of his philosophy, the first speech composed by himself:

Though in rather confining circumstances, I have now been living for over a year and a half in the Soviet Union, this land of present and future socialism. In these eighteen months I have made an honest effort to get to know this country, its people, and its socialism and above all the spirit, mind, and heart of the people and their whole culture. For this it has been necessary to make a thorough study of dialectical materialism, the theoretical foundation of this socialism, the great doctrine of Marx, Engels, Lenin, and Stalin. From this study I discovered what mighty minds created these works which formerly, I must frankly admit, were more or less unknown to me and without which I could not reach complete understanding. Today I bow my head in reverence before these great men who have paved the way for a better world. Dialectical materialism, as it has been created and developed by them —this I have come to realize through these studies—is without doubt one of the most progressive ideas in the world today. The Germany of the future, too, and in particular its social and democratic foundations, will be very, very greatly influenced by this dialectical material-ism and the socialism which is based on it. This socialism will therefore be one of the two main pillars of the new Germany.

However, the great, world-wide ideas of the future which will unite people and nations toward a common life and work cannot and will not be exclusively and one-sidedly based on the principles of dialectical materialism. I have the sacred conviction that humanity unquestionably needs the idealistic philosophy too and can never do with-out it if it is to achieve a true harmony of life and of the whole spiritual and material culture. Only if this is recog-nized will a lasting and truly peaceful community of nations be assured. The task before us is to achieve again a harmonious union of idealism and materialism. If I under-stand it correctly, the development in this country appears to be in that direction.

These definite insights of mine are undoubtedly influ-enced by the great experiences of a long and extraordi-narily active life. This life started in the year of the three Kaisers, 1888, which was of such significance for our German nation; but its decisive periods fall into the three decades from 1914 to 1944. The violent shocks of two world wars stood at the beginning and end of this period. The first World War began for me with the horror of the battle of Gumbinnen on August 20, 1914 during which I was wounded three times. Only being wounded for the third time, in the head and both hands, put me hors de combat. I looked as if someone had poured a bucket of blood over me. And when—on my birthday, thirty years ago today—I was the first wounded soldier to be taken to the hospital of my future father-in-law, my own father, who had been sent for, did not recognize me. The gay young lieutenant, who had so far not thought very deeply about the serious side of life, had turned into a different person. The second World War ended, for me, with the tremendous experience of the hell of Stalingrad. And then came my imprisonment with its valuable lessons which completed the whole experience. These were indispensable.

All these really big experiences shook me profoundly and have given me an insight of the kind which is perhaps given to very few people in their lifetime and which is only possible through great upheavals.

I now see clearly and without a doubt that transcendental and metaphysical forces have over and over again played an absolutely decisive part in determining my fate and life. It may be that my blood relationship with the greatest philosopher of idealism so far, Immanuel Kant, has played a role which though not exactly measurable was by no means minor in the idealistic emphases of my philosophy of life. So far as my blood is concerned I embody a racial ideal which is the complete opposite of Hitler's. In me, mixed with my pure Prussian stock, is the blood of ancestors from England, France, and Salzburg, who had all been turned out of their home countries on religious grounds and found refuge in Prussia, which was then a progressive and freedom-loving country. In addition, on my father's side there is no slight mixture by marriage of Slav, West Russian, Polish, and Lithuanian blood. Also in my family there is a branch which at some time went with the wind to America—the Mitchel branch, probably of Irish origin. Therefore like us all I am related by blood to all the great nations which are now at war with Germany. Only in my case everything can be proved. The picture will become even more complete if I tell you that I have lived several years in the places which have for centuries been bones of contention between Prussia-Germany on the one hand and Poland and France on the other: Danzig and Strasbourg.

The tremendous drama which we are witnessing today cannot in my opinion be understood if viewed only in the light of a materialistic conception of history. Rather I am inalterably convinced—in fact it is my faith—that higher forces are at work here. In this gigantic sequence of events things are completely upside down, paradoxical, and grotesque. So you must not hold it against me if, for once, I quote here the statement of a man whom I regard as the absolute incarnation of lies and falsehood, Joseph Goebbels. What he said was of course untrue; but since he had almost everything turned upside down, it was an exception when he predicted the following truth: "The day will come when the veils which now still cover events will begin to fall. In all the countries of Europe the great awakening will then set in."

Today we can lift only a corner of that veil. I do this by repeating the consecrational lines of Friedrich Hölderlin, which I quoted once before, on September 12, 1943 at the founding of the League of German Officers.

Apparently our newspaper *Free Germany* did not understand them as they ought to be understood, for they were not published then:

> "Messengers of victory descend,
>   Victory is ours!
>   O Fatherland, live above!
>   And do not weep!
>   For thee, O beloved,
>   Not one too many fell."

For according to *Faust* "All things transitory are but a symbol." Now let us remember the dead, and let us include in our thoughts the dead of those lands which today are still at war with us but tomorrow will be our friends. Here the pianist played "Ich hatt' einen Kameraden."

Then Seydlitz reviewed the situation. He touched on events such as the changed situation at the front, the attempt on Hitler's life, and the executions which followed. He made no commentary. Or was this the commentary?

And now allow me to conclude by quoting a few of the intellectual and cultural leaders of our nation who have spoken eternally valid truths. To contrast with these, one sentence by Hitler. Frederick the Great, "Testament" of 1781: "Those who assert that they can direct events are nearly always mistaken and will see their plans founder." Goethe, *Dichtung und Wahrheit:* "Child! child! no more! The coursers of time, lashed, as it were, by invisible spirits, hurry on the light car of our destiny, and all that we can do is with calm courage to hold the reins firmly, and to guide the wheels, now to the left, now to the right, avoiding a stone here, or a precipice there. Who can tell whither he is being borne? seeing he hardly remembers whence he has come." * When still a prince, eleven years after the victory over Napoleon, Kaiser William the Great declared that nothing but the memory remained of the wars of liberation. "If the nation had realized this as early as 1813, who would have sacrificed everything at the time for such a result?" And Adolf Hitler, *Mein Kampf:* "The German has no idea to what degree the people must be deceived, if the support of the masses is to be won." We say in the words of Goethe in the *West-eastern Divan:* "God is for everyone. Not for east or west, not for south or north." And with Schiller's Maid of Orleans: "Pain is brief and joy is eternal."

I am coming to the end. The conclusions which I have just drawn are conclusions of sober and clear reason. But if we look at the past with understanding and feeling, we must declare that the pact which Joseph Stalin concluded with Adolf Hitler on August 21, 1939 he concluded with the embodiment of deceit, dishonor, slavery, tyranny, disloyalty, lack of freedom and of peace—in fact with the devil. Whereas the agreements signed by Marshal Stalin on July 12 and 13, 1943 and on September 11 and 12, 1943 with the National Committee for Free Germany and the League of German Officers were agreements made with truth, honor, the spirit of concord, loyalty, freedom, and peace! He made them with God!

God—I don't know how I survived this speech, sitting at the speakers' table! I wanted to crawl under the table, and the others left the hall when they couldn't hold back their laughter any longer. Really we should have been crying.

The Russians sat through it all with stony faces. Paulus

* *Poetry and Truth*, trans. by M. S. Smith (London, Bell and Sons, 1913), 2, 312.

declared sarcastically that even the "Chatter Parliament" in Frankfurt * had been a scholarly gathering in comparison.

Seydlitz handed the manuscript of his speech to the radio editors. He wanted it broadcast to Germany. That is why I am able to reproduce it verbatim.

Looking at the newly arrived generals from the central front one no longer wonders why the men of the Putsch of July 20 were left in the lurch. Immediately after being captured they signed Red Army leaflets at the front and in the Lubianka prison, but when they were asked to sign an appeal in the name of the National Committee they suddenly got cold feet and thought they detected treason. Here in the headquarters of the National Committee they have forgotten their fear of being shot in the back and the uncertain fate which made them so pliable at the front and in prison. One of the generals declared: "My signature is null and void. It was extracted from me in prison at the point of a gun." Homann shouted: "You are lying! And even if you were telling the truth, it would be more dignified to keep silent. You are merely putting on record that you are actually a traitor." The general took this reprimand without batting an eye. A divisional commander declared that he had never even heard of the committee. And yet we are in possession of a long divisional order over his signature in which he made a more violent attack on the committee even than those of the official propaganda. It is clear from this order that he was accurately informed about our aims and that he believed in our existence. When we confronted him with this he denied his own signature.

Only two Bavarian staff generals stand out among these unimposing figures: Edmund Hoffmeister and Vincenz Müller. Hoffmeister was in the Soviet Union for six years as liaison

* The parliament of 1848–49 which failed to unify Germany. *Trans.*

officer of the Reichswehr. In Lubianka prison he immediately began a hunger strike, with the result that the next day he was moved to a comfortable country house. Vincenz Müller was once Schleicher's adjutant. He is considered one of the most capable staff generals. When he was taken prisoner on the central front he asked the Russians for permission to order his scattered units to stop all further senseless resistance in the White Russian virgin forests, which were overrun with partisans. He was therefore the first general to grant his troops the explicit right he had made use of himself.

In an excellent survey of the situation both before and during the Russian offensive, these two generals rejected Hitler's monstrous accusation that the collapse of the central front was due to the "treason" of the army command.

It is Müller and Hoffmeister again who have succeeded in getting the generals to sign a joint appeal for the committee. Both of them are politically experienced: Hoffmeister during the days of the Free Corps and the Kapp Putsch, and later as one of the organizers of illegal German rearmament in the Soviet Union; Müller as adjutant to Schleicher. They are both very active and are likely soon to have the other generals under their thumbs. Hoffmeister has already declared to the Russians at the front: "I put myself at the disposal of the National Committee and the Russian General Staff. March to the Bay of Biscay. Germany and Russia together—means world domination!" But on May 1, 1944 when still on the German side, he declared in a speech: "Red flags fly today from the Bay of Biscay to the Pacific Ocean, with only one difference: here the flag has the swastika on it, the sign of national renascence; and over there the Soviet star, the sign of Jewish internationalism."

The fact that he tells all this himself and laughs about it makes the whole thing engaging. He likes to dumfound his conversation partners by paradoxes and cynicism. Even in the Reichswehr he was well known for his disrespectful, witty, and pertinent replies to his superiors.

In the afternoon a truck arrived with the prisoners' orchestra from Camp 27. They played on the landing pier of the Kliasma river, where the younger officers and men were swimming. The generals and the émigrés went for walks in the garden and posed in groups for the photographers. Later they went down to the bridge to mix with the men. Pieck, in a dark suit—he normally wears a high-necked tunic cut like Stalin's uniform—stood with his hands on his stomach, beaming complacently in all directions. It was like a summer outing of a local Christmas club. There was no sign of class war in this summer idyll. Men from right and left were joined in happy unison: Pieck; Herr Steinkeller, commander of the Feldherrnhalle Division; SS Storm Leader Meier; the high-school teacher Rücker; Helmschrott, the son of a big farmer; and the left-wing radical, Zippel, a supporter of Neumann.*

The day finished with a party. This has happened several times before. At the request of the political authorities the camp placed a special allotment of food, wine, and liquor at the Germans' disposal. The tables in the dining hall were laden with hors d'oeuvres, sweets, and cigarettes and decorated with flowers. The store manager, Comrade Hirsch, kept running up and down the hall asking our senior officers, "Do you think there is enough? Will there be enough?" He is considerably more economical than the Moscow authorities. The reason is that he can sell everything he saves at high black market prices in the village and the rooms of the guards. The profits

* Heinz Neumann was one of the German Communists who in 1932 opposed the idea that the Social Democrats were a greater danger than the Nazis. After the Nazis came to power he fled to Switzerland, was lured to Moscow, arrested, and disappeared (cf. p. 242). *Trans.*

go into his pocket. But his special attention was concentrated on the tables laid for the VIP's and officers of the committee. Here everything was still more plentiful, especially the vodka. At their own parties, on the various political holidays, the degree of festivity is measured for the Russians according to rank. The commander receives more than his staff, the staff more than those next below, and these again considerably more than the sergeants and other grades. The latter are of course quite happy about this regulation as they contribute a good deal less of their pay.

Of course we do not have to pay. We are the guests of the Russians. This time Comrade Hirsch dipped further into his pocket, since the highest authority in the person of General Petrov, chief of the Administration for Prisoners of War, and his staff were expected.

As he drove up and rolled into the hall like a little, round, fat ball, we assembled too: the men of the National Committee in their black tank uniforms, mostly captured clothing which the house tailor had altered to look as far as possible like civilian clothes; the new generals in their field gray, still wearing their various distinctions and medals and swastikas the size of fried eggs, which we had scrapped long ago. The picture was no different from an evening at an officers' club with guests from the SS. The brown, ill-fitting uniforms of the Russians with their new, large, square epaulets were hardly noticeable among this crowd. Only Petrov's adjutant, the Caucasian Major Gagadse, carried on lively and adroit conversation with the generals. A Balt who once studied in St. Petersburg still remembered how as a prince in an elegant troika he had galloped along the Nevsky Prospect when the Court nobility had their parties or hurried to the great guards' parade on the Field of Mars. At the table this former prince looked down with a tinge of contempt on his chief, the former illiterate cowherd, as he speared potatoes with his knife and shoved them into his mouth or, pressing a large piece of meat onto his spoon with his thumb, gnawed at it from all sides, smacking his lips.

But before this Petrov drank the first glass of vodka on an empty stomach, according to the Russian custom, and proposed the health of Stalin. He skillfully combined this toast with an expression of hope that the war would soon be over and that Europe and all the belligerent nations might be reborn in a peaceful world. Thus the new prisoners could empty their glasses without hesitation. Such a banquet as this lasts several hours. It is interrupted by innumerable speeches and toasts and by long intervals between every course during which there is smoking and drinking. There were toasts to Seydlitz, to Latt-mann, to the Soviet Union, to the new community of soldiers and generals, to the fighters against fascism; to the leader of the German working class, Wilhelm Pieck; to the memory of Florin,* to the men of the resistance, and finally—this was proposed by Bredel—to Paulus, our new companion in arms. Weinert discovered that he had been in Korfes' company at the front during the first World War. The deserter and anti-militarist Max Emmendörfer exchanged toasts with Seydlitz, while the artillerymen shouted.

At this point Seydlitz rose to make a speech. His imposing, straight figure kept its balance with difficulty. He told how, being a passionate horseman, he always rode hell for leather to meet a difficult obstacle. But today his tongue was running away with him and taking all obstacles by itself. When he became too tactless and started making cheap jokes about the names of those present, troubling the apostles Peter and Paul for an allusion to Petrov and Paulus, Petrov simply interrupted him with three cheers. A little puzzled, Seydlitz sank back into

* Wilhelm Florin, Communist deputy to the Reichstag from the Ruhr before 1933. *Trans.*

his chair, overcome with emotion and alcohol. The orchestra began to play the "Seydlitz March" composed by a bandmaster. The meal was over. Weinert, who owing to an illness could take even less than the prisoners who were no longer used to alcohol, supported himself against a cupboard, babbling and trying to gather his flock for the bus to Moscow. Petrov disappeared with several chosen generals to continue the celebration in a small circle. The ordinary mortals joined the young Russian officers, who, now that their chiefs were gone, grew lively and began to sing and dance with all their artistic temperament. We too tried to wash down with a glass of Crimean wine the bad taste which Seydlitz' behavior had left in our mouths, and took part in the continuing festivities.

It was only after a Russian and a German soldier in the full swing of a mazurka banged their heads against a stove so badly that one of them lay on the floor with a large head wound that the party broke up.

A few days later there appeared in the newspaper *Free Germany* the statement: "On August 22, 1944 an important plenary session of the National Committee took place, during which, after careful consultation, important decisions were made to intensify the struggle against fascist tyranny." Among ourselves we have long had a name for these occasions: "showpieces."

Chapter Eight / The Collapse

FEBRUARY 15, 1945. "May God have mercy on us," I wrote a year and a half ago, when I had just thought of the possibility that the war might continue after the Red Army had crossed the German frontiers. That is what has happened. East Prussia is the first victim. But what is happening there surpasses my worst fears. It is beyond all conceiving and all describing. Yesterday we had a meeting with our sixty members at the front who advanced with Rokossovsky's army group into East Prussia. Sixty distressed, weeping, embittered, hate-filled people. They are mostly old Communists who until recently were ready to say everything bad about the German army and praise the Red Army to the skies in spite of knowing better. They are antifascists some of whom worked consistently for the National Committee for two years under the most difficult circumstances, without grumbling about the many humiliations and injustices they suffered at the hands of the Red Army officers, and without hope of recognition from any side for their dangerous work. But what they are now experiencing is more than they can bear. It is indeed too much even for some of the Soviet officers who, under the profound shock, forgot their party dogma and poured out their hearts to me about their soldiers' paroxysm of destructive fury which it seemed impossible to curb. But I must tell the story as it happened.

In Moscow New Year's trees were alight everywhere as our sleeper left for Minsk, packed with Soviet soldiers celebrating and drinking vodka in the glow of the fireworks and New Year salutes. Bechler and I were going to Poland as plenipotentiaries with the 2d White Russian Front, and it was an open secret that we were to go into Germany with the Red Army. Our comrades of the National Committee of course envied us keenly. Our pockets were full of addresses of relatives with whom we were to get in touch, in bombed towns or prisons and concentration camps. New arrivals among the prisoners had informed us that, since July 20, we had all officially been sentenced to death *in contumacia* and that our relatives had been put under family arrest. Our joy over our imminent homecoming was overshadowed by the thought that Germany was after all suffering the same fate as Stalingrad, as we had vainly foretold and warned for two years. In our luggage we had tens of thousands of leaflets, an appeal from Paulus, Seydlitz, and fifty other generals to their comrades on the other side to capitulate and spare their Fatherland the worst. But how many of us still believed in the effectiveness of such action? All we could hope for was to save as many lives as we could out of the chaos of military collapse.

Our journey, like all winter journeys in Russia, became an expedition: hundreds of miles in an open truck in a temperature of —4° F.; nights in east Polish woods, in deserted villages; attacks by Polish partisans, evenings passed singing and dancing with Russian soldiers over a glass of homemade vodka. Beside me was always the stiff figure of Bechler, who was still mentally wearing the white gloves and raspberry-colored tunic he had worn as adjutant to von Knobelsdorff, commander of the 19th Infantry in Dresden; he was quite unable to make contact with his fellow travelers, the Russian soldiers and noncommissioned officers, who though primitive were often kind and friendly. But he is not a bad fellow and, what is more important, not an NKVD informer such as have gained control of the National Committee—officers from the antifascist school or such prize Nazis as Colonel Lewess Litzmann, the grandson of the "Lion of Bresziny" and former staff officer of Field Marshall von Stumpf.

"I shall always do what Moscow says," Bechler told me once during a discussion we had after class about whether criticism of the party line would be possible within the Communist party in Germany after the war.

"You're in no position to do anything else," I snapped back at him, "but you're crazy if you think one can build a new world with a party of men who just take orders. How can the Comintern in Moscow, or any party for that matter, operate a reasonable policy if no opposition and no criticism are allowed inside it? The fact that life is a war of contradictions is being hammered into us all the time at the school. The party becomes a lifeless machine when it has no more internal contradictions."

Bechler was a battalion commander, respected by his subordinates as well as his comrades, and unwaveringly shared the official optimism at Stalingrad to the very last day. He was a pedant who, by his own account, weighed the small packages of his soldiers on a letter scale to see if they were two grams overweight. It is said that he was equally severe with himself. It takes all sorts to make a world, I reminded myself, and apart from occasional digs at one another we always got on pretty well together.

In the middle of January we arrived at the Narev front. Our chief, the Tulpanov of this front, was said to be a certain Lieutenant Colonel Saposhdansky, whom Bechler knew from a previous visit to the front. Bechler had told us enthusiastically of the "diplomatic" breakfasts they had enjoyed together. However, I was unpleasantly surprised to find that the man was a fat, opaque jellyfish in a brand-new show-window uniform.

Our first task was to arrange a conference with army divisional instructors from the Politburo, at which we were to give an account of the political work of the National Committee to eighty officers and members of the Bolshevik party.

Expectantly and with lively interest, we drove to this gathering. Here was an opportunity to do something for a German-Russian understanding and really get to know a large number of average Soviet citizens. But we were soon disappointed. We were received in icy silence, like enemies; and into this icy silence we spoke of the National Committee and its tasks. Then they let us have it. With unveiled animosity they put question after question: "What makes you call us your comrades? We have no German comrades. Haven't you read Ehrenburg's articles in *Pravda?* Only unborn children and dogs in Germany are innocent! . . . So you expect us to support your work? The work of reactionary generals, who only yesterday were still flogging their serfs? How many Jews have you shot? How many women have you raped?"

We were a match for them however, and gave those gentlemen a lesson in Marxism and internationalism which made their provocative questions stick in their throats. But it took our breath away. If this was not a planned maneuver to sound us out, we had better be prepared for a delightful collaboration with the Soviets in Germany. Compared with the political maturity of these eighty representatives of the "advance guard of the working class," Vansittart and Poincaré were progressive and full of understanding. But what was the use of all this grumbling? Events had passed us by long ago.

On January 14 the new Russian winter offensive began. We had done nothing from a propaganda point of view toward this offensive; our leaflets, appeals from generals, and our newspapers were used for other purposes by the Soviet staff officers. In order to preserve the element of surprise, Rokossovsky had forbidden all propaganda activity on his front. It was a needless precaution. The Germans knew, without this, that an offensive was imminent, and yet had no possible chance of preparing for it. Lack of gasoline, and the Führer's orders, nailed them to the spot, and lack of shells silenced their artillery.

But it made no difference whether our appeals landed in the Russian latrines or the Narev marshes between the fronts; fate took its course in any case.

I followed close behind the advancing Russian troops in a truck which I filled with prisoners. Several times I had to save them literally at the last minute from the automatic pistols of trigger-happy soldiers.

On the road of march I saw many clumps of people in German uniform who had been mowed down—allegedly men from Vlasov's army, but not all of them wore the badge of the eastern battalions. Sometimes near a small farm or settlement were scattered five, ten, or even twenty disabled Sherman tanks or T-34's. In the village would be a destroyed German antiaircraft gun, a tank left lying on the street, an uncoupled antitank gun, a heap of antitank mines, and a few dozen dead Germans who had sold their lives here as dearly as possible.

We met a column of prisoners, two to three hundred Russians in German uniform surrounded by Red Army men with whips. The prisoners had already been stripped of everything but their shirts, and their clothes lay in heaps on either side of the column. When I looked for Germans among them one man asked me in German:

"When are we going to be shot?"

"I hope never," I said, embarrassed.

The man shrugged this away and pointed at his bare feet in the snow, at his underpants and shirt. "I hope soon," he said. "It is terrible to freeze to death slowly."

Bechler and I with five other antifascists continued on our journey toward the encircled armies at Thorn. But when we got there the German force had already broken out. Rokossovsky's army group, basing its left flank on the Vistula, had turned northward and entered East Prussia. Allenstein and Elbing had already fallen. Southwest of the Vistula Zhukov was advancing toward the Oder, encountering hardly any resistance. A few divisions of his army group had also turned north and were marching on the other side of the Vistula toward Danzig. In this way a gap was created between the two army groups in which there were only a few Russian units. Nevertheless the position of the wandering encircled Germans seemed hopeless. Between them and the main German front lay the Vistula and a wide strip of land occupied by the Russians. Graudenz had already been cut off. In a large car, with a loudspeaker and tens of thousands of leaflets and letters from generals written in their own handwriting, I followed closely behind these encircled units as they retreated. The track along which they were escaping was littered for several dozen miles with dead bodies and destroyed equipment. The break-out was made after the manner of Cherkassy: the general and the commanders, together with the tanks and the rest of the heavy arms that could still be moved, rolled ahead, while the baggage and the units that were dependent on walking were left to their own devices.

But one night on the Vistula it looked as if the Germans

could go no farther. With difficulty I persuaded the Russians who had come with me, and their leader, a major who had been decorated with the Order of Lenin, to use the loudspeaker; they were really interested only in loot and vodka. Three or four times we tried to make contact with the German units in order to cross their lines and negotiate with their leaders. But all we found was two field sentries, although we spent hours wandering about the area which was presumably occupied by the Germans.

The next morning the mystery was cleared up. The previous evening the Germans had captured a pontoon bridge which the Russians had thrown across the Vistula, and had got to the other side. But at what price? A flat area of one to one and a half square miles in front of the bridge was covered with the ruins of trucks, cars, and arms, with piles of horribly twisted dead bodies among them. From the high banks of the Vistula the Russian artillery fired in the open on the columns as they lined up before crossing the bridge.

I climbed up the dam and looked across the river to the west. Not a living soul was moving. Dark puffs of smoke rose from the ruins of houses and munition trucks burning beneath the low clouds, which seemed to hang just above the dirty snow. The bridge creaked and swayed complainingly under the pressure of the ice. Behind me the Russians led by their major were looting the field of devastation. It was only when a Russian battery suddenly opened fire from the hills above, and shells with shrill whines blew the overturned vehicles into the air, that they abandoned their dreary activity and hastened back to Thorn in order not to miss their share of the booty there.

In the meantime Bechler had remained with an army staff and was occupied with prisoner-of-war assembly camps. We had no time to exchange views and experiences because as soon as we got back the major, without any warning, sent my five assistants to a prisoner collection point. His excuse was that they were cowards and had carried out their assignments badly. They had made three attempts to cross what was thought to be the German line. Three times the Red Army had recaptured them. They had been beaten and threatened with shooting, and yet they would have tried it a fourth time if I had asked them to. But I did not want to risk their lives senselessly.

The truth was that the major found it inconvenient to have these men as possible witnesses. After innumerable arguments about his lack of discipline, his drunkenness, and his quarrels which held up our work, I finally threatened to complain about him.

When all our protests to the major against his handing over our comrades failed, I asked Bechler to return with me at once on our own initiative to front headquarters, in order to plead for their release with Saposhdansky. Bechler was of the opinion that such independent action was too strong a protest, and we finally agreed that I should go alone while he—so that nobody could make any accusations against us—remained with the army staff in Thorn to which we were attached.

But Saposhdansky did not receive me until three days after my arrival, by which time Bechler had also returned to the front. Saposhdansky's answer to my complaints—which were but weakly supported by Bechler—about the impossibility of working with plunderers and marauders was that I had acted without self-restraint and should take an example from Bechler's behavior. As Bechler said nothing I left the two to breakfast alone.

Even this episode has now become very unimportant. During the last few days since my return to the staff at the front all our assistants from the divisions in East Prussia have gradually arrived here. They witnessed the end of East Prussia, the invasion of the Huns. They saw the Russian soldiers burn down towns and villages, watched them shoot prisoners and civilians, rape women, and turn army hospitals into death houses with the butts of their guns. They saw them drain kegs of potato alcohol and perfume bottles, plunder, destroy, and burn. They also read the orders of the new occupying power: all men between sixteen and fifty-five, all members of the Hitler Youth and the German Girls' League over the age of fourteen, all members of the National Socialist party or of any of its subsidiary organizations were to report to the Kommandatura with two days' rations, on penalty of being shot. They saw the camps into which these people were thrown and from there deported to Russia. They saw columns of refugees into which German and Russian artillery fired simultaneously and which were then rolled into the ditches by Russian tanks.

They witnessed an orgy of extermination such as no civilized region could ever have experienced before. Few of them were able to hold back their tears when they spoke of it.

I have always been afraid of the day when the Red Army would start fighting on German soil. But what is happening here goes further than I had thought possible in my blackest hours.

Even the Russian officers confirm what our comrades say. They are no longer in control of their troops. Commanders who try to put a stop to the activities of their own units are simply shot. The barbarism is so great that they fear for the fighting morale of their men.

Today I heard from Bechler that we have been asked to call a meeting of our sixty workers at the front, in order to talk over the events in East Prussia.

In silence we walked toward the neighboring village where the men were billeted, and in silence they gathered round us.

Two Russian officers attended the meeting, although I asked them to leave us alone so that the men should be able to speak freely. But perhaps it was better this way. At any rate they would hear for themselves what was said rather than have it reported by their informers, who were undoubtedly present, practicing "Bolshevik vigilance," as they have done in the National Committee and the antifascist school and as they do throughout the Soviet Union.

Once more our comrades unfolded before us a picture of the inhuman horror which has broken out in East Prussia. Suddenly I remembered that I had heard something like this before. Four weeks ago, when the Russian offensive had just begun, I came across a young farmer's son from the region of Goldap in a prisoner assembly camp. He had been a troop leader in the German Youth Movement. We were looking for volunteers to be trained in our school at the front, and had just delivered a lecture about our aims and intentions to a group of twenty selected prisoners. After the lecture we asked each one whether he was willing to join us in our work. With the exception of this boy everybody agreed to join. His reply was:

"Until a few months ago I was in the Hitler Youth. Maybe what you say about the Third Reich and its leaders is right. Events seem to prove it. But I can't change sides overnight. And do you think that the Soviets are better? What they have done in the towns and villages that they captured in the fall and we have retaken is worse than death. We East Prussians would rather die fighting than endure that without resisting."

This statement, made by the youngster in the presence of a Soviet officer, could not have been more courageous and clear. But at the time I tried to get over the shock that his report of the behavior of the Red Army had given me by trying to convince myself the boy's words were only the result of the usual Nazi propaganda.

Now there is no escaping the truth. Now we must face the fact that what the boy told us was the truth, though only about a small segment of the entire front.

When our comrades had finished their report Bechler rose, and without having previously discussed it with me made a speech obviously prepared in advance. Apparently he had instructions from Saposhdansky.

> Comrades, the war of the fascist conquerors is nearing its end. The Red Army, the army of the most progressive country in the world, the army of socialism and internationalism, has arrived on German soil to free the German people and the world from fascist slavery.

He continued in this vein for about twenty minutes, until he came to the concluding sentences:

> Comrades, the tone in which you have spoken about the conduct of the Red Army on German soil shows that you are still infected through and through with fascist poison and that you begin to wail when the Nazi crimes which have brought this catastrophe on Germany are finally atoned for. It shows that you are prepared to slander the Red Army and to build up an anti-Soviet campaign out of a few unavoidable excesses of war. It shows that you still succumb to fascist provocations if you blame the Red Army for arson and murders committed by the fascist "werewolves." In the name of the National Committee and the representatives of the Red Army, it is my duty to give you a severe reprimand and earnest warning. I close the meeting.

I felt as if I had received a blow on the head. Had Bechler lost his mind? I jumped up and began to speak myself.

What instructions Comrade Bechler has received from the representative of the Red Army I do not know, but I do know that he is not speaking in the name of the National Committee. I have something to tell you which is the exact contrary of what you have just heard. First of all I want to thank you in the name of the National Committee for all the care and trouble and grave conflicts of conscience which you have taken upon yourselves out of belief in the future of our Fatherland, and all this—as we see now—without any justifiable hope of recognition and understanding from any side. I must also tell you that I am, like you, deeply shocked by what is happening in these days in our country. I must remind you that many of you violently attacked me at the antifascist school when I voiced my opinion that the Red Army should not be regarded as the incarnation of all human and soldierly virtues but is an army whose soldiers are in the over-whelming majority uncivilized, brutal, primitive peasants who often wage the kind of war that was customary in other countries at the time of the Thirty Years' War. If we refuse to admit these facts, if we forget that, thirty years ago, 80 per cent of the population of the Soviet Union was still illiterate, that since World War I the Soviet population has known practically no normal and peaceful life but only civil war, hunger, political disorder, and a complete revolution in every aspect of life—which has not contributed to a stable conception of justice and humanity—we shall always have a false opinion of the Soviet Union. The grotesque attempt to show that the disaster which has befallen East Prussia is an anti-Soviet creation only goes to show to what downright idiotic political attitudes such a lack of objectivity can lead.

Having said this I tried to find an explanation for the behavior of the Red Army: the brutalization of war, the hatred pent up during the two-thousand-mile advance through their own ravaged country; the desperate, obstinate resistance of the German troops, who were still inflicting the heaviest losses on the Red Army; the necessity of intensifying hate propaganda at a moment when the war-weary Soviet soldiers had reached the boundaries of their own country and now had to be readied for the difficult final struggle; and finally the rage these soldiers must have experienced at our invading their country from a land with a standard of living which must have seemed to them the height of luxury.

In conclusion I said:

> Hitler has sown an excess of hate. It is not surprising that, while militarily senseless resistance continues on German soil, we also reap an excess of hatred from a nation which is fundamentally good natured and little given to aggression but has not yet learned to control its sudden emotional outbursts. We have often seen how the Russians can change suddenly from kindliness and sympathy to brutality and ruthlessness, and vice versa. If Bechler meant to point out in his speech that we started the war and so it is up to us to suppress the anger and sorrow we feel at the injustice which is being done now, to break the unfortunate chain of mutual hatred and revenge, and blot out the past, I agree with him on this point, but only on this.

My speech was not followed by discussion. But more or less furtively one comrade after another came up and thanked me for my reply to Bechler. Even one of the Soviet officers pressed my hand and said, "You spoke after my own heart. What Bechler said is incredible."

"He undoubtedly has instructions from your chief," I replied.

The Russian shrugged his shoulders resignedly. "Of course, I know."

This evening I was told that I have been ordered back to Moscow, supposedly by telegram. I suspect that the gentlemen of the staff at the front dislike my presence here!

FEBRUARY 25, 1945. I am still with the staff at the front. The Russians have not yet found means to send me and the other antifascists who have also become undesirable off to Moscow. In the meantime Bechler and Saposhdansky have started a propaganda campaign directed at the German units encircled in Graudenz. Bechler left for Graudenz with twenty comrades from our front school. This expedition again was not properly planned. Uniforms, arms, and passes were lacking. Nobody knew anything about the encircled units, their commanders, their position at the front, or about the minefields. Our men have no chance of getting safely through the lines and are sure to fall straight into the hands of the Secret Field Police with the encircled armies. But Bechler threw all my warnings to the winds. The lives of our people are being risked in an utterly crazy way just so that Saposhdansky can report proofs of his "activity" to Moscow.

Today four survivors returned from Graudenz. They tried five times to reach the encircled units. But as they had not even been allowed to look at a map, as they had no idea of the position of the front, the passwords of the Germans, or the location of the minefields, most of them fell at the first attempt or were severely wounded and remained lying between the lines. Only one group of four men, under a lieutenant from Bregenz, reached the encircled troops. This lieutenant had with him letters from Seydlitz to the commanders of the German units. But the next day we learned from new prisoners that this lieutenant together with his comrades was handed over to the SS for execution without having seen a single regimental commander. The Russians sent the four survivors to a prison camp as traitors and cowards.

I had one other sharp encounter with the Russians. When I taxed the head of our school at the front with the whole affair he accused me of having demoralized the men by advising them not to take part in this mad heaven-bent commando.

"We could just as well have ordered the antifascists to capture the commander at Graudenz," he mocked.

"In that case you might just as well have shot them here," I replied. "What you are doing is murder, senseless murder, and I shall accuse you of that in Moscow." I left the room without saluting.

The same young Russian lieutenant who has shown me sympathy on other occasions followed me and tried to calm me. "If the whole Red Army fought as badly as the political division works, we should have lost the war long ago," he said. "But they work particularly badly here."

I promised him I would do all in my power to get Saposhdansky's neck broken, especially as Bechler had promised to support my complaint with a written report. The lieutenant remained skeptical.

"I advise you to be careful. General Burtsev, Saposhdansky's chief in Moscow, was here recently. He went from one rabbit hunt and one party to another. The two of them are close friends. You won't accomplish much with him."

MARCH 3, 1945. The return journey to Moscow took five days. Sixteen men who had helped us at the front nearly collapsed under the weight of the loot which the two Russian officers who accompanied us carried for themselves and their comrades in Moscow: tins of meat, butter, rolls of material, tablecloths, dresses, stockings, tools, watches, and jewelry.

In Moscow we had to deliver the loot to their various relations, and in this way we had an opportunity to see the apartments of these Russians. One of the officers was a teacher in a ten-grade school in civilian life. He lived with his mother, his wife, his sister and her daughter in a dreary room about sixteen feet square filled with broken furniture and dusty plants. How these five people managed with two beds and a dilapidated plush sofa was a mystery to me. The lieutenant explained it as if it were the most natural thing in the world: they slept in shifts.

There were ten doors leading off the hall onto which this room opened, and behind each door lived such a family, often of three generations.

The lieutenant and I had a meal with one of the neighbors. The room was about half the size of an ordinary Berlin bedroom and was equipped as a workshop (which had not been cleaned for a long time), with a turning lathe, and full of metal scraps. Two metal workers camped here and they too slept in shifts on the floor, upon a pile of nondescript rags. I asked our host what his food ration was, for I was struck by the enthusiasm with which he greeted the tins of meat the lieutenant had contributed toward our meal. They were exactly the same rations that were prescribed for the officers' prison camps. I could not understand this. The man looked tolerably well nourished. But even considering the greater frugality of the Russians, he could not possibly exist on such food while doing twelve hours of piecework. Our host pointed to the turning lathe and the rag pile in the corner.

"We work privately for ourselves too. We have sold everything we could do without, even the bed, so as to buy on the black market."

"Isn't that dangerous?" I asked, remembering the struggle against black marketeers and speculators which *Pravda* was endlessly proclaiming. He made a disparaging gesture: "Nichevo. One must live. And as long as the gentlemen at the top buy on the black market—or they would starve too— nothing much can happen to us."

The lieutenant looked rather embarrassed while this conversation was going on. As an officer and party member, he had never talked to me about these things. Now he tried to interrupt.

"Better not talk like this," he said in Russian. "He's a German."

"My friend," the other replied, "what difference does it make? He is a German and I am a Muscovite. Want is the same everywhere."

The apartment of the other officer was no better: the room a little brighter, the house not quite so dilapidated, but wretchedly furnished too and packed with people. I had not realized that things were quite so bad. Yet *Pravda* said that everywhere in East Prussia the workingmen's flats were fitted out with furniture stolen from the Soviet Union.

At last we reached our objective, the Moscow office of the committee. But the reception that awaited us was surprising. We were locked in a cellar. At first I thought this was just a bureaucratic measure, as permission to go to Moscow and stay in the city even a few hours was difficult to get. But after all our arrival had been regularly announced to the Kommandatura and we had our delousing certificates in our pockets. There could be no further obstacle to our being received by

Weinert. Hour after hour passed. Nobody bothered about us. At last, in spite of the orders and curses of the guard, I left the cellar in order to get into the office of the National Committee. The cries of the guard brought the military sentries, and they tried to push me back into the cellar by force. Members of the National Committee rushed out, very excited, and tried to persuade me to have patience. I kept on shouting and struggling with the guards until finally I was standing before Weinert. Indignant and wrathful, I gave him a brief account of our experiences at the front and made all our protests.

"You must talk to our front workers at once. They are thoroughly disillusioned at the arbitrariness and injustice with which their years of work are being rewarded. The committee has accepted responsibility for these people; it can't simply drop them just because a corrupt lieutenant colonel wants to be rid of them."

Weinert promised everything. First I was to talk to General Burtsev. A table was set with caviar, vodka, canned lobster, white bread, and cold meat, in short with everything that makes real Russian *sakuska* or hors d'oeuvres. Then the general appeared with his adjutant, the son of the well-known graphic artist Heinrich Vogler, who died of starvation in exile in Central Asia.

"You have had difficulties?" the general asked me.

He was an uncouth fellow, whose fat jowls hung down to the collar of his uniform. He had been a glass blower, Weinert assured me quickly with pride, to prove that it was possible to rise in the social scale in the Soviet Union.

"I am sure you will agree, General," I answered, "that the work on the 2d White Russian Front has brought nothing but failure."

"I am not referring to the front, I am alluding to your difficulties here in this building," interrupted the general.

"Yes, they shut us up for hours in the cellar—and that was just the last of a long series of humiliations, injustices, and undeserved reproaches to which my comrades and I have been exposed. I hope to be able to give you a full report on all this, and I would like to point out that it concerns not only ourselves but the work that we should be doing and that Bechler and the other comrades are still trying to carry out."

The general interrupted me again: "Have a drink and some food; you've had a strenuous journey."

"I have waited so long, sir, that I can wait for my food a little longer. I must tell you, General, . . ."

"Later on, after you've eaten. Get rested first."

In the middle of the meal, as the talk came round again to conditions at the front, the general suddenly took his leave.

"I have work to do; we'll talk later."

And before this had been translated to me he was gone.

"What's all this comedy about?" I asked Weinert. "Why didn't you put in a word to back me up with the general? You're perfectly aware that things are just as I described them to you. Or don't you like to hear the truth about what is happening at the front and in Germany? Is it distasteful to have me inform the general that it was a year and a half before you managed to issue your first report about the work at the front, and only a few weeks before the end of the war? Why don't you talk with the workers at the front? If you don't believe me, they'll tell you things that will make my report look glowing."

Weinert listened to all this with an unmoved expression.

"The front workers have been sent away," he said finally. "The report shows clearly that they are not only demoralized but definitely hostile elements. As far as your report goes, Bechler is saying just the opposite."

He showed me the latest issue of *Free Germany*, which had

a large picture of Bechler, a whole-page report of his "successes" in Graudenz, and a conversation with the commandant of the fortress, General Fricke, after he had been taken prisoner. I put the paper aside.

"Well, that's for the newspaper. We know the behavior of the German generals. But where is Bechler's report? I am speaking in his name too. My complaints are his complaints. We decided that, and he expressly asked me to support him against Saposhdansky."

"We have no such report," answered Weinert.

"Then it must have been held back by Saposhdansky, just as our earlier reports apparently were," I said.

"Not at all," said Weinert. "There is a report on your attitude toward the behavior of the Red Army, and it is easy to see from it that you were not equal to the job."

"One man's word is nobody's word; both sides must be heard, Comrade Weinert. If this elementary principle is not to be respected, I could have saved myself a lot of trouble."

"Well, we have heard you now," said Weinert, closing the conversation. "The report on you was not at all exaggerated."

MARCH 26, 1945. I was held prisoner nearly a week in the office of the National Committee. They were probably discussing what was to be done with me. Finally I came back to Lunovo.

Naturally I have now become considerably more prudent in my reports. But the fact of my merely stating that things had happened in Germany which would unfortunately leave an irreparable breach for many years between Germany and the Soviet Union was enough to make me suspected of slandering the Red Army and of being anti-Soviet.

Chapter Nine / The Dissolution
of the National Committee

MAY 9, 1946. A year has passed since the armistice. How we longed for the last day of the war, and how complete was the disillusionment it brought! Nothing we worked for has been accomplished. The Third Reich came to an end in the very circumstances we had attempted to avoid; and this end did not even bring our return home.

The National Committee vegetated the whole summer of 1945. In June the first two members, Reyher and Willms, were allowed to go back to Germany. A little later a large number of the Communist émigrés followed, and with them all those who, like Bechler, were ready to carry out Moscow's orders unconditionally or, to be more precise, to carry out unconditionally what Moscow appeared to order. For it is in fact much more difficult to determine the official party line from the oracular hints about practical postwar policy than it was in the theoretical courses of the antifascist school. What was yesterday's party line could be a deviation today, and vice versa. In this way the official point of view on a federated Germany, the steel quota, the eastern frontier, dismantling, and reparations has changed three or even four times. Only those who can acclaim each of these oscillations fervently and unhesitatingly as the one saving and binding truth are disciplined Bolsheviks.

This situation reached its climax in the question of the Oder-Neisse line. Even though I recited to myself ten times a day the succession of ideas which would read into this policy fidelity to the principles of internationalism, of national self-determination, and of understanding between peoples, my emotions said no although my mind allowed itself to be persuaded.

But let me leave my feelings out of it. Dialectical reasoning shall prevail. It is a traditional principle of communism that the national question must be subordinated to the social revolution. For a convinced revolutionary, the claims of one's own nation must take second place if the strategy and tactics of the international class struggle require it.

If one starts with the premise that the Soviet Union as the first and only socialist state in the world is in fact the backbone of the revolutionary movement, and that the existence and success of the latter depend on the existence and power of the former, then as a German Communist one must subordinate the interests of one's own nation even on the question of the German-Polish frontier.

The annexation of the three eastern German provinces by Poland, or rather their delivery to Poland by the Great Powers, naturally decided the struggle between East and West for greater influence in Poland in favor of the Soviet Union. The London Poles thought they could undermine the pretension of the Polish Communists to be the exclusive representatives of the centuries-old claims of Greater Poland to the Oder boundary by making these demands their own. In this they received the support of the English who hoped thereby to prevent the transformation of Poland into a Moscow-oriented people's democracy; but it is clear that London missed the point that Poland, once it accepted these provinces, would be bound to follow Moscow's policy. How shall Poland defend this boundary against revisionist claims if she is not supported by the Soviet Union? September 1939 has shown what Western guarantees are worth to an anti-Soviet Poland which lives in enmity with Germany.

For the Soviet Union, this gift to Poland is doubly valuable because this is the only way it can hope to take the edge off the deeply rooted Polish hostility toward Russia—a hostility newly inflamed by the Soviet action with regard to the eastern boundary of Poland. Poland's gain not only means security for the Soviet Union on its western frontier but also guarantees its influence in all occupied territories even after the withdrawal of the occupation troops.

The German Communists find themselves today in a situation similar to that of the Polish Communists in 1939, when the Soviet Union participated in the destruction of Pilsudski's Poland. Like Poland then, Germany has now sat down between two stools. In both cases the Soviet Union profits. Communists of both countries can, with a certain justification, wash their hands of any responsibility, because they have always fought against expansionist desires in anti-Soviet guise, which in both cases led to the same result.

This whole Communist construction received a severe blow when it became known that more than twelve million Germans are to be moved from the new provinces of Poland and from all other East European countries. Which of us would ever have thought in his wildest dreams that the Soviet Union would be guilty of such a violation of the rights of national minorities established over centuries, when it had an opportunity here to give the world an example of the socialist handling of this problem and to demonstrate a lesson in applied internationalism? This unparalleled expulsion of millions of persons is bound to push Germany and the whole of Europe into mortal hostility toward communism and the Soviet Union. But here again the Moscow Communists have an explanation ready, which is not, in fact, really flattering to the Soviet Union but without doubt has very real foundations: one of the main reasons why the Soviet Union was not overrun long before this war by its capitalist neighbors lay in the contradictions and conflicts which made these neighbors incapable of united action to solve the social conflicts existing within the capitalist countries, and in the competition among them. Lenin's whole conception of the possibility of the victory of socialism in only one land rests on a skillful exploitation of these contradictions in the capitalist world. After this war one of the most important of these conflicts disappeared with the defeat of the Axis and of Japan. Moreover, a new and powerful bond appeared which holds the capitalist world together, namely, the undisputed rule of the world market by the dollar and the dominating power position of the United States. On the other hand it may take years for the Soviet Union to recover from the war's enormous destruction and sacrifice of lives. It may take it even longer to catch up with the still very large lead of the West in technical and scientific fields. So the Soviet Union has every reason to be cautious and to make sure that Poland and the Balkan states follow a line which is coordinated with her own, without being disturbed by foreign national elements, before it embraces the vague hope that the Communists may sometime come to power in Germany after a long and difficult political fight. It has to take into account the fact that the annexations and expulsions will make communism very unpopular at first in Germany. But in the long view both these measures will bring about such

a conflict in the rest of Germany between the need for imports
and the possibilities of export, such an intensification of unemployment and foreign trade deficits, that eventually these problems will no longer be solvable by bourgeois democratic methods. Unavoidable misery among the masses will prepare the
ground for Communist agitation, and even the middle classes
and big capitalists will finally be compelled to seek their salvation in an orientation toward Eastern markets and a planned
economy—in short, toward Moscow.

Certainly this strategy is so cynical and cold-blooded that
one shudders at it, but it is impossible to deny its logic and
far-sightedness. Sentimental revolutionaries should not even
try to put their ideas into practice. If one believes in the Soviet
experiment, in communism, one must have the courage to ac-
knowledge such consequences. That is the root of the matter.
We must not pursue our own trains of thought. The only
valid foundation for the Oder-Neisse policy must be considered Molotov's declaration that the three eastern German
provinces are the "cradle of the Polish state," once stolen by
the German aggressors and today returned to their rightful
owner by the magnanimous Soviet Union. In the whole Soviet
press, and naturally in *Free Germany*, history is misrepresented
in page-long articles in order to give a "scientific" foundation
to this story.

While Ulbricht, who with all his crudeness is very clever,
first disposed of this question in the Soviet zone of occupation
with the statement that "Hitler gambled away the eastern German provinces," we in the National Committee had to accept
the most insanely biased historical constructions that the Polish
chauvinists and fanatical Pan-Slavs could produce.

We are supposed to believe that a policy which violates the
principles of national self-determination in the crudest manner
is in the last resort faithful to the principles of nationalism. At

the same time we are supposed to defend it with the most insipid nationalistic and racist slogans, and arguments that falsify history dreadfully. After we have painfully made the first argument our own we are suddenly obliged to subscribe unconditionally and fanatically to the second if we do not want to be at once suspected of nationalistic deviations and fascist origins. The Communists in the house such as Zippel, Emmendörfer, Grandy, and Klement make it their business to incite the other inmates to protest these ridiculous articles so that they can immediately report their protests to the NKVD. Grandy, a former noncommissioned officer in the air corps who has now become editor of the central organ of the Communist party in Germany, when he was repatriated at the beginning of August 1945 left a notebook behind, either by oversight or in a spirit of cynical defiance. In this his comrades discovered accurate entries of all such heretical statements. In such an atmosphere the last traces of solidarity within the National Committee disappeared. Ulbricht's statement that only antifascists would be repatriated, as there were enough fascists in Germany, let loose in the middle of the summer what we called "the battle for return tickets." Everybody understood only too well that anyone who allowed himself something like an opinion of his own was considered a fascist.

In the first months after my return from Narev I was too depressed to let myself think about the criticisms which had been leveled against me. It was only gradually that I realized that these reproaches were not only designed to make me keep my mouth shut about my particular experiences at the front but also indicated that I had really fallen into disgrace. The party judged me to be politically unreliable and demoralized. I lived in a vacuum. With a few exceptions my comrades of the left wing of the committee—the Communist element, as it

were—with which I had always been closely associated, were
quick to loosen their personal ties with me.

The inner ring of this Communist element in the house was
formed by the triumvirate Homann, Vincenz Müller, and Arno
von Lensky. The two generals had attended the antifascist
school in the winter of 1944 and returned to Lunovo convinced Communists. Hoffmeister could not take this course
because his health had grown much worse. In the winter a
stroke put him out of action for good.

Müller aligned himself with the Communist way of thinking
with a speed that astonished even those of us who had personally experienced the attraction this theory could have on
people who by their origin and education belonged on the
other side of the barricade. He had been considered one of the
most capable General Staff officers of the Wehrmacht. Physically he somewhat resembled Vlasov. He could be polite,
smooth, and obliging as well as energetic and decided. He had
once been a Catholic and an ardent monarchist. As former
adjutant of Schleicher he had supervised the overthrow of the
Prussian Social Democratic government in the Third Army
District on July 20, 1932. Apart from Hoffmeister he was the
only captive general who had any political experience. It was
the kind of experience in the Reichswehr party which his
friend Hoffmeister had condemned so sharply in his articles and
it culminated in the Machiavellian ideas and the sober and
unprejudiced *Realpolitik* which were characteristic of von
Seeckt. Müller, like Hoffmeister, knew that the successes which
the Reichswehr party had celebrated behind the façade of the
Weimar Republic were inseparably linked with the military
and political activities that had brought the former imperial
officers and deadly enemies of the revolution together with the
leaders of the Red Army on the Soviet training grounds, in the

airdromes of the Red Air Force, and in the arms factories of Kharkov and Tula. He also recognized the dilemma of this policy, the lack of an ideology with a mass base. After a last attempt by Schleicher through the trade unions to renew the marriage of convenience between the military casts and the Social Democrats made in 1919 and soon dissolved, this lack finally resulted in capitulation before Hitler's demagogic triumphs.

So it is not surprising that in the present catastrophe Müller regards a renewal of the pro-Russian policy of the Reichswehr, reinforced this time with a Communist mass movement, as Germany's only political hope.

The most simple and straightforward of this triumvirate was Arno von Lensky. He embodied the tradition of the Prussian cavalry, both by origin and in his career. This elegant and chivalrous sportsman, whose graying head would have looked wonderful beneath the three-cornered hat of Frederick the Great's era, was captured at Stalingrad as commander of the 24th Panzer Division, a division labeled reactionary by the Nazis since its officer corps was composed primarily of bearers of old noble names. It was not until the spring of 1944 that he came of his own volition into the committee. He was able to give honorable reasons for his action in a sincere and manly statement. But he found no echo among his former subordinates in the officers' camp at Yelabuga.

It is possible that the influence of his aide Jesco von Puttkamer was just as important to his decision as the fact that the Russians had apparently experimented with him by treating him in a psychologically skillful and very correct manner, separating him from the other generals and lodging him for several weeks in a luxurious country house with Puttkamer. Hope for the national rebirth of Germany on the side of the Soviet Union brought him into our camp. Another motive for his behavior was his feeling of guilt at belonging to a class which had regarded the task of military and political-social leadership as its privilege but was clearly no longer equal to it.

Another group in the house, under the leadership of Martin Lattmann, we called the Christian Socialists. Korfes, Steidle, von Frankenberg, van Hooven, and Dr. Czimatis belonged to this group. Lewess Litzmann also claimed to be a Christian Socialist. They loved to call themselves non-Marxists or even anti-Marxists at every opportunity in order to follow the Communist line all the more surely. Lattmann clearly hoped to be of more value to the Russians as a non-Marxist; and this speculation entangled him in continual vacillations and con- tradictions. In general an astounding dishonesty with them- selves was a characteristic of this group. They were commonly called the "erasers" in the house, because in all political dis- cussions one always visualized them, internally and externally, sliding uncomfortably back and forth on their bottoms, under the pressure of Communist demands. The Protestant clergymen among us could also be considered as belonging to this group, although as ministers they were in a special position, and more- over all four were sent back to Germany during 1945. The Catholic priests, on the other hand, were the only ones in the house who, with all the tactical compromises they had made, were always ready to say no when anything was demanded of them which contradicted the principles of their Catholic view.

There were also a few men who had leanings toward social democracy. Among these were Captain Fleischer and his friends, and also, with vacillations, Major Hetz. They had to be even more prudent than the oppositional Communists, for to be a declared Social Democrat, and therefore "against the unity of the working class," was the most reprehensible heresy of which one could become guilty, even if as here it happened only in theory.

Why the National Committee was not immediately disbanded after May 8, 1945 we never found out. It was left dangling in air. But apparently the Soviets wanted to hold it in reserve as long as they were uncertain whether the Western powers might not favor the formation of a German government. From week to week and from month to month Pieck and Weinert promised that we should all be sent home immediately, except for the generals whose repatriation was impossible for the present for reasons of foreign policy. But when even the Potsdam Conference, to whose conclusion all dates were finally postponed, brought no change in our situation, and when radio and newspaper talked into a vacuum (since there was no contact with either the prison camps or Germany), six of us made a last attempt to re-establish solidarity in the house and obtain a clarification of our position by a united front against the émigrés and the Soviets. We sent a request to Weinert for the convocation of a plenary session in which we hoped officially to learn the intentions of the Soviet Government toward the National Committee. Moreover, we demanded that the committee discuss the proposals and demands which would be addressed to the Russians in case the committee were to continue to exist.

We proposed the following agenda:

a) Full information to the house from the president on the political situation in Germany and on the intentions of the Russians toward the National Committee [if necessary by calling in some suitable expert].

b) Discussion of the political situation in Germany and of the possibilities still open for political activity of the National Committee under these circumstances.

c) The establishment of a clear attitude toward the program of a united front in Germany and the program of the various parties. Clarification of the question whether members of the National Committee will be free to join the different parties and whether publicity can be given to their party membership.

d) Clarification of the question of providing up-to-date working material from Germany and the prison camps for political activity. Discussion of an urgent request about the possibility of being brought into contact with life in the Soviet Union [which we were promised hundreds of times would take place after the war].

e) Discussion of the composition of the National Committee and adding new working members. In this context it is necessary to determine:

1) whether the members of the National Committee who have been transported to different prison camps for other purposes cannot be brought back to Lunovo to bring the committee up to full strength;

2) what relations and connections still exist between the National Committee and those members who have been sent to Germany, and how they can be strengthened;

3) whether it is possible to resume preparing ideological memoranda [in the manner of the Education Commission] by calling on suitable collaborators from the camps and from the civil sector.

It seems to be high time for us to be more actively concerned again with our real tasks and more conscious of our responsibilities toward the members of our movement— however understandable in the present situation all personal calculations and considerations of the individual members may be. The proposers are of the opinion that a plenary session will not encroach upon the decisions of the Russian authorities. A clarification of the open questions from the German viewpoint will doubtless be welcomed by the Russian authorities too and will mitigate their attitude toward the view of the National Committee or perhaps toward its legal successor. Signed: Graf Einsiedel, Fleischer, Gerlach, Hetz, Kaiser, Steidle.

In the last resort it was a question of a clear and unambiguous decision: either to disband the committee with a guarantee to repatriate its members and collaborators (whose names would have to be published with the decision to dissolve the committee) or define its rights and duties as the official representative of prisoners of war in the Soviet Union. But we did well to formulate these intentions very cautiously. The initiators of the proposal were easily able to obtain the signature of Kaiser as a representative of the Catholic priests and of Steidle who, despite his oddness, was always upright and public-minded. But when we approached the Reverend Mr. Schröder, as the representative of the Protestant ministers, with a request that he sign our proposal, he literally went white as chalk. Trembling and stammering with excitement, he left the room immediately and ran to Major Homann to ask how he could best dissociate himself from our action. He was afraid he might become suspect by the mere fact of our considering it possible he might sign such a proposal. A few minutes after this consultation with Homann the rumor ran through the startled house of a new Huber affair, an attempt to split the committee, an extortionist provocation of the Soviet Union in a complicated foreign political situation. Now our circumstances were of course dangerous. If the Russians should snatch at this indirect denunciation we would have to be prepared for all kinds of things. It was fortunate that we initiated Schröder only the day before one of our regular sessions of the National Committee, so that fortified with our proposal formulated in writing we were able to lodge a formal protest with Weinert against these insinuations, before either the political officer in the house or Weinert himself could receive instructions from Moscow how to act in the business. There was nothing for Weinert to do but welcome our proposal as the "long-hoped-for democratic initiative by the members of the committee," and approve the convening of a plenary session of the committee. This session, it is true, was then postponed from week to week.

Finally, early in November, Weinert suddenly appeared in the house and came toward me with outstretched arms:

"Heinrich, in three days you will be home. Tomorrow the National Committee will be dissolved."

This clumsy manuever was enough to nip in the bud any discussion of the conditions for the dissolution of the committee. No single individual, or even minority, would dare to demand or to open such a discussion. The possibility that there might be some truth in Weinert's promise about going home in three days deprived the majority of the house of the courage to endanger their return at this moment through any untimely opposition. Hence the National Committee dissolved itself unanimously, and its members delivered themselves and all their supporters in the camps—indeed practically all the prisoners—voluntarily and unconditionally into the hands of the Russians.

With a wry smile the six signatories recognized that Weinert was putting the decision to dissolve the house to the vote by expressly referring to our proposal.

Night after night the members and collaborators of the committee were pulled out of their beds by the NKVD and, if they were on the list of aspirants, were examined closely as to their suitability for repatriation. Even people like Homann, who in the summer had arrogantly let Ulbricht know that he would expect a high price for his political collaboration in the Soviet zone of occupation, became more and more nervous.

The tension reached a climax when I was called one day to Commissar Saveliev who, because of his partial lameness, was generally called Club Foot. He was one of the NKVD specialists in dealing with officers of the conservative nobility and social strata closely connected with the army. During the past years he had won many of them over to an orientation of Germany toward the East. He received me in the presence of Lewess Litzmann, Major von Frankenberg, and Jesco von Puttkamer.

"So you are very dissatisfied, Herr von Einsiedel?" he asked me, weighing each word with care but not looking at me. I did not deny it.

"There are also trains that go east, Herr von Einsiedel!" His heavy eyeballs turned slowly toward me behind his fleshy eyelids, and a flicker of a smile played around his mouth. I looked at Puttkamer, who with a still poker face was watching Saveliev. Frankenberg turned red and then white as the wall. Lewess Litzmann could hardly conceal his pleasure at my discomfort. As for me, a terrible fear seized me. Nobody in the house had been the subject of such an unconcealed threat before witnesses, at least not so far as I knew. It was with difficulty that I managed to keep my composure.

"I have never doubted that, Herr Saveliev," I answered in the most casual tone I could muster.

"Very good," said Saveliev, and left the room.

"Well, that was clear," spluttered Frankenberg excitedly. "I have always told you, Einsiedel, you really will talk your head off. You have certainly got yourself into hot water with your proposal." And he too went out of the room. Franken-berg looked after the news service in the house. His greatest pleasure was to rush from room to room reveling in the effect of the news he could retail, whether of a sensation like this or the latest quarrel between two inmates of the house.

Litzmann amused himself trying to raise my spirits.

"That doesn't mean a thing. It's only meant to scare you. He doesn't really mean it."

"You should know what he means," I answered ambiguously. His roommate, Puttkamer, the only man in the house with whom I dared to speak openly, had long since told me of Litzmann's nightly conversations with the NKVD.

The public warning given to me did not fail of its purpose. From now on there was quiet in the house. Everybody tried to avoid, as far as possible, political discussions or conversations about our fate and that of the war prisoners. We played bridge, learned Russian, or wandered through the snowdrifts on the frozen Kliasma.

A last transport left for Germany. In it were the Protestant clergy—Bishop Krummacher, Schröder, and Sönnichsen—as well as Lewess Litzmann and, to everybody's surprise, even two of the signers of the proposal, Father Kaiser and Colonel Steidle.

The radio, our last link with the outside world except for *Izvestia,* was taken away from us. The newspapers which we had now and then received from the Soviet zone failed to appear. Weinert left for Germany. The National Committee was dead for good.

MAY 25, 1946. This morning we were suddenly told that the house of the National Committee must be closed down. The Government of the Soviet Union has revoked the special wartime laws, and the building in which we are living must be given back to the trade union whose convalescent home it was before the war.

The inmates of the house have been divided into two groups. We try in vain to understand the basis of the division, but we cannot discover whether it has anything to do with the trust and good will or the distrust that each of us enjoys with the NKVD. I am in the group which, besides Generals Seydlitz, Korfes, and Lensky, includes Homann, Stösslein, Frankenberg, Fleischer, Puttkamer, Paulus' adjutant Colonel Adam, and a few other officers. Our destination is rumored to be the generals' Camp 48, 185 miles northeast of Moscow near Ivanovo.

Two trucks appeared at our house, into which we were packed like herrings.

"The saviors of Germany are being wheeled off," I whispered to Puttkamer.

The eternal die-hards, under Homann's leadership, would have liked even on this occasion to compose a message of thanks to the Soviets for having "put the house at our disposal so magnanimously and without charge in our struggle for national liberation"; but even they at least kept silent and tried to make the best of a bad bargain.

Only one lost his self-control: the thwarted father of his country, General of the Artillery Walter von Seydlitz-Kurzbach. As the good-natured Russian commandant of the house, who in fact was in no way to blame for the whole business, came up and put the Russians' usual question, "How are things?" Seydlitz whispered "Ochin," and then shouted louder and louder until his voice cracked, "Ochin, ochin, ochin khorosho . . . very, very, very good."

Chapter Ten / The Ghost of Stalingrad

MAY 26, 1946. Von Seydlitz' outburst of rage yesterday was not brought about merely by his and our general humiliation. The day before our departure Vincenz Müller, whom Seydlitz hated so, was taken from Lunovo in General Petrov's car to the villa in Moscow where Marshal Paulus and General Buschenhagen have been lodged in relatively luxurious circumstances since testifying at the Nürnberg trials. It was the fact that his great rival Paulus, whom he so wished to outdo, lives in a villa and is allowed to visit the Moscow theaters, movies, and museums, while he, Seydlitz, was taken back in a shabby truck to the place from which he had been fetched in an elegant Buick, that made him lose his self-control.

Paulus' path is certainly very different from Seydlitz'. It is nearly two years since the marshal first came to Lunovo, on that August 22 when Seydlitz thought he was so near his own triumph. It was only last summer that Paulus was finally moved from the small country house, where he lived with several colonels and generals, to Lunovo. At first he met a very negative attitude there. The occupants of the house were nearly all former "Stalingraders" and nourished strong resentment toward the marshal. They reproached him in the first place with not having acted energetically enough against Hitler, and in the second with not having organized the defense of the encircled troops tightly enough; furthermore he had neither accepted responsibility for the capitulation nor gone down fighting with his army.

Paulus was a beaten man, tired, resigned, his face distorted by a continual nervous twitch. He kept aloof from all discussions and sought diversion in his favorite pursuits: drawing, wood carving, and playing cards with comrades from his homeland of Hesse.

It was impossible not to feel sympathy in one's personal dealings with this cultured and educated man, who in his outward appearance, gestures, and behavior resembled a scholar rather than a soldier. His opinions and judgments were considered, and were thought over from all angles. Generals who knew him before said that this cautious way of expressing himself and of making decisions occasionally won him the sobriquet "Cunctator." We learned from his entourage of Stalingrad days that he had let himself be extensively influenced by his energetic and unscrupulous chief of staff, General Schmidt—"Lying Arthur" as he was called in the Wehrmacht —who had taken control away from him. One had the impression at any rate that this Hessian minister's son was not a general like Reichenau or Air Marshal von Richthofen, whose unbridled temperament, ambition, and recklessness made them such feared commanders. Nor was Paulus a man who had sacrificed his army out of blind obedience. He appeared rather to have been overwhelmed by the whirlpool of events at Stalingrad, because his sharp intelligence realized the whole responsibility which fate had placed upon him and which he was simply too soft to bear. He was not able to make up his mind to break out of the encirclement against Hitler's orders because he did not believe that in his position he could judge whether, from the military point of view, the sacrifice of the 6th Army was not really the last chance to establish a stable front. Moreover he did not want to give anyone cause to accuse him of being responsible, through disobedience, for the failure of the Russian campaign. Nor, as he stated, had he been able to judge whether a premature surrender at Stalingrad would not have upset important political developments, such for example as the possible entry of Turkey and Japan into the war on the side of Germany against the Soviet Union. Paulus never told how far he was supported, in his conception of the untenability of the position, by his superiors, the chiefs of the army group and of the General Staff, at their conferences with Hitler, or how far these men, on the contrary, tried to lend the authority of their judgment to Hitler's promises of reinforcements and orders for holding on.

The army had rejected the Soviet suggestion of capitulation in an order of the day which read something like this:

"We all know what threatens us if the army ceases to resist. For the majority of us there waits certain death—either by bullet or by cold—hunger, or the sufferings of shameful imprisonment. There is only one way out for us: to fight to the last shot."

Among the members of the National Committee this army order was the cause of the severest criticism of Paulus. They blamed him for avoiding its final consequences and letting his troops passively lay down their arms only after enemy bullets, hunger, and cold had wiped out hundreds of thousands and robbed the remainder of all power of resistance to the sufferings of captivity. Paulus defended his action by declaring that he knew nothing of the order. Many people thought it credible

223

that Lying Arthur had given it behind his back. Did Paulus and the rest of the generals evade death on the battlefield, or the traditional action of captains of sinking ships, out of personal cowardice? The undisputed bravery which they personally, and the officer corps in general, had shown in two wars makes it unlikely. Perhaps their attitude is explained by a declaration made by a Stalingrad general during the last days of encirclement: "I refuse to put a bullet through my head for that scoundrel Hitler"—a statement that seems quite inappropriate in view of the 300,000 lives just sacrificed for this scoundrel, yet which one can understand if one thinks it possible that these generals did not recognize the real character of their Führer until his unparalleled betrayal of them and their armies.

During a conversation in the summer of 1945 Paulus was criticized for the fact that his decision to surrender, against Hitler's will and his own order, could have been fully justified only if from that moment on he had thrown all his authority into the scales against Hitler.

"It was more than a coincidence that Marshal von Witzleben and his comrades were strangled on Hitler's gallows the very day that you finally acted openly for the first time against Hitler," a young officer said to him. "If you had taken part in the activities of the National Committee a year earlier, you might have helped the men of July 20 to succeed."

Paulus refused to admit this. He said that he had acted neither too late nor too soon. Even if there may now be good reason to doubt whether any action of his would ever have had any influence on events, it was grotesque that he found an excuse for his hesitation in the diplomatic compliments made to him by Pieck and Weinert during those days in August 1944 when they were trying to win him over. A violent attack of his nervous facial twitch betrayed the embarrassment he suffered at the reference to the empty compliments paid him by these men with whom he had for so long refused to sit at the same table.

A few weeks after Paulus' arrival at Lunovo the Communists and the Russians made further serious attempts to win him over, using Homann and Vincenz Müller as their intermediaries. These two men, who were certainly equal to Paulus in intelligence but superior to him in will power, finally managed to persuade him to disclose what he knew about the preparations for the Russian campaign, in which he took a leading part as quartermaster general. What a decisive blow Paulus could have struck at Hitler's prestige as early as 1943, when large circles in Germany still believed in the thesis of a preventive war against Russia!

Now, when it was too late, he put all his knowledge on record, under great psychological pressure. This work, as we were soon to find out, served in the preparation of the indictments and also in his testimony in the Nürnberg trials. Several times during the winter the chief Soviet prosecutor, General Rudenko, appeared at the house to find out how the work was progressing. General Buschenhagen, too, was brought to the house. It was his evidence which gave the trial of "war criminals" in Finland such a sensational turn against his former Finnish comrades; and later he was also to give evidence at Nürnberg. The Olympic rider, von Wangenheim, who as the staff officer of a division had been taken prisoner on the central front, would show up with him. Since he had been assistant to the military attaché in Ankara, the Russians tried in hundreds of interrogations accompanied by chocolate and cigarettes, threats and promises, to extract incriminating evidence from him against Papen; but judging by the outcome of the trials they must have been unsuccessful.

Once during the weeks when Vincenz Müller was working

on Paulus I happened to be standing near our house in the
snow, hidden by some trees, beating the dust out of my uniform. Out of the door which also led to the offices of the Russians came Müller. He looked right and left like a wolf, but
without noticing me. Then he quickly stole back into the
house by the other door. I couldn't understand his behavior. At
—4° F. no man was likely to leave the rooms which had been
placed at our disposal, without a coat, merely in order to return
to them immediately through another entrance. It was also
possible to enter our rooms directly from the Russian offices
withhout going out of doors. Quite by chance I mentioned
the incident to a comrade and made fun of it.

"Apparently Müller has the prisoner's 'twitch,' too," I said.

But he put me wise. "Are you blind?" he said with some
surprise. "Müller hasn't eaten anything for days."

"What do you mean?"

"Since he's been working on Paulus, he's been getting
special rations over there. That's why he no longer likes
cabbage soup and porridge. He told us himself how he tried to
refuse it; but the Russians said, 'Eat, general; don't offend us.
You are fulfilling a great political task.' So of course he doesn't
want to be seen too often leaving the Russian quarters."

Since Müller was rewarded with caviar sandwiches, he was
not alone to blame for the pressure he put on Paulus, which
frequently made the latter break into fits of crying. It is all
part of the system. The Russians do not give up their methods
of corruption even in cases where they could achieve their
goals without them. What their idea is in all this is simply inconceivable. They must know, if they have any intention of
ever sending any of us back home, that this connection between
the Nürnberg trials and the caviar sandwiches is bound to come
to light. But it obviously doesn't matter to them. They really

seem altogether convinced that the "material basis" rules the "ideological superstructure."

Now that I have mentioned this, I must also relate my own experiences in this field. When I lay in the ice-cold hospital barracks in Krasnogorsk, worn to a skeleton and utterly exhausted by attacks of fever, a Russian officer appeared one day and brought me some white bread and lard. He said he had managed to obtain this for me from Moscow at the request of the head woman doctor. He came several times and these gifts, ridiculously small though they would have seemed in normal conditions, obviously helped me to get over my illness and recuperate. I was genuinely grateful to the woman doctor. It was only weeks later, when I learned that the Russian who brought me the food was Commissar Stern, that I began to doubt how disinterested this help had really been.

A similar thing happened to me at the antifascist school. Bechler and I were promised that when we completed our course we should be taken to Moscow for a few days to see the town. This promise, like all the other promises of being given an opportunity to see life in the Soviet Union outside the camp, was never fulfilled. Instead, I was kept under interrogation for days about my experiences as a fighter pilot. When I protested and demanded to be returned immediately to Lunovo, they tried to make me change my mind by offering me wine and food parcels. It was only when I complained to the head of the school that the NKVD finally left me alone.

It is an open secret in the camps that the NKVD at all their interrogations try to loosen tongues with food and cigarettes, a method which, considering the starvation conditions in the camps, is bound to meet with some success. Only those who have been for months on the point of dying of hunger can judge how much more effective, under certain circumstances, a plate of soup can be than threat or torture—if between this plate and the starving man lies the demand to denounce and betray.

The demoralizing effect of hunger and the methods of corruption used by the Polit officers and Communist émigrés in the camps, as well as the privileged treatment given to the inmates of the house and the committee delegates, created an inseparable fusion between the naked instinct for self-preservation and the founding of the National Committee. Sometimes it is even difficult to tell whether and how far this has influenced one's own actions, although one joined the antifascist group in the camp in circumstances and at a time when there was no question of deriving any advantages from the action.

At all events, I have the same unadmitted bad conscience that everyone who belongs to the group constantly has. So long as there was a war, and it was possible to look upon all this as a necessary evil and the outcome of circumstances one had to put up with, it was easy to justify oneself. But the Müller incident brought up all these misgivings again. I had the feeling that I needed a bath immediately, in order to wash off all the filth we had got ourselves into, come out of the twilight and get rid of the revulsion I felt toward myself and my entire surroundings.

A few weeks after Christmas Paulus and Buschenhagen were taken away. Soon after, the report of their testimony at Nürnberg appeared in *Izvestia*. "The ghost of Stalingrad enters the hall and testifies against the Nazi criminals," the Russian reporter wrote with fervor.

Chapter Eleven / The Return Home

APRIL 23, 1947. It is almost impossible to believe: I am on my way home to Germany. I am waiting at the White Russian station in Moscow for the train to Brest-Litovsk. Perhaps in three days I shall be in Berlin. I can hardly realize it yet.

It is over a year now since we arrived at the generals' Camp 48. It was a sensation for the two hundred German generals who lived there, together with forty Hungarian, four Rumanian, and two Italian generals. They watched us with derision as we settled down. With a few exceptions they strictly avoided all contact with us. Even most of those who, after July 20, had taken part in the various proclamations of the committee had now renounced such behavior, submitted to the "courts of honor," and begged for gracious reinstatement from the large group of generals who were taken prisoner in May 1945. What these generals have in common is an almost pathological hatred of the allies, especially the Soviets. The orders and insignia which were taken away from them by resolution of the Allied Control Council appeared, carved twice life size, on their walking sticks, tobacco containers, and ash trays. Their war experiences, from the front line to Maxim's and the Folies-Bergère, and the gossip of the officers' clubs of the last decades were their topics of conversation. The Third Reich was wonderful—if only Hitler had known a little more about how to run a war—that was their general line of thought.

They had no wish to realize that it was not our defection from Hitler but their own blind obedience, to the point where the Reich Chancellery lay in ruins, that had brought Germany to catastrophe and the enemy whom they underestimated as much as hated to the banks of the Elbe.

Quarrels, threats, and insults to us "traitors" were the order of the day. Only when we complained to the Russian commandant of the camp did they stop needling us.

There were many NKVD spies among the generals, chiefly among those who had something to fear from Soviet war trials and so were easily blackmailed. As early as the winter of 1945–46 about thirty German generals received death sentences and were executed. Often these were commanders of rear army areas who had been involved in partisan battles and reprisals against the civil population, and labor levies. The Russians carried out their investigations with untiring thoroughness.

Under the pressure of these generals we members of the committee recovered, at least on the surface, a certain solidarity. We did not want to and could not air our differences among ourselves or with the Russians in front of these men who persecuted us with deadly hatred. Our chief occupations were learning languages, working in the garden, playing volley ball and bridge.

The greatest burden for us, besides uncertainty about our own fate, was uncertainty about our families. We were almost the only ones in the camp who had not yet received any mail, and gradually the conviction grew within us that all our families had been destroyed because they were related to us. The first mail we got which dispelled our anxiety was in the autumn of 1946.

A small group among us had constantly tried to persuade the rest of the National Committee to make vigorous representations to the Russians and demand a definite decision about our fate. But fear that the Russians might misinterpret such action, together with the continual promises of imminent repatriation, brought all these attempts to nothing. In January 1947 I finally screwed up my courage and, ignoring the warning of well-meaning friends, addressed a letter to the Russians asking to be released or transported to an ordinary labor camp. I based my plea on a declaration made by Weinert in September 1945, according to which our repatriation and participation in the political reconstruction of Germany depended on the confidence the Soviet authorities had in the democratic attitude of each individual.

·I demanded to be told why, fifteen months after this declaration, and in spite of all promises, we were still kept in a camp. Of course I attached no great hopes to this action, but I was certain that such a written protest would at least reach the heads of the Administration for Prisoners of War and I was anxious to make these gentlemen aware we no longer appreciated their hospitality. We could not hasten our return by just waiting.

The reaction of the Russian camp administration to my proposal was certainly anything but reassuring and seemed to confirm the warnings of my friends. When the Russian political officer made his occasional rounds in the camp and talked to us he deliberately and provocatively cut me. I did not care. This officer was only small fry and it was in his interest to be able to report to his chief that all was quiet and everybody satisfied in the camp. For this reason he took my letter as a personal insult. But I was convinced that, in view of the sluggishness of the Soviet organization, one must open one's mouth wide to get results. If I should not get a reply to my appeal I had decided to go on a hunger strike on July 1. This measure had not only got General Hoffmeister out of the Lubianka prison but helped many a young officer who had been interrogated once or twice and then forgotten in his cell.

In the spring the foreign ministers met in Moscow. Their speeches, full of mutual reproaches, covered whole pages of Soviet state newspapers; and the Soviets, in their long-winded radio commentaries, made fun of the vain attempts of the West to revise the agreements concluded at Yalta and Potsdam. One day we heard the name of Seydlitz over the camp loudspeaker; they read Bevin's speech, in which he had reproached the Soviet Union for the so-called Seydlitz army.

Seydlitz understood no Russian. He came excitedly into the room of those who knew the language to ask what it was all about. "Your army is to be disbanded!" we told him, laughing. Deprived of one more hope, he slipped back into the log house built for him by the Russians, who feared an attempt on his life by the other generals.*

* According to my latest information—1951—General von Seydlitz has been missing in the Soviet Union since the end of 1949; that is to say, since that time no mail from him has reached Germany and mail for him has been returned as undeliverable. It is reported from the Soviet occupation zone that late in 1949, in a prison camp near Tambov, 250 miles southeast of Moscow, he categorically refused a last offer of a post in that zone which was submitted to him by former General Bamler of the Wehrmacht, and demanded repatriation to his family in West Germany so that he might justify his behavior in captivity before a regular court.

Field Marshal Friedrich Paulus remained a prisoner in the Soviet

Yesterday the Soviet officer on duty suddenly appeared in the camp and said:

"All set, Einsiedel, transport with all belongings; quick—in half an hour!"

Was it the train for the East? Who could tell? Everything was possible, from Siberia to Germany.

In the Kommandatura the camp commander told me that in four days I should be in Germany.

"I was promised that by someone else two years ago," I replied.

He gave me his "officer's word of honor." I was skeptical. It was only when I was actually in the White Russian station, from which trains leave only for the West, that the Lubianka prison receded into the background and I began to hope. Could it be really true?

I had someone buy a copy of *Pravda* at the station. Now I think I know what caused this sudden turn in my fate. *Pravda* in one of its articles mocks at the rumors prevailing in the West about the Seydlitz army and about the new Committee for the Military Restoration of Germany which is supposed to be meeting in Moscow under the chairmanship of Marshal Paulus, whose political adviser I of all people am reported to be. How can this rumor be more effectively refuted than by the release of one of the three men mentioned, even though the least important?

As I folded the newspaper, a Russian officer who sat next me in the waiting room spoke to me. He asked for a needle and thread. As I watched, surprised, he took off his coat and, sitting on his suitcase quite unembarrassed in his many-colored,

---

Union but was occasionally allowed to receive and to send mail. A prisoner recently back from Russia reports having seen Marshal Paulus in Russian uniform in 1950 and been told he was regularly employed as instructor in tactics at the Moscow Military Academy.

striped, sleeveless shirt, sewed a fresh white collar inside his coat.

When he noticed that I was watching he laughed: "People much civilized in Germany. You wear a clean collar or they look at you funny," he said in broken German.

All the Russians around me are returning from leave. Their joy at being able to go back to Germany glows in their faces. They are enthusiastic about Germany. It is not only the cleanliness and order, the restaurants, the theaters, and the shops that appeal to them. They are most impressed by the Germans' zeal for work and the independence and initiative they develop in it.

"Germans good workers," said the sewer. He is in charge of a telephone station somewhere in Thuringia. "You tell him once—he does his job good. You tell him twice—he's angry, thinks you don't trust him."

"Where is it better—here or there?" I asked cautiously. The Russians were indignant. "In Germany, of course."

This is really a surprising change of attitude. During the war one was lucky to find a single Russian who had a good word to say about Germany. And now this sudden change of heart, in spite of all the anti-German tendencies which still dominate Soviet propaganda. Is some sort of understanding breaking its way through in Germany, at least from below? Does the "plain Soviet man" realize that he still has a lot to learn from us as well as from the Western countries in general? Those I am meeting here are certainly completely cured of the insufferable complacency and boastfulness which sprang up after the war. With Russians such as these cooperation should be possible.

MAY 1, 1947. Transit Camp Brest-Litovsk. A cloudy, gray dawn is beginning to creep over White Russia. A cold, damp wind blows through the town. In the camp it stirs up the smells of latrines, barracks full of corpses, and kitchen refuse, and chases the prisoners as they go on the double across the camp square in their torn, threadbare field jackets. Only a few shivering figures linger in a corner of the kitchen barracks and with screwed-up eyes stare through an aperture at the food containers in the kitchen.

"Open up, you lugs," one of them cries to the cooks who lean against the warm tiled stove, leisurely smoking their morning cigarettes.

"The hungry pack," the cooks mutter contemptuously, and spit crumbs of tobacco out of the window.

"You bloody so and so's," the others swear outside, having learned the Russian words for it. "Look at the bloated swine lolling about."

"Quiet, you fellows! They won't eat up your nettle soup today, not even on May 1!" A tall, white-haired man calls his comrades to order, his mouth straight as a line, his eyes watchful and ironical. His teeth were knocked out in a concentration camp; the scar on his forehead he owes to a sentry outside the *Vorwärts* building. He was a Spartacist, a regular member of the German Communist party, an agent of the Comintern, and an officer in the Red Army, sentenced to death in Sachsenhausen concentration camp. From Penal Battalion 999 he deserted to the Red Army, went through Lubianka prison, the antifascist school, and was an active leader in the labor camp. Now he is waiting with his comrades for the transport to be made up which is to take them to Germany at the request of the Social Unity party, a priority group of 250 men, meritorious Communists, members of independent socialist groups, relatives of victims of fascism, and sons of Social Democrats who participated in the fusion of both workers' parties in the Eastern zone. I too am assigned to this transport.

The prisoners come from every corner of the Soviet Union. From Murmansk, Georgia, and Bessarabia, from the Donets basin, from Karaganda and the northern Urals, from Minsk, Asbest, or Omsk, and from Kaliningrad.

The mere story of their transport to Brest-Litovsk would read like a novel. A party of three men had to sit on the buffers of the train for 1,900 miles because the train attendants wanted to pocket their fares. One of them, a former socialist now almost sixty, who had contracted serious heart trouble during his time in concentration camp, had to be kept tied to the car by his comrades so he would not drop off out of weakness. An old Communist, shaking his head, told how some Russians started quarreling in his train, shot one of their own men, and threw him out of the moving train. None of the other travelers, among whom were some officers, took the slightest notice. Some others got only dry bread and water on a three weeks' trip because the guards had sold their allotment of food. As they had already been starved in camp, they arrived more feeble than I had been after my transport to Oranky in September 1942. Theft was so common in the trains that one in each group had to stay awake to prevent everything being taken from the others' pockets.

But this is nothing to what they tell about the camps—the endless, pathetic stories of hunger, corruption, terror, and exploitation to the last breath. Four hundred grams of soggy bread, half a liter of watery soup, as much watery porridge— that was their nourishment at best. And with this, ten to twelve hours' slaving in mines, road-building, blastfiring, cutting peat and wood, and floating timber. In some cases strong fellows wasted to skeletons in a few weeks. The lucky ones got transferred in time to a war prisoners' hospital, where they were built up in order to be worn down once more. The unlucky ones were removed from the camp only when they were dying, so that there should be no cases of death on the camp lists. But in many camps the administration did not even take that precaution.

The corrupt camp authorities filled their pockets with the proceeds of stolen food supplies or of articles made in the camp shops. There was a German officer, a former Communist deputy, who had spent twelve years in concentration camp, and whose wife was supposed to have written a deeply moving book in Germany about her own way through Nazi prisons. He lodged a complaint against a general's thieving adjutant, was jailed for ten days, and his name struck off our transport list of men to be repatriated. A German camp elder, a former officer of the secret police who had participated on a large scale in the Russians' blackmarketing, read aloud derisively the punishment which the hated Communist received from his Russian "comrades" for his honesty.

Sometimes the "authorities" interfered. Ten, twenty, forty Russians marched off in their wooden shoes, together with the German prisoners who had held minor official posts and who had encouraged and sometimes forced them into the black market, for ten to twenty-five years' forced labor in Siberia. Four weeks later the new camp administration was indistinguishable from the old.

A Communist dockyard worker who, before he deserted to the Red Army, had for twenty-five years gone through all the ordeals which party membership brought with it, was sent to a prison camp in White Russia in 1945. There the inmates died like flies, sometimes thirty a day. A gangster band of Russians and Germans ran the camp, stealing even the last crumb of bread from the prisoners. He felt it his duty to speak to the camp commandant as comrade to comrade and to call upon his

honor as a Bolshevik and his duty to the Communist movement. He was arrested at once and put in prison. He got less
than a hundred grams of bread a day. He was to be eliminated
through hunger and had only a few days to live. A commission
arrived from Moscow. A comrade smuggled the news to his
cell. When the commission was near the prison building he
began to scream. The cell was opened and he got the opportunity to complain to a general who set him free, reprimanding
the commandant. This protected him from revenge, and he
was actually appointed camp elder. But four weeks later he
began to realize that even as camp elder he was able to remedy
only the worst abuses, that the system of corruption was all-
powerful because it was total, because everybody was participating in it, because it was the means of existence of the
members of the camp administration and of the population
outside the camp. The situation was at its worst in the camps
which lay in the regions devastated by the war; the destitution
of the population there had removed their last inhibitions. In
the spring of 1946 conditions had somewhat improved, but the
catastrophic failure of the harvest through the drought made
the next winter a fresh disaster for the prisoners.

All spring home-bound transports have been passing almost
daily through Brest-Litovsk. The return of the war prisoners
has started at last. But what cargoes these trains contain!
Starved, emaciated skeletons; human wrecks convulsed with
dysentery; gaunt figures with slow-motion gestures, expression-
less gray faces, and dead eyes which brighten only at the sight
of a piece of bread or a cigarette; each a living indictment of
the Soviet Union, each a death sentence to communism. The
dead from homeward-bound trains are brought into our camp
by the truckload. We special repatriates are locked up meanwhile in our barracks. We are not to see this. What naïve
precautions! We see everything: the dead stripped to the under-

shirt by their comrades, dragged by the legs from the car, piled up in one of the stinking barracks which infest the whole camp with their stench, and carted at night to a mass grave. One of the poor wretches came to for a few hours as he fell from the truck; another one only when thrown into the grave. But they were dead when brought back to the camp. The Soviet doctor who had to certify each death was reprimanded for "lack of alertness."

This doctor also examines the men at the station and withdraws those who are too weak to travel or still too strong to be returned. Both categories meet again after a certain time in the Brest-Litovsk camps. Brest needs labor hands.

For what? The trains arrive every day from Germany carrying booty: dismantled parts, reparations from current production, the spoils of the administrators. All this has to be transferred to the Russian gauge railway. Steel frames for machine factories with the machines which belonged to them, telephone exchanges, pianos, furniture, toilets, bolts of cloth, radios, sacks of sugar, boxes of chocolates, rolls of paper, typewriters, barrels of butter, stockings, haberdashery, sewing needles—everything in fact that a modern industrial country can produce, and piles of foodstuffs besides.

Oh, for the happy time of the imperialistic Versailles Treaty! The "socialist" peace looks very different.

If all these things were to be put to a sensible use, one could still take this in stride. Nobody can deny that the Soviet Union has the right to reparations. But when ramps, pulleys, and other equipment for unloading these goods are not available, the valuable machines are simply rolled out of the train on two inclined beams and allowed to crash onto the rails. Levers and hinges snap, shafts and cylinders bend, contacts split and tubes break in pieces, expensive pieces of machinery are wrenched apart and dispatched in different directions. The consumer

239

goods are sold in great quantities by guards and prisoners on the black market in Brest-Litovsk. Or else they remain lying in the open for so long that everything becomes covered with rust or rots away. In this way a large portion of dismantled equipment and reparations deliveries is merely destroyed or wasted and is of no use to the Soviet Union. How absurd it all is, and how terrible for us this senseless waste!

"Railwaymen, help to realize and surpass the postwar five-year plan! Work for a better life and the further prosperity of your socialist Fatherland! Raise high the banner of socialist competition!" These posters with their slogans for increased production hang at every step within the working areas. "According to plan," our old Communists cry with bitter laughter when they see another lathe crash upon the tracks. And then begin the stories about the factories and mines where they have worked. The same picture everywhere. Figures, figures, and more figures, statistics, lists, rules, orders, and threats of penalties. "Plan achieved, overachieved by 93, 105, 110, 230, 320%. Great victories on the production front, 20% improvement in quality as compared with the past year." Paper is patient. Nobody is interested if up to 80% of the production is wasted, if hundreds of people die in the process, if material and labor are squandered irresponsibly. The important thing is somehow to come up with the figures laid down in the plan.

A machine shed was being erected in the Don basin. The German engineer refused to accept responsibility for the roof construction as planned. He proposed an improvement. No attention was paid to it. The building crashed in the first thunderstorm and buried Russians and Germans under it. A scapegoat was looked for and found—the German engineer! Sabotage! Sentence: twenty-five years' forced labor.

Hundreds of similar stories are told and the conclusions to be drawn from them are always the same. Tremendous efforts

are being made in the Soviet Union to build up a modern industry and raise production, the armed strength of the country,
and finally also the standard of living of the population. But
the very party, the very machinery of state, which is behind
the whole plan initiating, organizing, driving, and overseeing
often destroys with one hand what has just been built with the
other. Bureaucracy, distrust, and the blind obedience which the
center of this immense, inflated organization demands so
categorically paralyze the initiative of the people, kill their
sense of responsibility, make quick, objective decisions impossible, and stifle all constructive criticism. Is this a typically
Russian phenomenon which finds its origin in the backwardness and century-old stagnation of the country? Is it the result
of the overcentralization of the Soviet state or the inevitable
accompaniment of the socialist economic structure? Is the
policy of the Kremlin, the Bolshevik Politburo, responsible
for these defects, or is the Russian character, or socialist theory?

Today, May 1, the "holiday of the world proletariat," nobody worked. Tired and hungry, the prisoners twisted on their
bug-infested bunks. Now and then the nettle soup drove them
to the latrine. The camp was deserted and desolate. At the
corner of a barrack a croaking loudspeaker swung in the wind;
the speeches, the "endless storms of applause," the orders, the
salutes, the din of the tanks and airplane engines at the Moscow
May parade boomed eerily across the empty square of the
camp.

In the steam-bath and delousing shed officials nailed up
streamers with the "May 1 slogans" on the walls: "We thank
the Soviet Union for freeing us from fascism!" "Long live our
wise and beloved leader Stalin!" "Fight along with the Soviet
Union for a better, peaceful life!"

At noon whistles shrilled through the barracks: "Out for
the May festivities." Apathetic and compliant, the prisoners

crawled from their bunks, wrapped themselves up in coats and blankets, and shuffled along to the meeting hall. With curses and threats the "activists" chased the sluggards into the bath shed. "Come on, don't try to get out of it. Do you want to be taken off the list to go home, eh? Get along!"

At last everyone was ready. The "active" elder combed his hair again, had his aide brush his tailor-made coat, and strutted through the camp gate. He disappeared into the Kommandatura.

The prisoners were sunk in a stupor, some of them crouching on the damp floor. Like a fog the miasma of sweat, urine, musty underwear, and squashed bugs hovered over their heads. Now and then the shrill cry of the guards could be heard: "Put out your cigarette, you saboteur!" The old Communists had gathered in a corner. They smoked and chattered, paying no heed to the guards. The activists did not dare to go near them. "Did you hear that! Wanting to strike us off the list, the bastard. And the stinker makes it sound like a reward to be let stay here."

"Well, all I can say is, the first thing I do in Berlin is go to Wilhelm—I'll have something to say to him."

"The hell you will! He was here twelve years, he knows what the stakes are."

"He better have an answer for his old comrades."

"Have you gone crazy? Do you want to disappear like Heinz Neumann or Remmele or Hugo Eberlein and all the rest of them?" *

The white-haired Spartacist interrupted them: "Keep quiet, boys. You can argue at home. But first you've got to get there."

* For Neumann see p. 181 Eberlein was one of the founders of the Spartacus league and of the German Communist party (see also p. 268); and Remmele was a leading party member. All three were arrested in Russia and disappeared. *Trans.*

"God preserve us from our friends, we can preserve ourselves from our enemies," murmured one of them, and then he groaned: "For fifteen years every penny to the party, every free minute for the party, and then months in prison and years in a concentration camp. The hounds." He shouted this into the room.

The old man seized him by the arm. "Carl, don't go and make trouble. Pull yourself together. There's no sense in it. Don't do yourself in ten minutes before the end."

Endless minutes went by, an hour or perhaps two. Suddenly the door was flung open. "Attention!" cried the leader of the camp and reported in Russian to the commandant: "The whole camp drawn up for the May celebration, Major." The commandant took up his position under the poster of Stalin. The chorus of camp attendants sang the Soviet hymn. The "active" leader opened the meeting: "I call for the election of the honorary presidium. I propose as first candidate the genius and leader of the Soviet people, Generalissimo Stalin." He applauded. The commandant applauded. The activists applauded. "I propose . . ."

The commandant jumped up: "Why no *applaudissment?* Why no shouts? Rrrepeatt! Hurrah for Comrade Stalin!" The prisoners started up from their doze. Oh, applause is demanded. A few hurrahs were heard; thin applause dribbled through the room. The major got red in the face. "I order *applaudissment!* For the last time, *applaudissment.* Comrade Stalin, hurrah!"

This brought the old Comintern agent to his feet. "Come on, boys, for the last time! You have my word for it. For the last time! Comrade Stalin—hurrah!" He shouted as loud as he could and the others did the same. "Comrade Stalin, hurrah! Hurrah! Hurrah! Hurrah!" Two minutes, three minutes, five minutes, until the commandant signaled them to stop. "Enough, enough. Now, Comrade Molotov, hurrah!"

Little by little the men began to find it amusing. Shouting at least warmed them up. They called out names to the chairman. "Comrade Budenny, Comrade Voroshilov, Comrade Mikoyan, Comrade Ivanov, Comrade Stakhanov, Comrade officerrr, Comrade leader, Comrade major, hurrah and hurrah again!"

The commandant was radiant: "Good meeting, very good. Great success. Germans fine." And he called out: "Attention! The leader of the German working class, Wilgelm Pieck, hurrah, hurrah, hurrah!"

"For the last time!" cried the old Communists. "Comrade Pieck, hurrah, hurrah!"

JULY 15, 1947. I have the transport through Poland and the Gronenfeld camp behind me. With a pounding heart on June 26 I stumbled once again along Berlin sidewalks gnawed by bombs and grenades. Home at last after more than five years!

I hesitated a long while whether to give up this whole political business and go to my family in West Germany. But I could not bring myself to do so. It was no feat to subscribe to German-Soviet cooperation, to socialism and communism, while a prisoner; that meant simply being on the side of the strongest party. I can't desert my position now; I must act now, in freedom and against public opinion, in accordance with the principles I have increasingly recognized in the last five years.

Of course it is a hopeless undertaking to convince people in Germany of the correctness of this political conviction. The prisoner-of-war problem, the Oder-Neisse line, the deportations, the concentration camps, the spy abuse, and the unbridled lawlessness make almost all discussion impossible. It is my first general impression that the people here would have been prepared to forget the dreadful excesses of the Red Army when it marched in if it weren't for the terrible present. In the face of such facts every theoretical discussion of the bitter necessities of the revolutionary struggle and the difficulties in constructing a socialist order of society remains mere talk. One is looked upon as a naïve illusionist at best if one believes in these, and more often as a venal opportunist.

I had no great hopes about the conditions I should find in the Soviet-occupied zone. But even these were disappointed.

There can be no question of any independence for the German Communists. Just as in the committee, Ulbricht is the key man here, the apparatus that automatically registers Communist orders and carries them out. The Russians have coined the right word for his type: *apparatchik*. This man rules like a crowned toad over the party, poisons the air with distrust and fear, and trains his creatures while the NKVD stands behind them with all threads in its hands. Slavishly, without regard to historical, cultural, or political conditions, Soviet institutions are aped and forced upon us, often perhaps against the better judgment of Soviet occupation officials, who do not dare, however, to make any independent decisions adapted to German circumstances because that might make them guilty of a deviation, a sacrilege.

But what is the use?—if you say A you must also say B. If one is prepared to admit the logical necessity and the success in essential points of the revolution in Russia, if one has the courage to accept all the repellent phenomena as necessary evils, as the logical result of Russia's history, as a consequence of the blind hatred and lack of understanding which the rest of the world showed from the beginning toward the young Soviet state, and lastly as a consequence of Hitler's attack (which to a certain extent justified after the fact the uncompromising harshness of Stalin's dictatorship)—then one also must accept the situation in Germany.

I cannot help thinking how much more healthy, natural, and logical the whole development would have been if in 1918 the German working class too had completed the revolution. What pressure—which in turn produced counterpressure—would have been removed from the Soviet Union and what great creative forces would then have been unleashed in Russia! But this chance has been missed. The revolution was victorious only in this one backward country. It could be carried out there only with tremendous effort, iron discipline, and an unscrupulous use of power. And now that it is coming from Russia to Germany there is nothing to do but clench one's teeth and wait for better days, when we shall be freed from the rule of force and terror and at the same time from having to submit to the inhumanity and cruelty which every superhuman concentration of power entails. The day must come when the blinkers of a hopelessly limited party dogma will be removed and twice two will once again be four and Rilke no longer be ranged with the degenerate bourgeoisie.

Has the West found any better solution? Has anything been forgotten or learned since 1918 or 1932? Didn't the Western powers make almost all their decisions concerning the vanquished in conjunction with the Soviets? Aren't they using in principle the same methods in the reparations, the dismantlings, the war trials, and the de-Nazifications, except that in the West it is not a socialistic ultimate goal which is behind it but national and economic competition? Where in the West do they abide by the principles of freedom, self-determination of nations, and justice? Is there any sign that the capitalist world will not in the foreseeable future—after the destruction of the war is removed—land in the same catastrophe as before—economic chaos and mass unemployment?

It is terribly cheap to mock at the defects and difficulties of a socialist Russia when the most advanced industrial countries, with all the technical, material, and cultural advantages, proved unable to avoid the disasters of 1929, 1933, and 1939. Naturally it is more tempting to profess Western democracy, especially when it is accompanied by considerable dollar loans. It is more attractive than a socialism which, as now represented by the Soviet Union, is forced to appear as a starving, rapacious mercenary who cannot bribe but can only rape.

But is Americanism a future worth striving for? Haven't pursuit of the dollar, the conveyor belt, skyscrapers, crime thrillers, the jazz mania done more to demoralize the world and turn man into a mass creature than could a collectivist party dictatorship inspired by a socialist ideal? Where is the towering cultural achievement of America, which would lend inner justification to the wealth of its ruling classes? Don't the Russians' "thirst for culture"; the removal of illiteracy; the mass training of (admittedly still inferior) doctors, engineers, technicians, and teachers; the quantity editions of books by Tolstoy, Pushkin, Gorky, and Goethe; and the attempt to make technology really serve man in a planned organization of society spell a richer future, even if behind them all there is today totalitarian compulsion leading only too often to a state of rightlessness?

That is how I explained to myself the possibilities of further collaboration with the Communists in Germany.

So now I am working for the *Tägliche Rundschau*, a newspaper of the Soviet Military Administration in East Germany. When I reported to the Central Committee of the Social Unity party I was asked what I would like to do. Go to the university and earn my way as a journalist, I said. They wanted to ship me to Leipzig, to the new division of social science established there by the party. But I didn't want to go into that zone, not even for the price of a scholarship. I would have the feeling of being buried alive there. After five years in prison, five years of one-sidedness, I want to breathe air in which the winds do not always blow from the same quarter. Even Frida Rubiner, the old Communist fighter for women's rights who ordered Müller and Lensky about like schoolboys both in the antifascist school and in Lunovo, advised against it. All one could do in Leipzig now, she said, was starve, and the division was still in a state of chaos. So I followed her advice and recommendation and presented myself at the *Rundschau*. But there was another very cogent reason for this decision.

Johannes R. Becher * asked me to come and see him at Pankov. My "honorable" party leaders are living in luxurious villas behind barricades and Russian sentries. (Times have changed since Kuibyshev and other top officials of the Soviet state lived in Moscow on a maximum salary of 250 rubles a month in a two-room apartment.) Becher thought it would be a mistake for me to work directly with the Russians. With my name I could surely do much more effective work in one of the above-party welfare organizations of the Social Unity party, in the Kulturbund for instance. But I explained my attitude to him as plainly as possible.

"It is already clear to me, Herr Becher, that there is no independent German political work for us. If I cannot escape being a ward of the Russians I prefer to deal directly with my masters. We have not been very fortunate with our dear comrades as middlemen. Why should I, for the sake of a transparent disguise, voluntarily give up the possibility of being at the center of things? It is less dangerous and I should say more

* German expressionist poet who lived in Moscow from 1933 to 1945, when he was asked by the Soviet to organize the Kulturbund in the Soviet zone of Germany. *Trans.*

fruitful as far as work is concerned. They say that now and then there is a Russian who will listen to reasonable objections and criticism."

Becher nodded thoughtfully: "There is certainly something to be said for that point of view."

On the first day my new editor in chief, Colonel Kirsanov, took me with him to Lichtenberg, to the information department of the Soviet occupation forces. His chief, Colonel Tulpanov, wished to celebrate seeing me again. I sat for an hour in his waiting room listening with amusement to the talk of Russian officers about their chief. They had no idea that I knew Russian and did not mince their words.

"Is the old man in a good mood today?" each man who had to go in to see him asked. They were all the more surprised when Tulpanov sailed out of his room to welcome me with wide-open arms and embraced me heartily Russian fashion.

"I marched with him from Stalingrad to Berlin!" he explained to the dumfounded onlookers. He then broke off his daily routine and drove with me to his villa in Karlshorst.

After dinner we had coffee with his family.

"Well—how are things?" asked Tulpanov. This question is inseparable from a Soviet official. I didn't conceal my point of view.

"I've seen something myself, Colonel, of what happened when the Red Army entered Germany. We don't need to talk about it. But people in Germany would be ready to forget even that if there weren't so many other things wrong. For instance, the question of the Oder-Neisse line. That may not be acute as yet—but the line will never be accepted in Germany. Twelve million people expelled. The Soviet Union has given her enemies in the West a weapon that will stay sharp for decades. The worst of all, though, is the problem of the prisoners of war. Unless there is an immediate radical change in the treatment of the prisoners, unless Moscow reinstates order in the camps with an iron hand and protects the prisoners from starvation, tuberculosis, and exhaustion to the point of death, and guards them from the arbitrariness of local NKVD men, and establishes acceptable postal communication, and publishes the names of the dead—unless Moscow self-critically makes official apology for the present situation and promises a change—all wooing for the favor of the German people is wasted."

I described conditions in the camps in detail, gave the colonel the heartrending picture of the home transports, and told him how all directives of the central office were disobeyed by the local authorities. I spared him no details of the gruesome picture I had been given in Brest-Litovsk from almost 250 camps. Tulpanov did not interrupt, and his face betrayed that he believed what I said and was himself shaken and depressed by the vast scale and fatal consequences of these abuses.

"Are you sure the Kremlin is aware of these things?" I asked him. "Do you think Stalin and the men around him know what an irreparable blow this deals to the prestige of the Soviet Union and the Communist movement? I can't believe they do. Who is there to tell the Kremlin? Those responsible would be the last to. If anyone should be shot as saboteurs it is they."

I offered to give Tulpanov a written report on all that I had told him, especially on the effect of the prisoner problem on the atmosphere in Germany.

"You must be in a position to see that a report reaches the proper quarters!"

Tulpanov made a gesture of resignation. "It's no use. Even Moscow can't clean up this mess," he said.

His wife and daughter interrupted. "What did Einsiedel say?" they asked curiously.

I had talked for an hour without stopping and only now

realized that Tulpanov, contrary to habit, had spoken in German. He looked at me earnestly and said shortly to his wife in Russian:

"Einsiedel says the Germans are still fascists and that is why they hate us!"

Astonished, I started to correct him. But a glance silenced me.

We drove back to town without talking. Tulpanov got out at his office in Lichtenberg and even placed his car at my disposal to take me to the Western sector. But before leaving me he took me aside and put a hand on my shoulder.

"Thank you for your trust. If you have any difficulties come to me. As long as you are with the *Rundschau* I can do something for you—as far as is in my power."

Another reunion took place during those days. I visited Bechler. My anger with him had gradually died away and I was ready to attribute his behavior on the Narev front, and the way he stabbed me in the back with his doctored-up success reports, to crudity and thoughtlessness rather than malice.

With another comrade from the days of captivity I went to Kleinmachnow, where Bechler, as minister of the interior for Brandenburg, lived in a villa. Two police sentries stood before his door. Nearby, in another villa, lived the minister of education, Fritz Rücker. He and his wife came to see Bechler that evening. But it was no longer the Bechler I had known. It was not the rather limited but good-humored comrade, who blushed and did not know what to say if you made fun of him, who thought Tolstoy's novels were boring, who had once believed in Hitler and then discovered communism, who learned the catechism of the party by heart and then marched along the new road loyally and steadfastly. The official who now sat before me on the terrace of his villa, stuffing himself with ham sandwiches, had become an ice-cold careerist, a man who had power, who spread fear and terror around him and then mocked at his victims.

We had no opportunity to talk much about events on the Narev front. We were occupied with the present.

"Elections next year?" Bechler asked indignantly, while the mere thought made the timorous Rücker tremble with fear for his ministerial portfolio. "We aren't that crazy, we won't just let power slip out of our hands. Collaboration with the bourgeois parties—how mad it makes me when I hear that. Typical middle-class opportunism! We give the orders and they obey. The dictatorship of the proletariat!"

"Isn't there any resistance at all, then?" I interjected.

"Oh, of course they try to speak up. But the NKVD is usually better informed than I am. They have those gents under their thumb. The smug little fellows deserve to have to help dig their own graves. I assure you I've learned from the Russians how to deal with the cowardly swine."

Yes, he had learned that and more too. When he introduced his wife to me, I was taken aback. From his pictures and stories of her in Russia I had thought of her as a simple little Gretchen. This woman was a virago to whom the party jargon was second nature. Now I learned from him how this transformation had taken place. During the war his wife had heard from "black listeners" who secretly tuned in foreign stations that her husband was speaking on the Moscow radio. She wouldn't believe it. How could her humble Bernard who had so worshipped the Führer be capable of that? No, never, quite out of the question. There was something wrong there, she thought, and to be on the safe side reported it to the police. An official who was a Communist is said to have been arrested as a result. When the Red Army marched in it was Mrs. Bechler's turn to be arrested. She disappeared without a trace a few days before Bechler returned. He tried to intervene, or at least to find out what had become of her, in which camp she was, and what her sentence was. In vain.

"Your wife's case is so serious," a high official in the NKVD told him, "that we advise you to drop it."

"What else could I do?" Bechler asked me. "I had her declared dead, and married again. My present wife is OK, a former Young Communist, politically enlightened. My best co-worker, I can assure you."

Bechler spoke of other things. "You know, in Potsdam a whole Wehrmacht safe was lying in the street. Hundreds of thousands of bills fluttering about the pavement. Do you think I pocketed a single bill? Not I, I was too naïve then."

"Yes, yes . . ." I murmured uncomfortably.

"Well, of course," he broke in quickly by way of apology, "I had no idea we'd still be using Reichsmarks."

"Still, even if you didn't, you're doing all right without it," I couldn't help remarking with an ironical glance at his large terrace windows and ostentatious study.

"Oh yes, I can't complain. But I need it, you know. With all the responsibility, you have to have a real home or you wear yourself out."

Mrs. Rücker looked up at her husband's colleague admiringly. A little earlier we had been saying how you never can tell with the Russians, and how easily one burns one's mouth with a completely well-meant criticism; and I insisted that one must still be courageous and persevere because in the end one would be heard. She interrupted: "It's all right for you, you have no family. You can afford it. But not you, Fritz, no nonsense from you, do you hear!"

"Oh, I don't think there's any danger, Mrs. Rücker," I reassured her. "Even in prison Fritz showed determination only when Ulbricht was far away. And now he has you at his side."

My irony did not get across. "He certainly has," the resolute lady agreed.

"A charming evening at the minister's," I said to myself as I returned home. I had a bad dream that night. I think I am afraid.

Chapter Twelve / In the Eastern Sector of Berlin

JANUARY 12, 1948. Even in captivity I found the Russian newspapers terribly boring. But I am only discovering how boring it is to work on a newspaper of the "new type." I have always thought of journalism as interesting work. I considered the journalist a man who ferrets out the new, the exceptional, and important, and the newspaper a battlefield of opinions, a forum of criticism. There is nothing of all that in the papers licensed in the Eastern zone, and none at all in the *Tägliche Rundschau*. At first the work provided a certain excitement, but now that I have got used to the new surroundings and the new people, the clatter of printing machines and the atmosphere of press conferences, I feel more and more ill at ease. The work runs in the deep rut of an empty rhetoric which has no relation to reality. We concentrate on endlessly rehashing party dogmas, on a tasteless glorifying of the Soviet system, and on trying to dam up the flood of invectives which the

Russians use in their articles. Our "profession" is gross distortion of truth, restrained by no consideration for credibility or the common sense of the reader.

Recently Karlshorst * issued a directive that no parcels might be sent from the Eastern zone to West Germany. The German staff of the *Tägliche Rundschau* were tearing their hair. What did this mean? Nobody wanted to write a comment upon it. Nobody had the slightest idea how to account for the measure. Every sensible person was bound to see that it meant a new blow struck against the highly praised unity of Germany and was bound to embitter the population still more. The chief of the service, Major Weisspapier, jumped up from his seat at the editorial conference when he noticed our hesitations, and instructed us in shouts: "This is a blow to the saboteurs of the new order who want to plunder the Eastern zone by sending out parcels. This is a measure to unite Germany, because now people will see how poor the Western zone is and how rich the Eastern."

Even the Russian department heads shook their heads or looked down in embarrassment. The unfortunate man who was told to write the comment got malicious smiles from his colleagues. Very few had the courage, or were in a secure enough position, to say no to such instructions. The faithful Communists consoled themselves with "The end justifies the means." The cynic who had once produced as good a newspaper for the German People's party as he did later for the Nazis, and then wrote for the *Tägliche Rundschau* as badly as was expected of him, figured out the fee this would bring him.

For a long time I have avoided writing anything on current issues. But that too is self-deception. Articles on Marx's anniversary or the hundredth anniversary of the Communist

* Seat of the Soviet Military Administration. *Trans.*

Manifesto, on Sacco and Vanzetti or the history of May 1 may contain just as little original thought and must correspond just as little to reality as all the others. One can use no argument, no matter how pro-Soviet it may be, that deviates in any way from the official line. If the objection does not come from the Russian chief of the department, then it comes from the chief of the service, from the acting assistant editor, the editor in chief, or from Colonel Kirsanov himself. For the Russians in Berlin are in an even more deplorable predicament than we. They seem to be automatically suspected of Western tendencies by reason of being here. A crease in their trousers, a carefully knotted tie, a friendship with a German comrade, an affair with a secretary can be their undoing. How much more reason they have to fear taking responsibility for an article that may provoke the disapproval of the bosses or later on may serve as a proof of long-standing "treachery."

At the same time, no one knows what the official line actually is. Yesterday it may have been a crime to criticize the French attitude say on the Saar question. Today it is a high duty to accuse the French politicians of shameful annexations and to vituperate against them. The next day the same sort of article may be removed from the paper on an order from Karlshorst, even though it is already in type. The directives about newspaper contents come from some anonymous source, whose processes of thought are impossible to predict according to the laws either of logic or of reality.

The Russians are in mortal fear of their own bosses. The paper is read word for word in four different control points before the editor in chief sees it and initials the last proof. Sometimes a couple of hours are spent discussing whether a single word in an article deviates from the dogma.

My own chief, Captain Bernstein, normally a placid and sensible man, rushes back to his room four or five times when he is on his way to the editor in chief. He imagines he has forgotten something. When you ask him what he is looking for he can't answer but runs out, turns around, wipes the sweat from his forehead, and at last knocks at the editor's door as timorously as if he is searching for the fuse in an unexploded mine.

At last the Russian editors, because of the continual shrinkage of our circulation, began to wonder if things were going as they should. Our untiring and bitter criticism of the crude and one-sided reporting from the "workers' paradise" directed their attention particularly to this department. They themselves didn't dare to suggest a change of line in Karlshorst, though, so they arranged a conference instead. The luminaries of the Social Unity party press were invited to express their opinions. They were Becher, Abusch, Klaus Gysi, Hedda Zinner, Wolfgang Harich, Professor Kuczynski, Kantorovicz, and the general secretary of the Kulturbund, Willmann.

For a whole hour they hemmed and hawed over a clear statement. At last Becher threw himself into the battle. He can afford to be reprimanded by the Russians for being a nationalist. This clever orator and negotiator is needed in the Kulturbund, which is above parties. So he took the bull by the horns.

"Millions of Germans have been in the Soviet Union," he began. "You can't pull the wool over their eyes. The abuses, the defects, the backwardness they have seen must be explained to them, not just denied. A Russian worker who can compare his existence only with the time of tsarism may be aware of the progress that has taken place. A German worker who sees prisoners return from Russia as skeletons, who sees the undisciplined, drunken, dirty Red Army men in his streetcars, is bound to ask himself what this has to do with socialism. This is where reporting from the Soviet Union must start. The Soviet Union must be described truthfully, in its evolution and struggle against obstacles, against the indolence of the population, technical backwardness, against bad crops and lack of housing . . ."

After that the others became more courageous and subjected the work of the Russian department to annihilating criticism. The permanent staff of the *Tägliche Rundschau* listened in silence. They engage daily in guerrilla warfare on that front and have long since lost all faith in achieving anything there. Captain Silbermann, the responsible department head, is an unusually dogmatic and quarrelsome fanatic. He certainly operates with great skill and subtlety within the limits set for him. But dare to follow Becher's suggestions or ours, at a time when the Bolshevik party had entered upon the road of unrestricted chauvinistic propaganda? He would have to have suicidal intentions. Today every expression of respect for another country is branded Westernism and cosmopolitanism in the Soviet Union. There is no invention and no discovery which is not claimed by the Soviets for the Russian people. And while the rest of the world is presented to the Russians as one vast poorhouse, as the incarnation of rightlessness and lack of freedom, the slightest and least important institution of the Soviet state must be praised as the peak of all social, technical, and cultural achievements.

The conference might as well never have taken place at all. Changes can be made only for the worse.

But again it was typical of the strange situation in which we find ourselves. To offer criticism at such a conference is not very dangerous, even if it earns a reprimand. But there is no talking to the Russians individually. Then they become more orthodox than *Pravda*. They are afraid of finding an NKVD spy in every German colleague. So they reply to every critical remark with a counterattack and accuse the critic of all the mortal sins of heresy.

Major Weisspapier, foaming at the mouth, rushed at me with clenched fists when I turned down an article full of insults to André Gide and did not conceal my admiration for the writer.

"Gide? Gide is our deadly enemy. There is no place in the progressive world for this traitor," he shouted at me.

When I refused to write a report about the arrival of the alleged 500,000th German returning from the Soviet Union, maintaining that the Russians should take the consequences for their treatment of the prisoner-of-war issue, my Russian colleagues had no further doubts about me.

"You must be very sure of yourself, Herr von Einsiedel, to make such a statement," one of them said to me maliciously.

"Is that a threat?" I asked.

"No, it isn't a threat. You know very well what I mean."

At first I couldn't see what he was getting at. Only after long reflection over this remark and its author * did I realize its double meaning. Many of our Russian colleagues considered me, on account of my frank attitude in the matter of prisoners of war, to be an agent provocateur of the NKVD.

Among all the Russians on the editorial board Kirsanov is the most difficult to size up. His originality, simplicity, and breadth of nature can evoke admiration just as much as the sinister watchfulness which seems to hide behind his bearish familiarity and small, quick eyes inspires fear.

There is much that one cannot help loving about the Russians. In the rare unforced conversations that one has with them, when they forget for once that they are functionaries and behave like normal men, all the suspicions and doubts, the distrust and insecurity that one ordinarily feels with them vanish—until they once again take fright, remember that they

---

* He was arrested, together with eight other Russian editors, shortly after my departure from the *Rundschau*.

are Soviet men, and begin to agitate and make a political issue out of every harmless jest.

"Stalin, Mussolini, and Hitler were discussing world supremacy in 1940"—I told this old political wisecrack the other day in a laughing and joking company of Germans and Russians. "Stalin demanded world supremacy because he already governed the biggest country. Mussolini solemnly insisted that the Almighty had said world supremacy must spring from Rome. Then Hitler jumped and shouted: "Didn't I say so?" The Germans laughed. Several Russians laughed. But the others pulled official faces and warned me:

"That is no joke, Comrade Einsiedel. Comrade Stalin never discussed world supremacy with Hitler; that is a Trotskyite slander."

As I shook with laughter, the Russians grew really angry.

"You are politically immature, Comrade Einsiedel. You spread hostile propaganda and think you are telling harmless jokes."

In a moment the gay party became a pack of wolves each of whom watched the others and slipped away with suspicious eye so as not to get involved in unpleasant quarrels.

The editorial board reflects, in a small way, the jungle represented by the system. If you are guilty of an independent opinion you must fear the fanatics. If you stick to the party line, the hidden enemies of the party and of Stalin's dictatorship—who under certain circumstances act as the most rabid fanatics of all—use every opportunity to make you suspect in the eyes of the party. Friend and foe become indistinguishable. The doctrine of a monolithic party has not produced a disciplined fighting organization but only the secret war of every man against every man.

FEBRUARY 20, 1948. I have been invited to a birthday party in West Berlin but I am almost afraid to go. There are to be Western journalists there, American and French. But also people with pro-Soviet ideas. And that is where the risk lies. Only a few months ago I still did what I pleased and met all sorts of people irrespective of political persuasion and nationality. Wasn't I entitled to? Must I have a bad conscience?

A few weeks ago I was invited to a friend's and comrade's house in the Western sector. It was a miscellaneous company from both East and West which gathered there, Communists, Social Democrats, Trotskyites, and followers of Sartre, and an animated political discussion developed. Owing to the interest in my person, to my experiences in captivity, to my temperament, and the course the conversation took, I became the spokesman for the Communist viewpoint. I fulfilled this function to the best of my ability and conscience. I glorified nothing and did not deny what was undeniable. I admitted that I, too, could vanish tomorrow without trace, because of a spiteful denunciation, a misunderstood criticism, or a personal difference with a leading official. But as my conversation partners from the other camp had nothing positive to offer beyond criticism of the inevitable accompaniments of the dictatorship of the proletariat, as they had found no way out of the chaos of the last decades and did not themselves believe that the Western world had any future, my frankness made all the stronger impression. In the end they no longer laughed at the ardor with which a grandson of Bismarck went to bat for communism, but became very serious and thoughtful.

As for myself, I was in good spirits and returned to the Eastern sector strengthened in my conviction that I was on the right side of the barricade in spite of everything.

A few days later I was summoned to Colonel Kirsanov.

Unsuspecting, I walked into his room. There was no Kirsanov but two Russians in mufti, with the faces that are common to all the secret police in the world. In a friendly way they inquired—as usual—how things were and how I was. They wanted to know whether I had enough to eat and got along on my salary. They asked whether I was lonely, where my family was, whether I intended to marry, and who my friends were.

I had no reason to deny my acquaintances and friends. It would only have aroused suspicion if I concealed someone whose existence must naturally be known to the supervising organs. Slowly the questions of the two commissars concentrated on my host of that evening. What are his political views, they wanted to know. Who are his friends and what do they talk about in his house?

"Ask him yourselves. He works in the Central Administration, is a convinced Communist, and will speak for himself. I'm not an information bureau, after all."

"As a party member, it is your duty to answer," I was informed.

"That is not mentioned in the rules of the party to which I belong," I retorted.

"You know very well the unwritten laws of the party. Answer!"

"I have no intention to! I will answer unreservedly questions that concern me. Also questions of general interest to the party. But I refuse to play the spy on my friends."

"Ah, but these questions concern you, Comrade Einsiedel."

"What do you mean? Is this an interrogation?"

"Call it what you like. But tell everything that you said the other evening at your friend's house."

"That would lead into too many details," I said evasively.

263

"During a long discussion I defended and gave reasons for my political point of view. And not exactly clumsily or ineffectively, at that."

"You made no anti-Soviet statements?"

"Not that I know of," I replied lightly.

"Didn't you say that the NKVD caused people to disappear? Tell the truth!"

"Of course I said so. That is no lie and no anti-Soviet statement. Everybody knows it! But I both explained and gave reasons for it."

"But you said that innocent people are arrested too. Is that right?"

"I said that under the system there was no guarantee that only those guilty before the law would be arrested. Anyway, that was my meaning. And I tried to explain that too."

"Did you say that in the Eastern zone there are concentration camps, as in Hitler's time? Did you say that there are spies everywhere?"

"Yes. Unfortunately, I could hardly maintain the opposite without being laughed down."

"Well, are those anti-Soviet statements or not?"

"I see no hostile act in stating the facts. Everything depends on how one interprets them."

The commissar jumped up. "You are an enemy, Comrade Einsiedel!" he shouted. "You talk like a warmonger. You lie. You are a traitor."

I lost my temper too. "Don't speak to me like that," I shouted back. "No one can talk to me that way. I am not lying and I'm not a warmonger. This conversation, which I am now concluding, proves how true what I said is and how idiotic your suspicions are."

I jumped up in a rage and strode to the door. The Russian ran after me and seized me by the arm. I shook him off. "Don't touch me," I roared at him. "Are you arresting me, by any chance?"

It would not have surprised me at all if I had been arrested then and there. But I was determined to stick it out. If I were in danger the only thing that could save me was a counter-attack.

The Russian drew back. I lost all self-control and rushed at him with clenched fists.

"I won't stand for such treatment," I shrieked so that the windowpanes shook. I had the impression that the whole house would soon be alerted. The Russian's face, distorted with anger, suddenly changed. He smiled. He lifted his hands entreatingly. "Calm down, do calm yourself. I didn't mean to offend you."

"But you are!" I retorted, and tears of rage came into my eyes. "You must be crazy. If you're too stupid to realize that you can't use the same methods in Berlin you do in Kazan, why the devil don't you get back behind the Urals? Your spies are your worst enemies if they distort your comrades' words. I stand before the whole world and defend methods which I loathe, call things good when I hate them, only because I believe in the great goal; and then you go and abuse me because you are too stupid to understand that one can't push one's head through a wall, because your horizon on the Vistula is studded with Soviet stars. Who do you think you are?"

The Russian ignored my angry words; he kept repeating in Russian: "Calm down, be quiet. Sit down and have a smoke." He passed me his cigarettes. "We know you are a staunch comrade. Nobody wants to do you any harm. But you must realize we have to be on our guard. The enemy is strong. There are traitors and enemies everywhere."

"But I'm not an enemy!" I shouted again, banging my fist on the table. "I won't have this suspicion."

"All right, calm down. Nobody suspects you. We've heard

nothing but good about you. Forget what I said. It was a mistake."

The Russians were quite friendly when they let me go. I could say and do as I pleased, the commissar assured me, talk with and visit whom I liked. He was convinced of my loyalty. But yet ever since that day I have felt afraid, afraid to go to the Western sector, afraid to invite anyone to my house, afraid just to telephone to West Germany.

MARCH 12, 1948. In Moscow I often wondered why even such intelligent and educated communists as Friedrich Wolf, Alfred Kurella, and Fritz Erpenbeck were so timid in their descriptions of conditions in the Soviet Union. How completely Moscow émigrés seemed to have forgotten what life in a Western country was really like! How hard they tried to support official propaganda statements, against their better knowledge. But it is only here in Berlin that I have learned what awful pressure produced that attitude. I have learned it from people who are still unconditional 'Sovietists" but do not belong among the prominent Communist émigrés and who speak not without bitterness of their experiences in the Soviet Union. From all their stories together there is only one conclusion to be drawn: that the destruction of revolutionary Communists started by Hitler in Germany was completed in the Soviet Union. Actually only a small group of Central Committee members around Ulbricht, and prominent writers, were spared in the orgies of persecution that accompanied the purges of the 'thirties.

Night after night, for years, the patrols of the GPU marched through the corridors of the Hotel Lux, the Moscow residence of European émigrés. Night after night the émigrés lay awake in the horrible expectancy that the steps would come to their door, that by morning they would have disappeared and no news of them would penetrate the walls of their prisons to reach their comrades.

The men who told me this were themselves among the innocent victims of that terror. Some have spent as much as twelve years in concentration camps, or in the exile of "family arrest" where all suffer for one member. Others have lost father, mother, brothers and sisters. They were sentenced to death or years of imprisonment by the so-called *troikas*— tribunals of three men who "pronounced sentence" without trial or inquiry, taking their evidence from dossiers without granting any opportunity for defense. A former student at the German school in Moscow told me that he once begged his father, a prominent official in the Italian section of the Comintern, to intercede for three out of ten teachers who had been arrested and vanished from that school. It was impossible to believe that these old comrades should have been traitors. His father replied that no one is arrested unjustly in the Soviet Union. Six weeks later he himself fell a victim to the flood of arrests. His son saw him for the last time watched by two secret police with drawn pistols while he hurriedly packed the few things he was allowed to take with him to prison. The father called out to his son some names of high Soviet officials whom he should ask to intercede on his behalf. "I replied to my father," his son told me, "that no innocent man is arrested unjustly in the Soviet Union." Of course he did everything to try to help; but the high officials whom his father had advised him to see were either arrested soon in their turn or seemed never to have known their old comrade in arms. He vanished without a trace. Only after the war did the son learn, from someone lucky enough to have been released through one of those incomprehensible chance shifts of the machinery of terror, that his father had died of hunger after seven years in a forced labor camp. The son still swears by Moscow and is a devoted party functionary. For him, as well as for other victims, these things are just "mishaps" like the artillery firing on its own trenches by mistake.

"Does freedom exist?" I was asked by the son of one of the founders of the German Communist party—Hugo Eberlein, who disappeared in Russia—a boy who had spent ten years in Siberian exile and was completely Russified.

"There is no absolute freedom," he replied himself. "There is only realization of necessity."

All this is the logical result of the point of view I held myself in the discussion that pleased the NKVD so little. All right, maybe, in theory. But when one sees the people it affects, one is seized with horror. What has it all to do with communism?

Lenin said that the dictatorship of the proletariat recognizes no laws but those it has set for itself. But he certainly took it for granted that these laws would be established on the basis of democratic freedom, at least for the working class and its allies, that is for the majority of the population. Back in 1905 he stated clearly that socialization without democratization must lead to the most terrible results. Have we not seen these very results? Must one not admit that the party, state, and NKVD apparatus does not itself abide by the laws which it issues arbitrarily and without consulting a single authority? We are thrown defenseless into the hands of a more or less anonymous group of top officials who force their will upon millions of Communists throughout the world, subjecting those in the Soviet Union to the terror of their own secret police and, where the latter's arm does not reach, surrendering the disobedient elements to the police of the class enemy.

We must not even discuss the purpose of a tax law, the produce delivery dates for farmers, or football pools. So how can a party member who does not belong to the small Kremlin group express his views on any important political question such as the German-Polish frontier, the resettlement of millions of people, the relationship with social democracy, or the attitude to the Marshall Plan? We have to carry out orders issued by a government which we do not even know. I should like to see the comrade who can answer to his own satisfaction the question where party decisions are really hatched. In the Politburo of the Bolshevik party? Perhaps. But where is the Politburo? When, where, and under what circumstances was it elected? Are its members free in their offices and their decisions or must they fear the secret police as much as we? Who has the power of decision anyway—Stalin or a clique around him, or Beria or some totally unknown comrade Ivanov, pushed into the Politburo by the NKVD?

"Realization of necessity." Very well, I can see that one must agree whether to drive on the right or on the left, and this realization of necessity helps to achieve a far-reaching freedom in traffic. A criminal may perhaps realize that a confession is necessary and give himself up to the police. Yes, perhaps one may even realize that it may become necessary to suffer great injustice from the state or society, unless one wants to take matters into one's own hands.

But what has become of the revolutionary elite, who waged their war against the existing order in the name of justice for all and established the "dictatorship of the proletariat" which was to realize this justice? They exhausted themselves in internal struggles. To a great extent they became victims of the grotesque justice of the state they created. A group of despots took over their inheritance, who claim to possess the only saving truth by means of which the earthly paradise can be built. In the name of this alleged truth they demanded the absolute subjection of all other men whom—this is the most favorable interpretation possible—they wished to force into happiness even against their will. They can keep their power only through terror and extend it only through force. Because they claim they are achieving communism it is necessary to accept this concentration of unlimited power and its unscrupulous use. But when the free Communist society of free individuals will break through the hard shell of this dictatorship the gods alone know. Perhaps after five or ten generations, when, like animals born in a zoo, they have forgotten what freedom is, when they have become so modest in their needs, especially their spiritual needs, that they can really live according to the Communist slogan: "From each according to his abilities, to each according to his needs."

APRIL 5, 1948. I asked for leave to go to West Germany, but the *Tägliche Rundschau* looked unfavorably upon this trip. "They" had fears for my safety. The NKVD raised its voice again. I was summoned to the Buschallee in Weissensee at 8 P.M. On the outskirts of the city on a dark street corner a commissar was waiting for me who took me by devious ways to a small villa. There, during a dinner with plenty of vodka, he asked me to give him reports on the foreigners I saw frequently. I was to sign a pledge to work for the Soviet News Service and to talk to no one about it. The next day a large parcel of food was brought to my apartment: a hunk of butter, four pounds of salt herring, a bag of barley and one of sugar, a huge piece of meat that stank so terribly I threw it straight into the garbage can. In a fortnight I was to go again to Weissensee and write down what I had learned in the meantime.

Well, I will play the game. I will give them a few unimportant bits of information. Quite by chance I discovered that the NKVD is ready to help me travel to West Germany. Purely out of fear that my request for leave to go there might be misinterpreted, I told the NKVD commissar about it of my own accord. To my astonishment he was quite pleased.

"Go and give us a report. Try to talk to former officers and find out about rearmament in West Germany."

It's really a joke that I should be helped by the NKVD to go where I can breathe freely again. And I need it! I must talk to people again with whom I don't have to weigh every word, whom I don't need to distrust, and be free of the fear and hypocrisy which are our constant companions here.

MAY 22, 1948. There are limits even to the power of the NKVD. I haven't yet received my interzone passport. But at least my request for leave has been granted by the *Tägliche Rundschau*. Altogether I am suddenly very much courted again in the editorial offices. I am one of three German staff members invited as guests of honor to the anniversary of the Soviet press in the Press Club at Weissensee. And on the third anniversary of the *Tägliche Rundschau* Colonel Kirsanov sang my praises in the principal address in the House of Soviet Culture, in the presence of the "heads of the party and of the army," pointing to my "exemplary efforts in the cause of the people." If one wants to get on here, all one has to do apparently is give the NKVD one's little finger.

As I was opening the quadrille with the colonel's wife at this jubilee, a Russian officer invited me to come out to a table behind the bushes in the garden. It was the same young lieutenant, now a captain, who once interrogated me at Stalingrad. Tulpanov had told me back in 1943, in the Ukraine, that he had been killed. I was delighted to see him again. Before long he asked me plainly to act as a spy for him.

"If you have the courage," he said, "come and see me in Potsdam."

I made an excuse of my coming journey to the West.

"All right, I'll see you about it when you come back." And with that he left me.

When I come back?—sometimes I shiver at the thought, yet I can't make up my mind to go without thought of return. How enthusiastically I embraced the idea of communism. What confidence and security it gave me. How clear and simple the future seemed, in spite of the hardships, the destruction, the suffering, the injustice. Was that all an illusion? An all-too-simple, patent solution? Today I can feel only sadness and anger when I think of all the stupidity, the clumsiness, the distrust and barbarity which poison everything, which create artificial enemies upon whom the perpetual conspirators can vent their mania for persecution. I rack my brain vainly to understand what people around me are really thinking. I don't mean Ulbricht or Pieck, the unscrupulous careerists and other corrupt elements. There are others after all: Ackermann, Friedrich Wolf, Erpenbeck, Kantorovicz, Bredel, and some of the friends and comrades from prison. They are not all fools or cynics. Don't they see these informers, spies, opportunists, and criminals around us? Don't they see or don't they want to see?

Or is it all necessary, after all? Is it perhaps the only way to establish a new and better order, which will do justice to man and his system of production? Perhaps I am really too soft, too sentimental, too "petty bourgeois" as they so handsomely say in the party jargon, to be on the side of the revolution. I have repeated to myself a hundred times that a pistol in the hand of a policeman is different from one in the hand of a criminal. A hundred times I have counted over all the crimes and abominations committed by the other world—the coffee burnt in Brazil, the potatoes destroyed in America, the bombing of Dresden, the chicanery with patents, and the armament profits.

And yet I can't believe that one can justify Soviet methods with this "dialectics." A rat remains a rat even if he is ten times a Social Unity party minister and "objectively" helps the cause of progress. Dialectics must take its orientation from reality or it becomes sophistry—an idea of Lenin's which seems to have been completely forgotten.

OCTOBER 3, 1948. For four months I have been sitting in solitary confinement, occupied only with myself.

On May 24 I arrived in Frankfurt-am-Main by the interzone train, and after registering with the police drove out pleasantly in a horse cab to the Bockenheim Highway where a friend had invited me to his villa. The next day I went to see my mother in Wiesbaden. We had arranged to meet in the Taunus Hotel. As we left the hotel a hand came down on my shoulder: "You are Count Einsiedel?" Two American officials demanded my papers. They regretted they could not examine them on the spot and must ask me to follow them to their office. On the terrace of a villa we had to wait a long time for the document specialist. We were politely offered sandwiches and drinks. One of the officials proudly showed a photograph of me, which he had foresightedly put in his pocket. Then it turned out that I had to go with them to still another, higher office. They asked my mother to name a place where she could meet me in half an hour, and a car drove me away from Wiesbaden.

In Oberursel the gates of the United States military prison were flung open at the sound of our horn. Without any explanation, and in spite of all my protests, I was locked up in a cell. Days and weeks went by. I was completely cut off from the outer world. No interrogation, no response to my protests, either oral or in writing.

I appealed in vain to the law of habeas corpus which had just been extended to the Germans. I went on a hunger strike when I learned through the newspaper that my imprisonment was known in Berlin. But what could the hunger strike of one individual achieve? Was I to let them resort to forced feeding? After eighteen days, when I could hardly raise myself from my camp bed, I gave up.

In the large barracks with hundreds of cells there was only a scattering of prisoners—a few SS officers, with whom I had a chance to speak once, and some dubious characters whom I watched through my quietly opened window as they proceeded in single file on their daily walk.

At last, after three months, I was interrogated for the first time.

"What are you going to do when we set you free?" an American officer asked me.

"Finish my leave and then go back to Berlin," I replied.

"Do you think we'll release you so you can send out horror stories about us in the *Tägliche Rundschau?*"

"All I have to do is write the truth; that is enough to give you a black eye."

"We'll make things hard for you if you're as stubborn as that. Give us a written statement that you have fled from the Russian zone. Then we'll release you. If you want time to think it over we can transfer you to a better place where we can put you in touch with men and material that will enlighten you about the Soviet Union."

I shrugged my shoulders. "I need no time to think it over. I insist on my immediate release."

"That's your last word?"

"Yes."

"Think about it carefully."

I made no further answer. The officer rose angrily.

"Your last word?" he asked once more, sharply.

I suddenly had to laugh. Saveliev's frog-like eyes appeared in front of me: "There are also trains that go east, Herr von Einsiedel!" Yes, that one was a real threat. But this American officer would have burnt his fingers badly if he had laid hands on me.

I looked thoughtfully after the American as he left my cell. Would I have been as "brave" as that with an NKVD man in Buchenwald? No, even here in Oberursel the mere thought of such a possibility filled me with terror.

A few days later I was transported to the prison at Frankfurt-am-Main, guarded by two armed civilians. In the course of a so-called "period of examination while under arrest," which according to the law should have been set within twenty-four hours after the arrest, I was handed a bill of indictment: "in possession of false papers, and espionage."

The trial was fixed for September 10. Three days before that date the lawyer appointed by the court for my defense was allowed to talk to me. The trial was not public. A few minutes before it opened the twenty-one-year-old prosecuting attorney attached to the United States intermediate military court, a German law student in his third semester, tried a little blackmail on me: if I pleaded guilty on the first indictment they would overlook the second. The judge dropped the second indictment even without my agreeing to this proposal.

An official of the United States Military Government swore that I was not entitled to my papers. In vain I pointed out to the judge that they had been issued legally by the Berlin Municipal Council, which was recognized by all four occupying powers.

At noon there was a recess. I learned privately that my sentence would be six months' imprisonment.

Two hours later the judge pronounced the sentence without looking up: it corresponded exactly to my information.

I have waited four weeks for the result of my request for retrial. The records proving the authenticity of my identity papers have been secured from Berlin. It can be only a matter of days now until I am released.

Why the Americans arrested me is a mystery to me. If they really suspected me of working for the NKVD, why didn't they first have me watched for a while so they could prove it? Why did they never once question me about that? Why now, instead, this rather clumsy attempt at blackmail and this curious trial?

Strangely enough this farce has provoked no ill feeling in me. Although they do not know it and cannot prove it I am, theoretically, an agent of the NKVD. While on leave, heaven knows, I had something better to do than spy on former officers and the supposed rearming of Germany. But how many tourists and men on leave from the Eastern zone are actually collecting information for the NKVD? Out of a hundred people in East Germany who receive an interzone passport, some eighty surely have orders to act as spies in one way or another. Even in prison camp anyone who had ever paid a visit to a foreign country was suspected by the Soviets of espionage. They can't see it differently, since every person who leaves their country has a spy assignment.

No, I don't bear the Americans a grudge, however endlessly the minutes stretch out in solitary confinement. But the question of what I am to decide when I get back to Berlin weighs on me more heavily than ever. The Tito affair was the latest blow. When Tulpanov six years ago asked what I knew about Karl Marx, I felt ashamed at not being able to answer him. But that was nothing compared with the embarrassment I felt when the Americans at Oberursel asked my opinion of the conflict between Tito and the Kremlin! Not until they thrust newspapers from the Eastern zone under my nose did I believe such a conflict really existed.

Only a few months ago two special correspondents of the *Tägliche Rundschau* returned from the much praised people's democracy of Yugoslavia. Only a few weeks ago their report about this model socialist country was concluded in the newspaper and it is supposed to appear soon in book form. Since the end of the war Soviet-Communist propaganda has been tireless in praising Tito's state as the prototype of the people's government.

But the propaganda magicians of the Kremlin overnight transformed a system of typically Soviet stamp into a fascist state, and rulers who had figured as the most popular heroes of world communism became fascist reptiles and traitors. Without the slightest knowledge of the matter, without examining the facts, without even reflecting, the Communist parties of all countries followed suit.

Pravda itself no longer sees any difference between fascism and Sovietism, beyond whether or not a government will dance to Moscow's tune, whether it will put up with Soviet secret police controlling its country as they please, or wants to shape its own destiny. No wonder I too find it difficult to detect any other difference.

"You must see things dialectically." Under this motto the war which the English and French fought against Hitler became nothing but skillfully camouflaged cooperation with him; and the Stalin-Hitler pact, which gave the latter his chance to control Europe, the Mediterranean, and the Near East, became an act of antifascist heroism.

"The end justifies the means." From this half-truth they claim the right to elevate to martyrdom any Communist who has been under arrest for a few days, while on the other hand tens of thousands of innocent people disappear without a trace.

"Liberation of the individual from exploitation, want, and ignorance." In the name of this propaganda thesis millions of people are subjected to a small group of drilled, fanatical, and callous party officials, are isolated from every intellectual exchange of opinion, and are forced into a labor system unequaled in history for its lack of social rights.

"Development of the creative powers of the people." Yes, there was a great poet, Maiakovsky, who in his poems clamored for the planning commission to determine his duty as a poet, and who swore to stifle the song in his own throat and devote his art to socialist water faucets and Parisian woman lavatory attendants. He ended by committing suicide. The lesser poets of the "Soviet epoch," however, managed to accomplish what their great model did not achieve: they warped their personalities to the rules of the planning commission and party orders, placed their talent at the service of a propaganda of lies which strangled all genuine sentiment, all genuine expression, in a mesh of tactical expediency and ideological dogma. Films as bad as any patriotic trash produced in the world in the last thirty years are labeled masterpieces of "socialist realism." Novels which once received the Stalin prize have to be rewritten to order. Statues representing the victorious Soviet man are equipped with bathing trunks and sport shirts, then disrobed, and finally robed again—and for each of these months of zigzagging "artists" receive 14,000 rubles, whereas a workman receives barely 400. Gorky's complete works are published in de luxe editions in German, with the author's head stamped on the binding, and in less than three weeks the whole edition is reduced to pulp because a flattering remark of Lenin's about Trotsky, which Gorky quoted in an article, had slipped into the book unnoticed. In the Moscow libraries the works of Traven and other "progressive" writers, who did not toe the party line precisely, are blotted out for pages by the censor because they contain criticism of the Soviet Union; and Plievier's *Stalingrad* is not printed because it would reveal the wholly fabricated Stalingrad myth of Soviet propaganda, because the Russian people would see the adversary in this book as he really was, would learn that the three hundred tanks that attacked the tractor factory and were repulsed by a small infantry detachment were not German tanks, but that the balance of forces was actually reversed. It is apparently seriously believed that it is possible to produce by party order works like "The Creation of Adam," the Strasbourg Cathedral, or the "Pathétique," and to regulate the intellectual, spiritual, and religious needs of man according to so-called "social necessity."

I am more and more preoccupied with the origin of this fantastic disregard for human conscience, for truth and life; with how it is possible for the socialist movement in its Communist aspect to have degenerated so far and achieved precisely the opposite of what it originally wanted, that is, to free men from the fetters of money and power, to master and control matter, technology, and the techniques of organization.

How is it possible for people who have written reason, logic, mathematics, and usefulness on their banners to come to worship pictures of Stalin and watch the platitudes and oracles of their party press more fearfully than a primitive tribe listens to the incantations of a witch doctor?

A few weeks ago I still tried to find the causes in external circumstances—for instance in the fact that the social revolution in Russia was a premature birth and had been distorted by the forced measures with which it had to be reared. Marx once said that one social order could be supplanted by another only when the possibilities of development of its productive powers had been exhausted. And that was not the case in the Russia of

1917. I regretted that Lenin died too soon. His knowledge of Europe and of the international labor movement would, I believe, have made him avoid the fatal mistakes of the International led by Stalin. But who can be sure the master Lenin would not have been swallowed up by his own creation like his best disciples Bukharin, Trotsky, Zinoviev, Kirov, Tukhachevsky, and the rest who, as revolutionaries and autonomous personalities, could never make their peace with Stalin's undialectical doctrine about the monolithic party?

I become more and more convinced that the roots of the evil lie much deeper. If it were true that man is nothing but a product of economic conditions, the highest form of development of organic substance, if the mystery of life could be explained scientifically, the soul proved to be only a sentimental expression for class consciousness, conscience a mere parson's invention which could be replaced by party decision, then it would be right to place utility above morality, and for reasons of expediency to slaughter men by the million or use them up in forced labor. After all, man slaughters cattle and harnesses oxen under the yoke.

But what is so fatal is precisely this apparently scientific materialistic interpretation of man and his history, which once fascinated me so with its many undeniable truths and now appears to me to be the starting point of the degeneration of the system, in that the truths which are contained in it have been made absolute in the Soviet Union.

It is not enough to nationalize the means of production and distribute the products of society according to plan. These measures would perhaps achieve their aim if they sprang from man's free choice, from his conscience and out of ethical maturity. But when they are imposed upon men by force they are just as valueless as refraining from murder out of fear of punishment.

280

For hours, for days, for months I paced up and down my cell, tormented by these ideas. And when I made this discovery, which is probably as old as the Bible, I felt like a shipwrecked man who discovers land.

For here I have found the key to why the road chosen by the Soviet Union can never lead to freedom and justice, never to communism.

The Soviet rulers will never abandon terror and force, will never be able to risk introducing intellectual freedom and freedom of conscience, though one may assume that is their intention and imagine Soviet society becoming the model of a genuine socialist society, the nucleus of communism. The force with which this order is imposed upon people has no educational value, it can never produce the ethical maturity which is needed for men to live together according to the Communist ideal. When there is no more choice between good and evil, true and false, right and wrong, these concepts lose their meaning. Even if it lasts for centuries, this forcibly imposed way of life can produce only a human herd which will perform social functions without knowing why and for what, an ant state, governed by a person in the Kremlin and dependent upon him, doomed to destruction as soon as this person ceases to exist, like a nest of ants deprived of its queen.

For this, too, is dialectics: whoever wishes to banish unhappiness from the world must also banish happiness; whoever destroys evil also destroys good. Who kills the devil kills God as well.

In this way the conscience of the revolution has been executed with the tens of thousands of revolutionary Bolsheviks who have fallen victims to purges, and its intellectual aims have been wrecked through the moral consequences of the methods with which they were implemented. The men in power who pretend to fight exploiters and warmongers, to

281

banish all need, fear, and injustice from the world, are inspired by the same drives that they accuse their enemies of embodying: lust for power, distrust, envy, and fear.

How can it be otherwise? How can so tiny a minority as that always represented by the Communists deprive millions of people of their freedom while retaining their own? That would be impossible even if this minority were defending a truth. A party which suppresses other parties is not free itself. This is a variant of Marx's words on national freedom. How can the rulers in the Kremlin who have liquidated millions of their real and imaginary enemies, followers, comrades in arms, friends, and companions be free of fear, of mistrust, and mortal anxiety? How can a party whose functionaries and members are told: You have no conscience, your conscience is the order given by the party; you need not think, the Politburo thinks for you; you must not criticize, but use self-criticism according to the directives of the party—how can such a party or its members develop further, perfect themselves intellectually and morally, know the truth, and act justly?

The greatest attraction which communism can still exercise lies perhaps in the critical truths of Marxism, to which it always refers in its propaganda. But the truth of the critical part of a program does not necessarily extend to its positive aims. This is another of those fallacies of which I too have been guilty.

The biggest lie of communism is the assertion that it is an absolute truth and hence has the right to force its program on the world.

Once again I ask myself: who are these people who pretend to possess the wisdom of a god? "We are not saved by any higher being, god, emperor, or tribune . . ." Who would want to shut his ears to these self-assured, rousing, and forceful words? Perhaps their very lack of humility has produced the grotesque situation today of men marching by Lenin's tomb singing the "Internationale" and carrying like ikons the heads of dictators demanding adoration.

I can hear the mocking, indignant cries of the "comrades" at the mention of such thoughts: "Look at the hypocrite preaching humility, modesty, submission to the power of the exploiters —opium for the people!"

But I feel that I am nearing the core of the problem here. Their whole system is vitiated not because of the nationalization of industry, the collectivization of agriculture, or the liquidation of private enterprise—not even because they impose these by force. Their guilt lies in attributing ultimate truth to all their measures, pretending to have solved the mystery of life and of living history, denying the beyond and the inscrutable, and forcing people to act against their conscience, against the law with which each of us is born. They want to force the mighty stream of life into the narrow channel of their ridiculous reason and steer history according to the drill regulations of their system. They wish to dominate the world and perpetuate their supremacy. Therein lies their terrible presumption.

For this they marched out to dethrone the gods and made the NKVD commissar their idol who presides over life and death, though he in his turn is a mere trembling idolator who can be destroyed tomorrow by one of his superiors.

They have announced the omnipotence of intellect and falter wretchedly in the mystical jungle of their dialectics.

What detours I have made in order to understand these simple things! Only here in the Frankfurt prison have I realized that there is no better comparison for the Soviet system than prison itself. People divided into prisoners, trusties, guards, supervisors, deputy wardens, and wardens. No crises, to be sure, but neither intellectual nor economic competition. The directors determine the work, the soup norm, the punishments and rewards, the reading material, and the prayers. But what may still have a meaning here in prison, because prison fulfills only a limited function within a free society, because the warden depends upon written and unwritten laws, because there are defense attorneys and hope of freedom, becomes meaningless in the Soviet system, which exists only for its own sake and leaves man no hope of salvation. An unemployed tramp may solve his problems by getting himself into jail for some small misdemeanor so that he can snap his fingers at the cold. But when a whole people, all mankind in fact, is to submit to the regime of the penitentiary for the sake of apparent security and freedom from crises, then this renunciation becomes insanity. This is exactly the path the Russian revolution has now taken. Yes, I must make a decision—one way or the other.

DECEMBER 7, 1948. In the middle of October I was released. In mid-November there was a retrial before a United States military court. The prosecutor dispensed with indictments. By this means, through a legal device, he avoided a clear acquittal.

Then I went back to Berlin. I had not yet found the courage to break with a world which I found very hard to return to. But though I told myself it was unlikely I would remain in the Communist camp much longer, I wanted to put myself once more to the test. I did not wish to avoid talking with those among my Communist friends who had traveled the same road as I and whom I could trust not to betray me even if they disapproved of my resolution to break with the party.

I also wanted to make it quite clear that I thoroughly disapproved of the behavior of the Americans toward me. For though they had not harmed me in any way and though their methods could not be compared with those of the NKVD, their procedure was far from correct.

My comrades and colleagues of the *Tägliche Rundschau* soon realized that a great change had come over me. I was asked again and again the very evening of my arrival: "What's the matter? You've changed completely."

The report I made at a press conference on my arrest and sentence by the Americans was not "sharp" enough, and was much too objective for them. Their long-winded advice to overcome my "modesty," and as a "victim of the American secret service" "tear the mask" off Western imperialism, revealed the distrust awakened in them by my unconcealed reluctance to let myself be used for their propaganda. My decision could not be put off longer. Either I had to capitulate completely or break with the party.

Today I have packed my suitcases and left the Eastern sector of Berlin. In two letters, one to Colonel Kirsanov and one to the central secretariat of the Social Unity party, I gave notice to the *Tägliche Rundschau* and resigned from the party.

APRIL 25, 1949. *New Germany*, central organ of the Social Unity party, sent me a letter saying that though I had been a genuine antifascist, yet "as an impoverished nobleman" I remained "a petty bourgeois who, as soon as the class war becomes acute, wrings his hands in despair, begins to cry, and finally deserts to the other camp."

Even if *New Germany* were right and I was only a sentimental bourgeois, I considered it more honest and forthright to admit it, instead of hanging on to the party line and artificially building up an inner resistance which would make me a menace to all because I would not be equal to the demands placed upon me.

The aggressive fanaticism of so many of my former comrades is caused only by a need for constant effective self-propagandizing. When betraying the wavering comrade to the NKVD with the gesture of a martyr—"Look, I am sacrificing my best friend to the party"—they actually wish to sacrifice themselves. The hatred and rage with which they attack their opponents is merely hatred of their own conscience which gives them no peace, wrath against their own rebellious ego which they suppress for the sake of the collective in which they long to be absorbed.

When I ponder the inner reasons which caused my break with the party, I also have to ask why I ever joined it. In the weeks when I faced the decision which brought me this obituary notice in *New Germany*, a group of former members of the National Committee who had been released from prison camp arrived in Germany. They had undergone a special course in the Krasnogorsk camp before their return. High Soviet officials instructed them in groups of seven on their political mission in Germany, the building up of a National Democratic party in the Eastern zone. Special commissars of the NKVD examined every one of them on their readiness and fitness for collaboration with the Soviet secret police. Once more ideological infiltration, coercion, and bribery marched hand in hand. Those who resisted the offer of high posts and additional funds had pressure applied by being accused of imaginary war crimes. Those who remained firm were sent back to the camps to face an uncertain fate, threatened by the Soviet legal machine.*

The most fanatical Communists among them, such as

* Those who were sent back, with a few exceptions, returned only in April 1950, after having been tried or waited for trial many months in prison.

Vincenz Müller, Heinrich Homann, and Arno von Lensky, were chosen to form the Politburo of the National Democratic party, together with the émigré and Soviet citizen, Dr. Lothar Bolz; they were to serve at the same time as point of contact for the representatives of the NKVD sent to West Germany. The fellow travelers—Egbert von Frankenberg, Colonel Adam, Colonel Ludwig, and many others—were given smaller posts in this branch of the Social Unity party. Other officers and generals filled the ranks of the People's Police.

All these men, as well as the friends with whom I discussed my break with the party in Berlin, believe they are on the side of the victors of the future. The fall of Peiping, the putsch in Prague are events which fill them with enthusiasm. What an offer of a position and security means for the fellow travelers a sense of having and of exercising power means for the active workers. In the turmoil of the German collapse, and from the perspective of a Soviet prison, the victory of communism has seemed inevitable for years. Reared in the concept of power politics, they regard the link with the Soviet bloc as the only way for Germany to play her role as a power again and, with her technical superiority soon win a leading position in a union of Soviet states.

The hope of sharing power in a privileged position exercises a special attraction for the most determined and active among them. They know how to transfigure their personal interest by the idea of taking part, as hammer rather than anvil, in a world-wide historical struggle (which, according to Bolshevik dogma, must end with the victory of communism).

No doubt a mixture of misunderstood patriotism, misguided faith in progress, ambition, and more or less conscious opportunism played an important part for us all in our decision in favor of communism. But this does not altogether explain why we fell such easy victims to Bolshevik ideology. It was rather the fear of "not being able to believe anything any more," the fear that overcomes people in chaos, the desire to find a psychological support in a strongly disciplined collective which made us cling to the Bolshevik party dogma and to the violent theory of class war as to a life anchor.

In this world which is out of joint and empty of faith the desire to exorcise fear by a cult of power was the temptation to which we fell.

It is not the break with Sovietism but the refuge in it which betrays psychological lability, petty bourgeois hesitation and weakness.

AUGUST 7, 1950. If success in power politics is the criterion, then the naïve faithful, the fanatics, and the unscrupulous theorists of terror in the Communist camp may actually appear stronger than the defenders of freedom of conscience and the spirit, who are inhibited with doubts and moral scruples. Who can deny that large numbers in the Western world move aimlessly between the extremes of ridiculously underestimating the enemy and panic-like fear of him, between the desire for a preventive war and pronounced defeatism?

But is the Soviet danger, with its fifth column all over the world, really as great as the spread of communism since Stalingrad might lead us to believe?

The military victory over Hitler undoubtedly meant the provisional end of the uninterrupted series of crises that have accompanied the existence of the Soviet Union from the very beginning: civil war and intervention, riots, hunger, economic crisis, disintegration of the Comintern, interparty strife, military opposition, and finally the attack of National Socialism— these crises were in great part the direct results of Stalin's personal ambition, and of the abandonment, under his influence, of the principles of revolutionary internationalism and democracy within the party. They characterize the protracted process during which the dictatorship of an intellectual elite *for* the proletariat was replaced by the dictatorship of a terrorist group, personified in Stalin, *over* the proletariat. It was none other than Hitler who gave Stalin the final decisive help in this process. His attack on "Holy Mother Russia" brought results which no Bolshevik propaganda could have achieved—the wretched morale of the Red Army at the beginning of the war was proof enough of that—it made Stalin a national hero in the eyes of the Russian people. If the first stage of the war, the offensive up to the Volga and the Terek carried out by the Wehrmacht against superior numbers, revealed how hollow and sterile Stalin's dictatorship really was and what an abyss separated it on the political and social plane from the people, it nevertheless helped the Stalinites to bridge this abyss on the national plane. It was the Nazi district commissars, the SS extermination commandos, and Rosenberg's and Ribbentrop's greed for annexation which drove the Russian people into Stalin's arms. The hesitant attempts linked with the name of Vlasov, which generals and the German Foreign Office made to give the attack on the Soviet Union the character of an act of liberation, did not alter this fact. They were paralleled in their insincerity only by the National Committee on the other side, and like the latter were hampered by the terror which the Nazi party exercised against the prisoners and population of the country that was to be "liberated." Thus the political opportunity to overthrow Stalin's regime was missed. In the military sphere alone Germany could not achieve victory— that was simply beyond her power.

This does not mean, however, that the thesis often repeated at the beginning of the war—that in this motorized era Russian space lost its value as a weapon—was wholly false. Nobody knows this better than Stalin himself, who described the attack of the Wehrmacht, though undertaken with inferior strength, as almost fatal to the Soviet Union. If the Wehrmacht could reach Stalingrad, then it is clear the Soviet armies would be defeated by any force which equaled them in numbers, was not so limited in its supply of guns and other material as the German army had been, and could draw on the technical superiority of the Western world even though the Russians should withdraw behind the Urals. For in the meantime space has shrunk further as compared with the strength and range of motors. The aggressiveness of Soviet policy since Potsdam seems to prove that the masters in the Kremlin are of a different opinion and believe themselves to be very strong. But every psychiatrist knows that people suffering from feelings of fear and inferiority tend to be aggressive. This is perhaps the explanation of Soviet aggressiveness. Almost every analysis of official and unofficial state propaganda must come to the conclusion that its initiators find it essential to pump up their own and their subjects' courage and to simulate strength.

Here lies a very real danger. No one can guarantee that one day the leading officials of this regime will not succumb to their own propaganda and lose all measure of the actual balance of power. No one can guarantee that they may not suddenly take flight from the inner sterility of their own organization and grasp for tempting successes abroad. Every totalitarian regime can use the surprise attack.

This danger will become particularly great if they succeed in causing panic in the free world and spreading fear and terror through their pretense of being all-powerful. No one can deny that they have already achieved a fair measure of success in this field already.

They are helped too in their attempts at intimidation by two factors. The first is the considerable overestimation, especially by the Western allies, of the military achievement of the Soviet counteroffensive from Stalingrad to Berlin. It is all too easily forgotten by both East and West that this offensive was directed against an overextended opponent who was able to oppose only a fraction of his reserves in men and weapons to the Soviet mass attack. The Soviet army crushed the Wehrmacht with its weight but did not defeat it by means of strategy. And owing to the clumsiness of the Soviet strategic leadership, the lethargy of the middle and lower officer corps, and the lack of initiative in all ranks, the cost in blood of this advance was disproportionately high. Even the battles of annihilation which the Red Army won were in no instance, even in the case of Stalingrad, due to its initiative. Rather they were presented to it by Hitler through his disregard for the most elementary laws of strategy. In the areas where the insane corporal did not have his finger in the pie, similar threats were successfully met by even mediocre General Staff officers through tactical and strategic maneuvers of evasion.

These facts cannot be dismissed merely by claiming that the person who raises them intends to create a new legend of the invincibility of the German army in the field. The Wehrmacht was defeated because it took on impossible tasks ordered by its political leaders, and in trying to carry them out had to suffer, in addition, the interference of a dilettante. These facts must be taken into account if one is to assess the achievement of the victors correctly. Generals always like to have conquered as strong an opponent as possible. Nor do the Western countries like to recall how much they were bluffed by Hitler in 1939–40, and how long they hesitated before they engaged in decisive hand-to-hand battle with an enemy already bled white. This hesitation gave the Red Army time to sweep on to the Elbe. In this respect Herrnstadt was quite right in his cynical analysis of the political and military situation after July 20, 1944.*

The second factor that favors the Soviet pretense of power is that the democracies are necessarily always demonstrating their own weakness. Every dollar intended for rearmament can be extracted from the taxpayer and the politician only after endless debates. This may be fortunate, as otherwise the bitter enders and lunatic fringe would long since have built up a "defense" which would have made the preventive war inevitable. But this "talk of the Soviet devil" in the battle for rearmament budgets must not go so far as to encourage him one day to appear. How would it look if the devil were suddenly to appear: that is if the Soviet Union were in fact to cross the boundary clearly drawn in Korea through the intervention of United Nations forces, and thereby provoke a world conflict?

Through Europe with her industrial potential, her numerous ports, and her communications, lies the nearest and easiest means of access to the Soviet Union. Therefore the Soviet's first military action would be to occupy Europe and even a portion of the North African coast. However, it is unlikely that the divisions necessary for such a step could be secretly massed in the Eastern zone, in Czechoslovakia, in Hungary, and in the Balkans. The attack would be launched against an inferior but not unprepared opponent. Assuming that the Soviet Union is fully mobilized, there can be little doubt of its success. But this success would bring the Soviet leaders face to face with their real problems for the first time. Under Soviet conditions an inconceivable military and political organization would be required to defend and control the occupied territories and make them of use in the war. The Soviet masses who have been strictly isolated for decades would come by the

* See pp. 159–161.

million into the defamed, prohibited, and thus all the more tempting capitalist world. They would thrive as conquerors. Yes, they would thrive so much that the "Agitprop" would be unable to prevent a noticeable demoralization. The fighting morale of the Red Army men was none too high even when they were defending their own home soil. Would it be any higher when they were removed from their homes many thousands of miles to partly hostile, partly enticing surroundings, and were infected by the inevitable realization that everything was not so wonderful and unique in the "workers' paradise"? This time the Red Army men would not roll to the front in Dodges and jeeps, they would not march in American clothes and boots, they would not eat powdered eggs, corn, wheat, pork, and tinned food from countries overseas. In the sky they would not see five hundred to a thousand of their own aircraft matched against one of the enemy's. This time the partisans would stand behind their backs, not their enemies'. And the Soviet command would have its actions dictated to it by a free world prepared to strike back.

Is it not more than doubtful that the Kremlin would consider such a state of affairs desirable? Its experiment in Korea is no counterproof. There the Western occupation forces abandoned a rump state, nine-tenths of whose industry lay behind the Iron Curtain, whose twenty-one million poverty-stricken peasants had to feed four million unemployed; a state that was practically without arms, while enormous stocks of United States arms were being scrapped; a state in which the nearby events in China caused just as much illusion as despair. Why should the Kremlin not have believed that the United States and the free nations had one way or another written Korea off as a lost cause, and that it only remained for them to create a fait accompli? That the speculation was a miscalculation makes it unlikely they intend to repeat it in Europe.

The political line followed by the Soviet Union in respect to Germany is the same by which the Soviet émigrés tried to make the Oder-Neisse boundary acceptable to the Communist proselytes of the National Committee in 1945. As regards Berlin, the Politburo of the Social Unity party was still of the opinion in May of this year that the Western position could not be held economically and therefore morally, in the long run, and that one day the city would fall like a ripe apple into the lap of the Eastern zone. This development could, if necessary, be hastened by repetitions of the Whitsunday march.* Owing to the panic in Berlin business circles this march caused more damage than could ever have been hoped for.

All the same, Berlin is a beacon which brings light into the darkness of the Eastern zone and whose power of illumination reaches far into the Soviet Union. For this reason they will keep on trying to put it out.

On the whole, however, Soviet policy is still dominated by the tenet that the internal contradictions of the capitalist world will of themselves lead to its collapse. The Bolsheviks still believe that the "ruling classes" have only one possibility of delaying this collapse: war, war against the Soviet Union. They are still much too frightened of such an attack to think themselves of attacks whose aims are wider than safeguarding and strengthening their present positions.

The hot war can be avoided. It is a matter of keeping one's nerve in the cold war, resisting all maneuvers of the totalitarians with the utmost toughness, watchfulness, and self-confidence, and above all of not betraying the principles of justice and freedom of conscience for the sake of tactical advantages. Stalin will not live to be a hundred, and the "Soviet paradise"

* Held by the Communist and so-called Free German youth. The threat that they would storm and "free" West Berlin made business people reluctant to stock goods or extend credit.

is not a "thousand-year Reich." The history of the Soviet Union and of the Communist parties proves that human conscience is in the last analysis an unassailable element and will again and again produce "traitors," renegades, and true revolutionaries in all ranks of this power apparatus. The more the apparatus swells and expands, the more play these forces will have. The sole possibility of the system is to kill itself with victories.

But even if the Western world no longer mustered the inner strength to meet the threat in freedom and without—consciously or unconsciously—resorting to preventive war; even if it failed to develop a new form of human living and working together; if technology and the machinery of power triumphed over mind and freedom for centuries; if the detour by way of the Soviet or some other totalitarianism became inevitable— one could still be happy if one knew that mankind would one day rediscover its conscience and its soul and faith in those values which lie beyond the reach of a secret police.

Index

West Berlin (Western sector), viii, xii–xiv, 262, 266, 294

West Germany (Western zone), 256, 266; NKVD representatives in, 270–271, 276, 287

Western world, future of, 262, 288–295

Willms, Lt., 66, 205

Wolf, Dr. Friedrich, 80, 81, 90–91, 108, 109, 122, 124, 126, 266, 272

Yelabuga, officers' prison camp at (Camp 97), 79, 82–92, 137–142;

antifascist group at, 64, 91; Nazi influence at, 138–139, 139–140; political conditions at, 64, 82–83, 137, 139, 212; treatment of prisoners at, 62–63, 138, 139

Yorck, Count von Wartenburg, 67, 74, 97

Youth Movement, free, 29, 68, 85–86

Zaisser, Wilhelm, 80, 157–158, 162–163, 165–166, 169–170

Zippel, Hans, 67, 96, 106, 136, 210